BACKROADS & BYWAYS OF
UPSTATE
NEW YORK

BACKROADS & BYWAYS OF

UPSTATE NEW YORK

*Drives, Day Trips, &
Excursions*

CHRISTINE A. SMYCZYNSKI

THE COUNTRYMAN PRESS

A division of W. W. Norton & Company

Independent Publishers Since 1923

Manufacturing by Versa Press
Book design by Chris Welch
Production manager: Lauren Abbate

The Countryman Press
www.countrymanpress.com

A division of W. W. Norton & Company, Inc.
500 Fifth Avenue, New York, NY 10110
www.wwnorton.com

78-1-58157-440-1 (pbk.)

10 9 8 7 6 5 4 3 2 1

To my family:
Thanks for all your love and support as I wrote this book.
I also dedicate this book in loving memory of my parents,
Joseph and Adele Kloch, who sparked my love of local travel,
and my in-laws, Stanley and Alice Smyczynski,
who were big fans of my writing.

Contents

LEFT: FRENCH CASTLE AT OLD FORT NIAGARA, FORT NIAGARA STATE PARK, YOUNGSTOWN

Acknowledgments

I wouldn't have been able to write this book without help from friends and family who supplied me with moral support as well as information. First, I'd like to thank God for giving me the ability to write as well as the strength and patience to finish this project.

Next, I'd like to thank my husband Jim, who offered love, support, and encouragement as I worked long hours on the book. Jim, along with our two youngest children, Jennifer and Joe, spent his summer vacations traveling with me to the eastern part of New York State. An extra special thanks to my daughter Jennifer, my partner in crime, for going with me on day trips closer to home and overnight girls' getaways. There was always lots of eating and retail therapy involved in our trips!

While our older two sons, Andy and Peter, didn't travel with us, they did help out by taking care of things at home when we were gone and making sure our dog, Franklin, was fed and happy.

I want to thank my friends Mary, Linda, and Annette, who were willing to read through some of the chapters about places that they are far more familiar with than I, to make sure I captured the essence of that particular place and didn't leave out anything important.

People working at area chambers of commerce and visitor bureaus, as well as shopkeepers, innkeepers, and restaurant owners, were very helpful in providing me with information. I wish I could thank everyone by name, but space does not permit. A sincere thank you if you helped in any way.

Finally, I'd like to thank the folks at The Countryman Press (a division of W. W. Norton & Company) for asking me to write this guidebook for them. It was a lot of work, but quite an adventure!

LEFT: HIGH FALLS GORGE, WILMINGTON

Introduction

New York: When most people hear that, they envision New York City, or perhaps Niagara Falls and Buffalo on the western end of the state. However, there is so much more to New York State. There are many interesting places located on the backroads and byways of the state, often just a short distance from major cities.

While this guide covers something from every region of upstate New York, from mountains, lakes, and beaches to everything in between, it is by no means a comprehensive guide of all there is to see and do in this vast area of the state, which, for the purposes of this book, is defined as everything in the state except the New York City area and Long Island. Information about those two areas could fill an entire book by itself! The nine regions that make up the upstate area are: Adirondacks, Catskills, Chautauqua-Allegany, Greater Niagara, 1000 Islands, Capital-Saratoga, Central, Finger Lakes, and Hudson Valley.

Writing about everything to see and do in upstate New York would be an impossible task, and even if one could accomplish that, the sheer volume of information would overwhelm most readers. This book offers a sampling of some of the most intriguing places to visit in upstate New York, some of them off the beaten trail, others close to some of the larger towns and cities. Some well-known destinations are mentioned, as well as places you may have never heard of before. This book includes areas along the Hudson River, Lakes Erie and Ontario, the Saint Lawrence River and the Erie Canal, as well as the scenic regions of the Adirondack and Catskill Mountains.

When I started brainstorming places to include in this book, I had well over 50 ideas for chapters in mind. However, I quickly realized a book with that much information would be as thick as a phone book! Plus, I would never be able to visit all those places and get the book done on a timely basis. So I

LETCHWORTH STATE PARK

whittled it down to 20 drives and destinations, perfect for day trips, weekend getaways, or even a week's vacation if you're so inclined.

I've tried to include something for everyone: history buffs, shoppers, boaters, wine and beer aficionados, outdoor enthusiasts, families with kids, car and motorcycle fans, and everyone who wants to learn more about New York State. Some of these drives will take you partly on the highway, while others will take you into the middle of nowhere. Some of the routes I've included have definite themes, such as a wine trail, while others string together a variety of attractions and sights along the way. Some are established scenic byways, while others are routes which I thought would be interesting to travel personally.

At the beginning of each chapter you get the basics of each drive: where to begin your trip, estimated time and mileage, and an overview of what to see and do on each drive. I'll even offer suggestions of side trips to take off the main route.

Please note that information in any travel-related book can change quickly, especially in rural, out-of-the-way places. While in general museums and other attractions don't go out of business that often, restaurants and stores frequently change ownership or close, so try to call ahead if you are traveling a long distance to a particular business.

Lodging prices in Upstate New York can range from very reasonable to extremely pricey. Here is a per-night guide to accomodations listed. Rates fluctuate seasonally.

$	$100 or less
$$	$101–$200
$$$	$201–$300
$$$$	$301 or above
**	Call for pricing

Fast Facts about New York

- One of the 13 original colonies
- Four US presidents from the state:
  - Martin Van Buren, 8th president, born in Kinderhook
  - Millard Fillmore, 13th president, born in Summerhill, lived in East Aurora, buried in Buffalo
  - Theodore Roosevelt, 26th president, born in New York City, inaugurated in Buffalo
  - Franklin Delano Roosevelt, 32nd president, born in Hyde Park
- The state has 62 counties
- 54,474 square miles
- 27th largest state by size

OVERLOOKING LAKE ONTARIO AT SODUS POINT

OPUS 40

If you want to learn more about the western region of New York State, my first book about the area, *Western New York: An Explorers Guide* (2008) is a good source. An updated version of the book, focusing mainly on Buffalo and Niagara Falls, is scheduled to be published in early 2018.

Here are some books by other Countryman Press authors that might be helpful if you want to explore some of the areas mentioned in more detail. For information about the Erie Canal, read *The Erie Canal* by Deborah Williams. The Finger Lakes region is highlighted in a book by Katharine Dyson, *Explorer's Guide Finger Lakes*. Read about the Adirondack region in *Explorer's Guide Adirondacks* by Annie Stoltie, and the Catskills and Hudson Valley in *Explorer's Guide Hudson Valley & Catskill Mountains* by Joanne Michaels, who is an expert on that region.

Christine A. Smyczynski,
Getzville, NY

TRAIL TO CHIMNEY BLUFFS, WALCOTT

TUSCARORA HEROES MONUMENT, CENTER STREET, LEWISTON

1

ROUTE 104:
THE COBBLESTONE TRAIL

From Lewiston to Rochester: Cobblestone Architecture, Wineries, Farm Markets, and More

ESTIMATED LENGTH: 75 miles

ESTIMATED TIME: 1–4 days

HIGHLIGHTS: The route, once a Native American footpath and later a stagecoach route used by the pioneers, is referred to as the Cobblestone Trail, as it has the distinction of having the most buildings of cobblestone construction of any highway in America. There are about 900 cobblestone buildings still in existence in North America; about 90 percent are located within 75 miles of Rochester. The "ridge" had been the shoreline of glacial Lake Iroquois; during the Ice Age, as the glaciers retreated, vast amounts of smooth round stones, known as cobblestones, were deposited in and around this region.

Of course you'll find more than just great architecture. Enjoy shopping, dining, history, and entertainment in Lewiston and the historic Erie Canal in some of the many towns and villages just south of Ridge Road. Mix in some wineries from the Niagara Wine Trail, along with farm markets and antiques shops, and you have a great way to spend the day, or several days if you choose to explore all the stops along the way.

GETTING THERE: This route runs west to east, from the Niagara River to the Rochester area. From Niagara Falls, follow the I-190 expressway north to Lewiston (Exit 25) and follow the signs to the village of Lewiston. This drive concludes in Spencerport, just west of the city of Rochester.

This route, which takes you through small quaint villages in rural Niagara, Orleans, and Monroe Counties, reflects the agricultural nature of this area. The drive begins in the historic Village of Lewiston, located along the Niagara River about 7 miles north of Niagara Falls. This walkable village was proclaimed the "Most Historic Square Mile in America" by then president Jimmy Carter in 1976. Established in 1798, it was named after Morgan

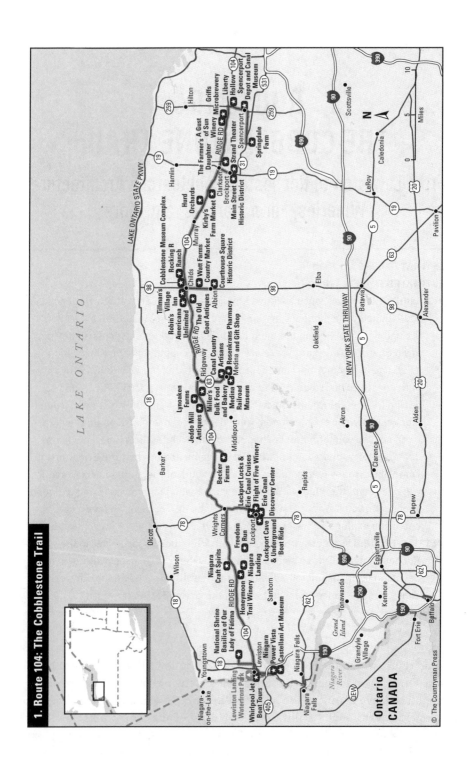

1. Route 104: The Cobblestone Trail

FREEDOM CROSSING MONUMENT BY LEWISTON WATERFRONT

Lewis, the third governor of New York State. Many buildings in the village date back to 1813, when the village was rebuilt after being burned down during the War of 1812. According to local legend, the cocktail was invented in Lewiston by Catherine Hustler when she stirred a gin mixture with a tail feather from a cockerel.

You'll want to explore the village on foot, so park your car in the lot at the foot of Center Street and take in the view of the Niagara River from **Lewiston Landing Waterfront Park**, one of the most scenic spots in town. The bronze Freedom Crossing Monument depicts the role Lewiston played in the Underground Railroad movement. There is also another bronze sculpture at the other end of town, at the corner of Center Street and Portage Road. The Tuscarora Heroes Monument depicts the Tuscarora Indians defending Lewiston against the 1813 British attack on the village.

If you enjoy thrills, go down to the docks and take a ride on the **Whirlpool Jet Boat Tours** through the lower Niagara River rapids.

Overlooking the river and the Lewiston Landing Waterfront Park is the upscale **Niagara Crossing Hotel & Spa**, a 67-room boutique hotel and spa.

Artpark State Park, a 200-acre state park, is just a short walk from the

NIAGARA CROSSING HOTEL AND SPA

village. Here you can experience natural beauty as well as performing arts during the summer months.

Strolling along Center Street you'll find many boutique shops, including **The End of the Road Boutique**, which has a variety of jewelry and accessories, **Canterbury Place**, which has all sorts of gift items and home decor, and **The Country Doctor**, which specializes in antiques.

There is also a nice selection of restaurants, including the **Brickyard**, which is noted for barbecue; **Carmelo's**, serving upscale contemporary cuisine; **Casa Antica** for fine Italian dining; and family favorites at **Apple Granny**. If you crave steak, check out the **Center Cut** steakhouse. Don't forget about **Water Street Landing**, which overlooks the river, as well as the **Lewiston Silo**, a very casual eatery, also on the water's edge. For coffee and sweets, check out **Orange Cat Coffee**, **Mangia**, **DiCamillo Bakery**, and the **Village Bake Shop**. For a more health-conscious selection, visit **700 Center Street Juice Bistro & Café**.

Annual events taking place in the village include the **Lewiston Arts Festival** and the **Lewiston Jazz Festival**, both of which take place in August. **The Lewiston Tour of Homes**, which benefits the **Historical Association of Lewiston**, takes place in early December. It features local homes decorated by professional decorators; a great event to get holiday decorating ideas. The annual Christmas Walk also takes place this same weekend.

Several attractions are located just a short drive from the village. The **Castellani Art Museum**, located on the campus of Niagara University, has permanent and special exhibits by local, national, and international artists. Right next door to the campus, the **New York Power Authority Niagara Power Vista**, located on the rim of the Niagara Gorge, has all sorts of interactive exhibits that demonstrate how electricity works.

Just north of the village, the **National Shrine Basilica of Our Lady of Fátima**, which was inspired by the Sanctuary of Fátima in Fátima, Portugal, was built by the Barnabite Fathers, an Italian religious order, in 1954. The focal point of the 20-acre shrine is the basilica, a dome-shaped church 100 feet in diameter and 55 feet high that depicts the Northern Hemisphere. A 13-foot statue of Our Lady of Fátima rests atop the dome. If you have the opportunity to visit the shrine in November or December, their annual Festival of Lights transforms the grounds into a wonderland of lighted displays that depict the true meaning of Christmas: the birth of Jesus. Almost all the items on display have been designed by Father Julio, the shrine's rector, and built by the shrine's maintenance staff.

When leaving Lewiston, head east along Route 104 and soon you will be

LEWISTON SILO RESTAURANT OVERLOOKING NIAGARA RIVER

TOP: NEW YORK POWER AUTHORITY NIAGARA POWER VISTA
BOTTOM: NATIONAL SHRINE BASILICA OF OUR LADY OF FÁTIMA, LEWISTON

in wine country, passing vineyard after vineyard. There are a number of local wineries on or close to Route 104 where you can sample the fruits of the vine. The soil and climate in this area just below the Niagara Escarpment are both ideal for growing wine-producing grapes. There are currently 22 wineries along the **Niagara Wine Trail**; however, that number will most likely continue to grow. Refer to the wine trail's website for a complete listing and map of the trail. Some of the wineries located on or near Route 104 in this area include **Honeymoon Trail Winery,** which has a cozy tasting room with a wood-burning fireplace. A short distance away, also along Route 104, you'll find **Niagara Craft Spirits,** a distillery. Other nearby wineries include **Freedom Run,** which has a light and airy tasting room; **Arrowhead Springs Vineyards,** just around the corner from Freedom Run; and **Niagara Landing Wine Cellars,** one of the oldest established wineries on the trail.

Continue on Route 104 until you get to Wrights Corners. You can continue

SIDE TRACKS

Lockport got its name from the famous "flight of five" twin set of locks on the Erie Canal, which was built between 1817 and 1825. Although one set of five of the original locks was removed in the early 1900s when the canal was modernized, the remaining set of five was left as a landmark, which is currently in the process of being restored to reflect its appearance during the Civil War era. Lockport's urban winery, aptly named **Flight of Five Winery,** which overlooks the historic flight of five, is located in Lockport's old city hall.

FLIGHT OF FIVE WINERY, LOCKPORT

Learn about Lockport's history at the **Erie Canal Discovery Center,** a state-of-the-art, multimedia interactive museum, or at the **Niagara County History Center.** The best way to see the Erie Canal is to take a cruise with the **Lockport Locks and Erie Canal Cruises.** Your two-hour narrated journey

(continued on next page)

includes "locking through" locks 34 and 35, the only double set of locks on the entire canal. Cruises are offered daily, May through October. Still another way to view Lockport is to take a tour with the **Lockport Cave and Underground Boat Ride**. This tour, which lasts about 75 minutes, begins with a view of both the modern locks and the flight of five. You then proceed to the cave, which was originally a water power tunnel used by industry in the mid-1800s. The cave tour concludes with an underground boat ride.

If you prefer more artistic endeavors, visit **Art 247**, which has an extensive gift shop with items made by local artists, along with artist studios. The nearby **Kenan Center** also has art exhibits and theater productions. Live per-

ERIE CANAL LOCKS, LOCKPORT

formances and first-run movies are featured at the historic **Palace Theatre**, which opened its doors in 1925.

When hunger strikes there are a number of great restaurants right in the city of Lockport, including **Danny Sheehan's**, **Garlock's**, and **The Shamus**, all noted for seafood and steak. More casual fare, like burgers, hot dogs, and ice cream, can be found at **Reid's**, which is open seasonally. If you wish to spend the night in Lockport, there are a number of options, including the **Lockport Inn & Suites**, family owned since 1968. There are also several national chain hotels, including Quality Inn, Best Western, and Hampton Inn. When you're done exploring the city of Lockport, head north up Route 78 back to Route 104 and continue east.

east on Route 104 or take a side trip south down Route 78 to the City of Lockport, located on the Erie Canal, which offers a perfect blend of history, art, and recreation.

If you have the time, make a right turn off Route 104 onto Quaker Road when you get to Gasport and check out **Becker Farms**, a 340-acre fruit and vegetable farm which has been run by the same family for five generations. In addition to having a large seasonal farm market where they sell fruits, vegetables, baked goods, jams, and more, including U-pick fruits in season, they also have a winery, **Vizcarra Vineyards**, and brewery, **Becker Brewing**, both open year-round. The farm is a popular place for weddings and other private parties. In the fall, families and school groups love to come here for their annual Pumpkin Fiesta.

Since this area is known for agriculture, you'll also find a plethora of farm markets along Route 104; some of them include **Harris Farm Market** in Gasport, **John B. Watson Farm** in Middleport, and **Fisher's Farm Market** in Medina, which has mini golf and a small restaurant in addition to seasonal produce. In that same area, **Miller's Bulk Food and Bakery**, an Amish-run business, has spice, jams, nut butters, baked goods, and a deli. **Jeddo Mill Antiques** can also be found on Route 104.

As you continue driving on Route 104, start looking for cobblestone structures. You'll notice three of them between Quaker Road and Route 63

SIDE TRACKS

Many of the buildings in Medina, which date back to the 1860s, are made of locally quarried Medina sandstone. Check out **Canal Country Artisans**, a craft co-op that has a large selection of handcrafted items and gifts. You can also find a nice selection of gift and household items at **Rosenkrans Pharmacy and Gift Shop**. There are also a number of restaurants to choose from, including **Zambistro**, known for upscale Italian dishes. You can also enjoy Italian dishes at **Avanti Pizza and Grill**. If you're in the mood for sandwiches, coffee and sweets, stop by the **Shirt Factory Café**, which is located in the former Newell Shirt Factory building.

Railroad aficionados will want to visit the **Medina Railroad Museum**, which is located in a 1905 wooden freight house that's 300 feet long and 34 feet wide, one of the largest buildings of its kind in the United States. All sorts of railroad memorabilia are on display, along with one of the largest HO-scale layouts in the country. Rail excursions are offered from the museum on a limited basis.

While you're in Medina be sure to check out the Erie Canal Culvert on Culvert Road, the only place along the canal where motorists can drive under the canal. It was built in 1825 to avoid the expense and time needed to build a bridge.

COBBLESTONE MUSEUM, CHILDS

in Medina. A cobblestone can be defined as a small round stone; these were very prevalent in this area as the result of glaciers retreating millions of years ago. Cobblestone masonry was developed by rural masons in this area during the early 1800s, shortly after the building of the Erie Canal. At that time it was considered a status symbol to be able to have a house built out of cobblestones.

Numerous cobblestone buildings can be found right along Ridge Road; however, most are private residences, so please just view them from the roadside and don't trespass. A good reference guide to bring along is the book *Cobblestone Quest*, by Rich and Sue Freeman, which has information about all the cobblestone buildings in the area, as well as maps and suggested driving tours.

In Medina, **Lynoaken Farms** retail market, which is located right on Ridge Road, is best known for its apples. In addition to apples and cider in the fall, they also sell a variety of locally made foods, candies, and arts and crafts. They also have a winery and tasting room, **Leonard Oakes Estates**, which features a number of wines, including whites, reds, fruit wines, and ice wines.

When you reach Route 63, turn right if you want to explore the village of Medina, which has a very quaint downtown area adjacent to the Erie Canal.

Return to Route 104 and continue traveling east. You'll see a couple of

SIDE TRACKS

Taking another side trip off Route 104, head down Route 98 toward Albion, stopping first at **Watt Farms Country Market**. Their gift shop features 25 flavors of homemade fudge, along with an ice cream parlor. On weekends visitors to the farm can enjoy a ride through the orchards on a 70-foot passenger train.

In the village of Albion, the Courthouse Square Historic District is on the National Register of Historic Places. The centerpiece of the district is the 1858 Greek Revival–style county courthouse, which is surrounded by 34 architecturally significant buildings, including seven churches. Albion, the Orleans county seat, was incorporated in 1826, just after the completion of the Erie Canal, which flows just north of the village.

antiques shops: **Robin's Americana Unlimited** and **The Old Goat Antiques**. You will also see many cobblestone structures between Route 63 and Route 98, including a cobblestone barn. When you arrive in Childs, at the intersection of Route 104 and 98, be sure to stop at the **Cobblestone Museum Complex**. There are eight historic buildings in this complex, three which are of cobblestone construction and designated National Historic Landmarks. These include the 1834 Universalist Church, which is the oldest church of cobblestone construction in North America; the 1840 Ward House, which served as the parsonage; and an 1849 cobblestone schoolhouse.

Around the corner from the museum is a wonderful restaurant, **Tillman's Village Inn**, which opened in 1824 as a stagecoach stop; it has been open almost continuously since then. They are noted for their prime rib. Tillman's also offers overnight accommodations in its **Fair Haven Inn**, which has four unique antique furnished rooms in an 1837 house plus four modern hotel rooms in a separate building. There is also an antiques shop, **Cobbleridge Antique Co-op**, across the street from the museum complex.

Get back on Route 104 and head about 10 miles east to the village of Holley, which was named after Myron Holley, one of the canal commissioners. One of the best known farm markets in Orleans County, **Hurd Orchards**, is located on Route 104 in Holley. The Hurd family has been in the farming business for seven generations. At this market you'll find a variety of in-season produce, baked goods, and the market's own gourmet jams and jellies.

After crossing into Monroe County, continue on Route 104; you'll see a couple more farm markets, **Kirby's** and **The Farmer's Daughter**, as well as **The Rocking R Ranch Market and Café**, which features organic and local meats and other foods. When you reach Route 19, turn right and head south to the village of Brockport, which has been dubbed "The Victorian Village on the Erie Canal." Many of the Victorian-era structures that line Brockport's Main Street, a designated historic district, were built during the Canal's construction period

APPLE TREE INN, BROCKPORT

in the early 1800s. You might want to take a walking tour of the village; maps can be found on the village's website, www.brockportny.org. If you walk all segments of the tour, it will take about an hour.

Since Brockport is a college town (home to SUNY Brockport), there are a number of interesting small shops and cafes in town, as well as the Strand Theater, a historic 1916 landmark theater which shows first-run movies. Some of the shops include **Bittersweet**, which is located in a former bank building, complete with the original counters and wooden floors. They carry a variety of jewelry, pottery, gift items, and natural fiber clothing. **Seaward Candies**, which has been in business since 1976, features handmade candies and other confections. **Lift Bridge Books** features two floors of books and toys. There are also a couple of antiques shops in the village.

Dining options include the **Red Bird Café**, which has wraps, paninis, and soups. **Stoneyard Brewery**, located right by the canal, offers pub fare along with house-made brews. The **Brockport Diner** serves up classic diner foods. One of Brockport's more popular restaurants, **The Apple Tree Inn**, located on Route 104 between Brockport and Spencerport, is a great place to stop for lunch. The restaurant, located in a circa 1839 farmhouse, is decorated with antiques and seasonal decor. They are noted for their chicken pot pie.

If you are looking to stay overnight in Brockport, the **Victorian Bed & Breakfast** offers five guest rooms in an 1890s Queen Ann Victorian, located just three blocks from the main shopping district.

One unique place in the Spencerport area is **Springdale Farm**, located in Northampton Park, off Route 31 just west of the village. Springdale Farm is a 200-acre working demonstration farm featuring historic farm buildings and a variety of animals. Two points of special note: First, Springdale Farm is operated by Heritage Christian Services, which offers assistance to developmentally disabled people, many of whom work at the farm. Second, it is home to the first robotic milking parlor in the Northeast that is open to the public for tours. Plan on taking the tour, as the robotic milking is fascinating to witness.

Return to Route 104 and continue east toward Spencerport. There are a number of interesting places along the way, including **A Gust of Sun Winery** and **Griffs Microbrewery**, which are located next to each other. There are a couple of large antiques stores in this area, including **Americana Accents** and **Liberty Hollow**. Restaurants located here include **Abe's** and **Sullivan's Charbroil**. Take Route 259 south to get to Spencerport; where there are a few shops and restaurants right in the village by the canal. Of special interest is the **Butterfly Kisses Sweet Shoppe**, which has 50 varieties of chocolate, retro candies, fudge, and bulk candies. **Café Macchiato** has local merchandise and a small café.

SPENCERPORT DEPOT & CANAL MUSEUM

Visit the **Spencerport Depot & Canal Museum,** located along the canal. The building served as the depot for the Rochester, Lockport, and Buffalo Suburban Trolley Line from 1908 to 1931. After trolley service stopped, it was a private home for many years before being donated to the village of Spencerport in 2002 and moved to its present location. It opened in 2007 as a museum with exhibits on local history and the Erie Canal. It also serves as a visitor center, offering restroom and shower facilities for boaters staying overnight at the docks. The depot is open during the canal season, May through mid-October.

IN THE AREA

Accommodations

FAIR HAVEN INN, 14369 Ridge Road, Childs, 585-589-9151. www.tillmans villageinn.com. $.

LOCKPORT INN & SUITES, 315 South Transit Road, Lockport, 716-434-5595. A 90-room hotel, family-owned and family-operated since 1968. $.

NIAGARA CROSSING HOTEL & SPA, 100 Center Street, Lewiston, 716-754-9070. An upscale 67-room boutique hotel that overlooks the lower Niagara River. www.niagaracrossinghotelandspa.com. $$.

VICTORIAN BED & BREAKFAST, 320 Main Street, Brockport, 585-637-7519. www.victorianbandb.com. $.

Attractions and Recreation

A GUST OF SUN WINERY, 5324 Ridge Road, Spencerport, 585-617-3000. www.agustofsun.com

ARROWHEAD SPRINGS VINEYARDS, 4746 Town Line Road, Lockport, 716-434-4136. www.arrowheadspringvineyards.com

ART 247, 247 Market Street, Lockport, 716-404-9884. www.theart247.com

ARTPARK STATE PARK, 450 South Fourth Street, Lewiston, 716-754-4375. www.artpark.net

BECKER FARMS, 3760 Quaker Road, Gasport, 716-772-2211. Farm market; winery, **Vizcarra Vineyards**; and brewery, **Becker Brewing.** www.becker farms.com

CASTELLANI ART MUSEUM, Route 104 on the campus of Niagara University, Lewiston, 716-286-8200. Open Tuesday–Saturday 11:00 AM–5:00 PM, Sunday 1:00–5:00 PM Admission is free. www.niagara.edu/cam

COBBLESTONE MUSEUM COMPLEX, 14389 Ridge Road, Childs, 585-589-9013. Open late June–early September, Tuesday–Saturday 11:00 AM–5:00 PM, Sunday 1:00–5:00 PM www.cobblestonemuseum.org

ERIE CANAL DISCOVERY CENTER, 24 Church Street, Lockport, 716-439-0431. www.niagarahistory.org/discovery-center

FLIGHT OF FIVE WINERY, 2 Pine Street, Lockport, 716-433-3360. www.flightoffivewinery.com

FREEDOM RUN WINERY, 5138 Lower Mountain Road, Lockport, 716-433-4136. www.freedomrunwinery.com

GRIFFS MICROBREWERY, 5324 Ridge Road, Spencerport, 585-617-3843. www.griffsbrewery.com

HISTORICAL ASSOCIATION OF LEWISTON, 469 Plain Street, Lewiston. 716-754-4214. www.hstoriclewiston.org

HONEYMOON TRAIL WINERY, 4120 Ridge Road, Cambria, 716-438-3255. www.honeymoontrailwinery.com

KENAN CENTER, 433 Locust Street, Lockport, 716-433-2617. www.kenan center.org

LOCKPORT CAVE AND UNDERGROUND BOAT RIDE, 5 Gooding Street, Lockport, 716-438-0174. www.lockportcave.com

LOCKPORT LOCKS AND ERIE CANAL CRUISES, 210 Market Street, Lockport, 800-378-0352. www.lockportlocks.com

LYNOAKEN FARMS AND LEONARD OAKES ESTATES WINERY, 10609 Ridge Road (Route 104), Medina, 585-798-1060. www.oakeswinery.com

MEDINA RAILROAD MUSEUM, 530 West Avenue, Medina, 585-798-6106. www.railroadmuseum.net

NATIONAL SHRINE BASILICA OF OUR LADY OF FÁTIMA, 1023 Swann Road, Lewiston, 716-754-7489. www.fatimashrine.com

NEW YORK POWER AUTHORITY NIAGARA POWER VISTA, 5777 Lewiston Road (Route 104), Lewiston, 716-286-6661. Open daily from 9:00 AM–5:00 PM. (Closed Christmas Eve, Christmas Day, New Year's Eve, and New Year's Day.) Admission is free. www.nypa.gov

NIAGARA COUNTY HISTORICAL SOCIETY, 215 Niagara Street, Lockport, 716-434-7433. www.niagarahistory.org

NIAGARA CRAFT SPIRITS, 4408 Ridge Road, Cambria, 716-438-7418. www.niagaracraftspirits.com

NIAGARA LANDING WINE CELLARS, 4434 Van Dusen Road, Lockport, 716-433-8405. www.niagaralanding.com

NIAGARA WINE TRAIL, www.niagarawinetrail.org

PALACE THEATRE, 2 East Avenue, Lockport, 716-438-1130. www.lockportpalacetheatre.com.

SPENCERPORT DEPOT & CANAL MUSEUM, 16 East Avenue, Spencerport, 585-352-0942. Open Tuesday–Saturday 11:00 AM–5:00 PM. www.spencerportdepot.com

SPRINGDALE FARM, 700 Colby Street, Spencerport, 585-349-2090. Open year-round. Free admission to grounds, fee for milking parlor tour. www.springdalefarm.org

Dining and Nightlife

Lewiston

700 CENTER STREET JUICE BISTRO & CAFÉ, 700 Center Street, Lewiston, 716-754-2277. www.700centerstreet.com

APPLE GRANNY, 433 Center Street, Lewiston, 716-754-2028. www.applegranny.com

BRICKYARD, 432 Center Street, Lewiston, 716-754-7227. www.brickyardpub
.com

CARMELO'S, 425 Center Street, Lewiston, 716-754-3211. www.carmelos
-restaurant.com

CASA ANTICA, 490 Center Street, Lewiston, 716-754-4904. www.casa
anticarestaurant.com

CENTER CUT: THE VILLAGE STEAKHOUSE, 453 Center Street, Lewiston, 716-246-2023. Open Sunday 4:00–9:00 PM, Monday–Thursday 5:00–10:00 PM. Friday and Saturday 5:00–11:00 PM. www.thevillagesteakhouse
.com

DICAMILLO BAKERY, 535 Center Street, Lewiston, 716-754-2218.

LEWISTON SILO, North Water Street, Lewiston, 716-754-9680. www
.lewistonsilo.com

MANGIA, 621 Center Street, Lewiston, 716-754-1517.

ORANGE CAT COFFEE, 703 Center Street, Lewiston, 716-754-2888.

VILLAGE BAKE SHOPPE, 417 Center Street, Lewiston, 716-754-2300. www
.villagebakeshoppe.com

WATER STREET LANDING, 115 South Water Street, Lewiston, 716-754-9200. www.waterstreetlanding.com

Lockport

DANNY SHEEHAN'S, 491 West Avenue, Lockport, 716-433-4666. www
.dannysheehans.com

GARLOCK'S, 35 South Transit Road, Lockport, 716-433-5595. www.garlocks
restaurant.com

REID'S, 150 Lake Avenue at Clinton Street, Lockport, 716-434-3105.

THE SHAMUS, 98 West Avenue, Lockport, 716-433-9809. www.theshamus
.com

Medina/Albion

AVANTI PIZZA AND GRILL, 500 Main Street, Medina, 585-798-1100. www .iloveavanti.com

ROCKING R RANCH MARKET & CAFÉ, 14877 Ridge Road, Kent, 585-283-4239. www.myfatcattle.com

SHIRT FACTORY CAFÉ, 111 West Center Street, Medina, 585-798-2633. www.shirtfactorycafe.com

TILLMAN'S VILLAGE INN, 14369 Ridge Road, Childs, 585-589-9151. www. tillmansvillageinn.com

ZAMBISTRO, 408 Main Street, Medina, 585-798-2433. www.zambistro.com

Brockport/Spencerport

ABE'S, 5232 West Ridge, Spencerport, 585-617-3000.

THE APPLE TREE INN, 7407 West Ridge Road, Brockport, 585-637-6440. www.appletreeinn.us

BROCKPORT DINER, 11 Erie Street, Brockport, 585-637-4060.

CAFÉ MACCHIATO, 123 South Union Street, Spencerport, 585-617-4912. Open Monday–Friday 7:00 AM–8:00 PM, Saturday 9:00 AM–8:00 PM.

RED BIRD CAFÉ, 25 Main Street, Brockport, 585-637-3340. www.redbird cafeandgiftshop.com

STONEYARD BREWERY, 1 Main Street, Brockport, 585-637-3390. Open Monday–Saturday 11:00 AM–2:00 AM, Sunday 12:00–10:00 PM. www.stone yardbrewingcompany.com

SULLIVAN'S CHARBROIL, 4712 West Ridge Road, Spencerport, 585-352-5860.

Shopping

Lewiston

CANTERBURY PLACE, 547 Center Street, Lewiston, 716-754-4818.

THE COUNTRY DOCTOR, 549 Center Street, Lewiston, 716-754-2614.

END OF THE ROAD BOUTIQUE, 335 Center Street, Lewiston, 716-754-2350.

Medina/Albion/Holley

CANAL COUNTRY ARTISANS, 135 East Center Street, Medina, 585-798-7460. www.canalcountryartisans.com

COBBLERIDGE ANTIQUE CO-OP, 14462 Ridge Road, Albion, 585-283-4009. Open all year, Wednesday 12:00–4:00 PM, Thursday–Sunday 10:30 AM–5:00 PM.

FISHER'S FARM MARKET, 11074 Ridge Road, Medina, 585-332-9167.

HARRIS FARM MARKET, 8475 Ridge Road, Gasport, 716-772-5229.

HURD ORCHARDS, 17260 Ridge Road, Holley, 585-638-8838. Open May–December. www.hurdorchards.com

JEDDO MILL ANTIQUES, 10267 Ridge Road, Medina, 585-735-3535. Open Thursday–Sunday 11:00 AM–5:00 PM. www.jeddomillantiques.com

JOHN B. WATSON FARM, 9413 Ridge Road, Middleport, 716-735-3286.

KIRBY'S FARM MARKET, 9739 Ridge Road, Clarkson, 585-637-2600.

MILLER'S BULK FOOD AND BAKERY, 10858 Ridge Road, Medina, 585-798-9700. Open Monday–Saturday 8:00 AM–5:00 PM.

OLD GOAT ANTIQUES, 14069 Ridge Road, Albion, 585-298-6167.

ROBIN'S AMERICANA UNLIMITED, 14007 Ridge Road, Albion, 585-589-2380.

ROSENKRANS PHARMACY AND GIFT SHOP, 526 Main Street, Medina, 585-798-1650. Open Monday–Friday 8:30 AM–8:00 PM, Saturday 9:00 AM–5:00 PM, Sunday 10:00 AM–1:00 PM. www.rosenkranspharmacy.com

WATT FARMS, 3121 Oak Orchard Road (Route 98), Albion, 800-274-5897. Open seasonally, Monday–Saturday 10:00 AM–8:00 PM, Sunday 11:00 AM–8:00 PM. www.wattfarms.com

Brockport/Spencerport

AMERICANA ACCENTS, 5319 Ridge Road, Spencerport, 585-352-1920.

BITTERSWEET, 41 Main Street, Brockport, 585-637-4774. www.bittersweet brockport.com

BUTTERFLY KISSES SWEET SHOPPE, 12 Amity Street, Spencerport, 585-349-4441. www.butterflykissessweetshoppe.com

FARMER'S DAUGHTER, 8089 Ridge Road, Brockport, 585-431-3267.

LIBERTY HOLLOW, 4975 Ridge Road West, Spencerport, 585-349-4500. www.libertyhollow.com

LIFT BRIDGE BOOKS, 45 Main Street, Brockport, 585-637-9200. www .liftbridgebooks.com

SEAWARD CANDIES, 7 Main Street, Brockport, 585-637-4120.

Other Contacts

LEWISTON ART FESTIVAL, www.artcouncil.org

LEWISTON JAZZ FESTIVAL, www.lewistonjazz.com

LEWISTON TOUR OF HOMES, www.lewistontourofhomes.com

LOCKPORT, www.discoverlockport.com

NIAGARA RIVER REGION CHAMBER OF COMMERCE, 716-754-9500. www.niagarariverregion.com

NIAGARA TOURISM AND CONVENTION CORPORATION, 10 Rainbow Boulevard, Niagara Falls, 1-877-FALLS-US. Information about Niagara County. www.niagara-usa.com

ORLEANS COUNTY CHAMBER OF COMMERCE, 212 North Main Street, Albion, 585-589-7727. www.orleanschamber.com

ORLEANS COUNTY TOURISM, 14016 Route 31, Albion, 800-724-0314. www.orleanscountytourism.com

SPENCERPORT CHAMBER OF COMMERCE, 129 South Union Street, Spencerport, 585-617-0200. www.spencerportchamber.org

VILLAGE OF BROCKPORT, 49 State Street, Brockport, 585-637-5300. www.brockportny.org

2

LAKE ONTARIO'S SHORE
From Youngstown to Chimney Bluffs

ESTIMATED LENGTH: 115 miles

ESTIMATED TIME: 1–2 days

HIGHLIGHTS: This route follows both the Lake Ontario shoreline and part of the Great Lakes Seaway Trail, a 518-mile-long scenic route that runs from the Ohio/Pennsylvania border to Massena, New York. If you make only a couple of stops along the way, you'll be able to cover this route in a day. However, if you want to explore all the towns and attractions mentioned in this chapter, allow two days or more. It's best to take this drive on a sunny day, as many of the stops are best visited in nicer weather.

GETTING THERE: This drive starts in Youngstown, New York, located at the end of the Niagara Scenic Parkway, which begins in Niagara Falls. From Youngstown, follow Route 18, which is part of the **Great Lakes Seaway Trail**. You'll travel on the Lake Ontario State Parkway, a scenic route, into the Rochester area and continue along the Great Lakes Seaway Trail until your drive concludes at Chimney Bluffs State Park in Wolcott.

Start your journey in Youngstown, which is at the mouth of the Niagara River. The main attraction in this area is **Old Fort Niagara**, located in Fort Niagara State Park. Structures in the fort include the French Castle, a designated National Historic Landmark which is the oldest building in the Great Lakes region. Costumed docents demonstrate 18th-century military life, and special reenactments take place several times a year. Allow a couple of hours to tour the fort.

Continue your journey east on Route 18, heading toward the village of Wilson. You'll first pass **Wilson Tuscarora State Park**, a 395-acre park that

OLCOTT LIGHTHOUSE ALONG LAKE ONTARIO, OLCOTT. THIS REPLICA WAS BUILT IN 2003

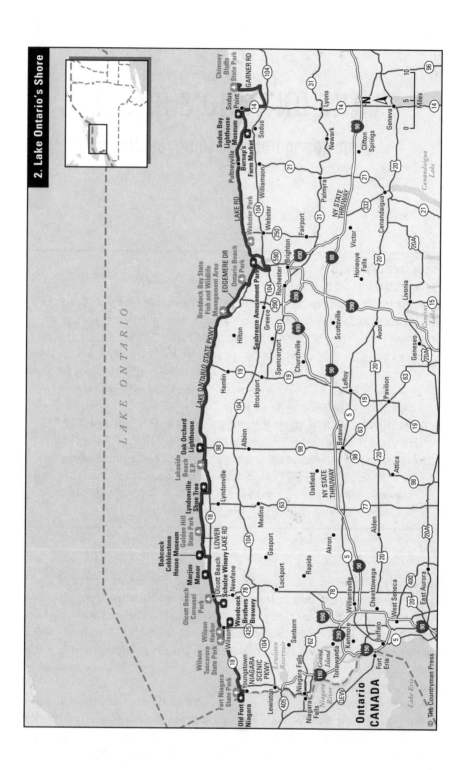

LAKE ONTARIO

Chimney
Bluffs
State Park

GARNER RD

104

96

31

Lyons

10

Sodus Point

Sodus Bay
Lighthouse
Museum

14

Sodus

14

Geneva

5

Miles

14

N

Pultneyville

Burnap's
Farm Market

Williamson

Sodus

90

Clifton
Springs

0

LAKE RD

104

Webster
Park

21

Palmyra

Newark

20

21

Webster

250

Fairport

31

NY STATE
THRUWAY

332

Canandaigua

21

Canandaigua
Lake

EDGEMERE DR

Ontario Beach
Park

590

Brighton

490

Victor

20A

Braddock Bay State
Fish and Wildlife
Management Area

104

Rochester

390

90

Honeoye
Falls

Seabreeze Amusement Park

Greece

390

Livonia

15

531

490

Scottsville

390

Conesus Lake

Hilton

Spencerport

Churchville

Avon

Hamlin

19

Brockport

19

LeRoy

90

Geneseo

20A

104

5

Pavilion

63

Albion

98

Batavia

63

19

Lakeside
Beach
S.P.

Oak Orchard
Lighthouse

98

Attica

20

98

Lyndonville
Shoe Tree

Lyndonville

Oakfield

NY STATE
THRUWAY

77

Golden Hill
State Park

18

Medina

63

Alden

20A

Babcock
Cobblestone
House Museum

LOWER
LAKE RD

104

Gasport

Akron

5

Marjim
Manor

Olcott Beach
Carousel
Park

Olcott Beach
Schulze Winery

78

Newfane

Rapids

90

Lockport

400

West Seneca

East Aurora

Woodcock
Brothers
Brewery

Sanborn

78

Williamsville

20

Wilson
Tuscarora
State Park

425

Wilson

104

62

Cheektowaga

Kenmore

490

Wilson Harbor

18

290

Buffalo

5

Fort Niagara
State Park

Youngstown

NIAGARA
SCENIC
PKWY

Lewiston
Reservoir

Grand
Island

190

Fort
Erie

Ontario
CANADA

Old Fort
Niagara

Lewiston

405

Niagara River

190

Tonawanda

190

Lake Erie

Niagara
Falls

Niagara
Falls

LAKE ONTARIO STATE PKWY

© The Countryman Press

has hiking trails, a boat launch, picnic areas, playgrounds, and a swimming beach.

Stop at Wilson Harbor, which is very picturesque. There are a number of small seasonal boutique shops in the harbor area along with the **Wilson Boat House Restaurant**, which is located directly on the water. It has the largest covered outdoor patio in the area. Enjoy a variety of foods here, from sandwiches and burgers to steak, seafood, and even rack of lamb. Just around the corner is the Wilson Pier, which has access to the waterfront and public restroom facilities.

Take a short detour down Route 425 to **Woodcock Brothers Brewery**, the first brewery in Niagara County to brew beer on-site and serve it in their restaurant. It is located in a historic old building that was once used for cold storage.

SIGN ALONG MAIN STREET IN YOUNGSTOWN

Head back to Route 18, where you can visit a few of the wineries that are part of the **Niagara Wine Trail**. Some of these include **Victorianbourg Wine Estate**, which specializes in European style wines. They have a lovely rose garden with over 40 varieties of roses, all with

FORT NIAGARA STATE PARK ENTRANCE, YOUNGSTOWN

WILSON PIER, WILSON

the word *Victoria* in their name. A little farther down the road, **Black Willow Winery** produces several artisan wines along with a selection of mead (honey wine). Just a short drive down Coomer Road is **Schulze Winery**, which has won awards for its ice wines.

Our next stop on the journey will be the quiet lakeside community of Olcott Beach. Stop in the red caboose at the corner of Routes 18 and 78, where you'll find all sorts of regional tourism information.

Check out the **Lakeview Village Shoppes**, a collection of small boutique gift shops on a boardwalk overlooking the lake. These shops carry a variety of merchandise, including nautical items, jewelry, chocolate treats, home decor, and more. If you have young children, they will enjoy the **Olcott Beach Carousel Park**, which has a restored 1928 Hershell-Spillman carousel and several other vintage kiddie rides. The park is open seasonally and rides are only 25 cents! This unique attraction offers today's visitors a glimpse into Olcott's golden era, when it was *the* place to be back in the early 1900s. Krull Park, overlooking Lake Ontario, contains a small beach and has good fishing.

Back in the day, the town had several hotels with grand ballrooms attracting the top musical acts of the time. The largest of these hotels was the 100-room Olcott Beach Hotel, located right on the water's edge, where the present-day beach is. During the Great Depression people couldn't afford to come, so the hotels and other attractions fell into disrepair and were eventually demolished. Olcott Beach saw a brief revival in the 1940s, with two amusement parks opening for a short period.

In 1999, a group of area citizens restored the 1940s-era carousel building from the former Olcott Amusement Park and were able to acquire and restore the vintage carousel, manufactured in 1928 in nearby North Tonawanda. Volunteers have also restored five other rides, including a 1940s vintage kiddie car ride from Olcott's New Rialto Amusement Park.

Looking for a bite to eat? Locals enjoy the **Park Place Restaurant**, which has an old-fashioned diner atmosphere, with good, reasonably priced food. Other places to eat in town include **Captain's Gallery** for casual dining and **Mariner's Landing**, a seafood restaurant.

Before leaving Olcott, take a short drive down Route 78 to get some freshly made popcorn, either traditional or caramel corn, from **Bye's Popcorn**, an Olcott Beach tradition since 1923. The roadside stand is open seasonally. The former Olcott fire station, also on Route 78, has been converted to a hotel, **Old Olcott Beach Fire Station**, with several guest rooms and a restaurant on the lower level.

Continuing driving along Route 18, you may want to stop for wine tasting at **Marjim Manor**, a charming winery located in an 1854 mansion, which is purportedly haunted. The winery produces a variety of fruit wines, each having a unique name and label related to the history of the home.

If you're traveling on a Saturday or Sunday, stop by the **Babcock Cobblestone House Museum**. This 1848 cobblestone home, built by farmer Jeptha Babcock, is maintained and furnished by the Town of Somerset Historical Society. It has been restored to reflect 19th-century life.

Right down the road from the museum is the Somerset Power Generating Station. Turn left at the first road just past the station, Hartland Road, which turns into Lower Lake Road. You'll have a much better view of the lake from this road than if you remained on Route 18.

Black Bird Cider Works, part of the Niagara Wine Trail and the only producer of hard cider in Niagara County, is located in this area. Stop by to sample a glass or two of their hard ciders, which range from sweet to dry. Their ciders are made from apples grown in their own orchards.

Another place to stop on a summer weekend is the **Thirty Mile Point Lighthouse** at **Golden Hill State Park**. The 60-foot-tall, circa 1875 lighthouse, made of hand-carved stone, was built to warn ships of a rocky shoal in Lake Ontario: the site of at least five shipwrecks before the lighthouse was built. You can even stay overnight at the lighthouse in the original lighthouse keeper's quarters. This second floor, two-bedroom apartment is available for weekly rentals during the summer and two-day minimum stays the rest of the year.

As you drive along Lower Lake Road, the road twists and turns several times. At one of the turns (Lyndonville Road), you'll see a dead end to the left; head down there to a parking area for a nice view of the lake. A historical marker says that this was once the location of the Yates Pier, a 275-foot pier built in 1875, which was used when shipping lumber and grain and also for passenger ships.

An interesting roadside attraction at the corner of Lakeshore and Foss Roads is the **Lyndonville Shoe Tree**. This row of four ash trees has hundreds of shoes hanging from its branches and nailed to its trunks. It started in 1986, when a young lady had some old shoes to get rid of and heard of a Canadian tradition of making a wish and then throwing a pair of shoes up into a tree to help make the wish come true. She enlisted her boyfriend to help her do this and then encouraged their friends to also add some of their shoes. People continue to add to the collection to this day.

Your next point of reference is **Lakeside Beach State Park**. This 743-acre park on the shores of Lake Ontario offers a panoramic view of the lake. There are 274 campsites, all with electric hook-ups, located in this scenic park. Facilities include picnic areas, playground, hot showers, camp store, and laundry facilities. The park is open for camping late April–late October and in winter for hiking, cross-country skiing, and snowmobiling.

Once you see Lakeside Beach State Park, start looking for the signs for **Lake Ontario State Parkway** and enter the parkway. This 35-mile-long parkway, part of the Great Lakes Seaway Trail, runs through Orleans and Monroe Counties. It was built in the 1960s as a scenic highway. There are many parts of the roadway that travel almost at lake's edge, and there are some great views of the lake. Note that the road can be quite bumpy in spots.

Head back to the parkway and continue east. The next stop you'll want to make is at **Braddock Bay Wildlife Management Area**, a popular spot to view hawks, owls, and other birds of prey during spring migration. Get off the parkway on East Manitou Road and follow the signs to Braddock Bay. There is a hawk-viewing station, as well as a nature trail, playground, and picnic area.

From Braddock Bay, take Edgemere Drive, which runs along Lake Ontario for several miles past small beach cottages. There are a lot of places to fish in this area. Just make sure you have a fishing license, as officers do check for them. If you want a bite to eat, both the **Charbroil House** and **Schaller's Drive-In** offer hot dogs, burgers, and more. Edgemere Drive turns into Beach Avenue, where your next stop will be **Ontario Beach Park**, which is

BABCOCK COBBLESTONE HOUSE MUSEUM, BARKER

SHOE TREE OF LYNDONVILLE

said to have the best natural sand beach in the Great Lakes region. It is a great place to stop to take a break to stretch your legs if you've been driving for a while.

Back in the early 1900s there was a huge amusement park here, which drew 50,000 people each day during the summer. While the amusement park is long gone, Ontario Beach Park is still a popular place. In addition to the beach, the park has a 1905 Dentzel carousel and a very long fishing pier, which is great for taking a stroll on. There is a concession stand in the park and several restaurants located along Lake Avenue.

To get a unique view of the lake, walk west down Beach Avenue to the "secret sidewalk." The sidewalk's entrance is located between the driveways of 490 and 510 Beach Avenue. This public walkway along the shore of Lake Ontario offers great views of the lake, as well as the chance to see the manicured lawns and gardens of area residents.

Another interesting attraction near Ontario Beach Park is the **Charlotte-Genesee Lighthouse** (off Lake Avenue, behind Holy Cross Church), a 40-foot-tall Medina sandstone lighthouse which overlooks the Genesee River and the Port of Rochester. Built in 1821, it is the second-oldest lighthouse in the Great Lakes Region. The Lighthouse is open for tours Friday through Monday, May to October and weekends only in November.

Continuing your journey, cross over the Genesee River on the Stutson Bridge and follow Pattonwood Drive to Lake Shore Boulevard, which goes

SIDE TRACKS

If you like lighthouses, exit the parkway at Point Breeze (Route 98) and drive toward the lake until the road ends in a parking lot. Here you can walk along a long pier, popular with fishermen, or visit the **Oak Orchard Lighthouse.** The original was built in 1871; this replica, which houses a museum, was built in 2010. The museum is staffed by volunteers and is generally open Friday evenings and weekend afternoons.

Stop for a bite to eat at the **Black North Inn**, a casual restaurant and bar located near the lighthouse. Around the corner on Route 98, **Breeze In Again** is open for breakfast, lunch, and dinner, as well as for ice cream.

through **Durand Eastman Park**, an over-1,000-acre park which has an 18-hole golf course, arboretum, and hiking trails. Exit the park, then turn left on Culver Road to make a stop at **Seabreeze Amusement Park**. It is the fourth-oldest amusement park in the United States; it originally opened in 1879 as a picnic grove. Today it has over 75 rides and waterpark attractions. The Jack Rabbit Roller Coaster at Seabreeze is the oldest continuously operating roller coaster in America. There are also several casual, seasonal restaurants, referred to as Hot Dog Row, along Culver Road. Also on Culver Road is **Whispering Pines Miniature Golf,** America's oldest miniature golf course; it opened in 1930, operated by the adjacent **Parkside Diner**, which is open for breakfast, lunch, and dinner.

When you're done in this area, take Culver Road south to Route 104 east and cross over Irondequoit Bay. Turn left on Bay Road to Lake Road. Turn right on Lake Road; as you travel, be sure to glance through the trees to see some truly magnificent homes.

Webster Park. A 550-acre park with a fishing pier and campground, as well as several hiking trails, can be found along Lake Road. If you are looking for upscale dining with a great view of the lake, check out **Hedges Nine Mile Point Restaurant** in Webster, which is open seasonally for lunch and dinner.

In Sodus you may want to stop at **Burnap's Farm Market**, which has been selling homegrown fruits and vegetables since 1970. They also operate the **Garden Café**, which serves sandwiches, soups, and salads for lunch, as well as baked goods and ice cream.

The Village of Sodus Point has a few attractions to check out. The **Sodus Bay Lighthouse Museum**, operated by the Sodus Bay Historical Society, is located in a circa 1879 lighthouse which was in service from 1871 to 1901. The museum has exhibits on the maritime history of the lake and lighthouse keepers who served here. There is a park next to the museum which has a great view of Lake Ontario. Concerts take place in the park by the museum Sunday afternoons from July to Labor Day.

Just a short walk or drive away from the lighthouse museum is Sodus Point Beach Park, a small but well-maintained beach which has a playground right on the sand and a fishing pier.

Looking for a bite to eat and maybe a drink or two? Check out **Captain Jack's Goodtime Tavern**, a full-service restaurant, open year-round, which serves everything from burgers to steak and lobster. They also have an upstairs deck, open seasonally, with views of Sodus Bay and Lake Ontario.

Before leaving town, be sure to take a look at the three murals located on the Sodus Point Firehouse. The mural on the west side of the building depicts the Underground Railroad and the role it played in the area. On the east side of the firehouse, one mural depicts Native Americans fishing near Chimney Bluffs in the 1450s, while the second mural depicts the Battle of Sodus Point that occurred during the War of 1812.

An interesting phenomenon takes place involving the two eastern murals and the shadow of the cross from the Sodus Point Episcopal Church across the street. The shadow of the cross moves across the murals during the summer months in a transition referred to as "the blessing of the murals." Read more about it at www.historicsoduspoint.com/blessing-of-the-murals.

If you want to stay overnight in this area, consider the **Maxwell Creek Bed & Breakfast**, which is located on 6 acres of land. There are five guest rooms in the main house, which is of cobblestone construction; there is also a private cobblestone cottage available. The **Carriage House Inn**, located right by the lighthouse museum, offers large, comfortable rooms, all with private baths. It is within walking distance of the beach and restaurants.

The final attraction on this drive is **Chimney Bluffs State Park**. The centerpiece of this 597-acre park is the line of large bluffs along the lake; the clay drumlins were formed by a glacier, then eroded by weather and waves from the lake.

There are several hiking trails throughout the park, including the Bluff Trail, which hugs the edge of the cliffs as you hike to the bluffs, a unique sight to see. From the main entrance parking area on Garner Road, hike about a half hour to actually see the bluffs up close; the view is spectacular

A Word of Caution

Use extreme caution when hiking the bluffs; a sign in the parking lot warns, THE VIEW OF THE BLUFFS SHOULD TAKE YOUR BREATH AWAY, NOT YOUR LIFE. The Bluff Trail is right on the edge of a very steep cliff; there are no railings, and the ground is very uneven. The bluffs are unstable and the top of one of them could collapse without warning, so don't get close to the edge and stay on the trail.

CHIMNEY BLUFFS STATE PARK, WOLCOTT

and unworldly, so be sure to bring a camera. You can also access the Bluff Trail from the East Bay Road parking area. In addition, you can hike along the lakeshore at the base of the bluffs.

After the stress of hiking the Bluff Trail, you'll probably feel like you need a drink. **Thorpe Vineyards** is located just a half mile east of the park. Operating since 1988, it is the oldest winery in Wayne County.

IN THE AREA

Accommodations

CARRIAGE HOUSE INN, 8375 Wickham Boulevard, Sodus Point, 315-483-2100. www.carriage-house-inn.com. $$.

COTTAGE RENTALS There are a number of cottages for rent in the Olcott area; see www.olcott-newfane.com for a complete listing. **.

LAKESIDE BEACH STATE PARK, Route 18, Waterport, 585-682-4888. Open year-round, dawn to dusk. There are 274 campsites, all with electric hook-ups, located in this scenic park. Facilities include picnic areas, a playground, hot showers, camp store, and laundry facilities. The park is open for camping late April–late October. $.

MAXWELL CREEK BED & BREAKFAST, 7563 Lake Road, Sodus, 315-483-2222. www.maxwellcreekinn-bnb.com. $$.

OLD OLCOTT BEACH FIRE STATION, 1573 Lockport Street, Olcott, 716-778-4443. www.oldolcottbeachfirestation.com. $.

THIRTY MILE POINT LIGHTHOUSE AT GOLDEN HILL STATE PARK, 9691 Lower Lake Road, Barker, 800-456-CAMP. www.nysparks.com/parks/143/details.aspx. $$$.

Attractions and Recreation

BABCOCK COBBLESTONE HOUSE MUSEUM, 7449 Lake Road, Barker, 716-795-9948.

SODUS BAY LIGHTHOUSE MUSEUM

SODUS BAY BEACH PARK

BLACKBIRD CIDER WORKS, 8503 Lower Lake Road, Barker, 716-795-3580. Open Monday–Saturday 11:00 AM–5:00 PM, Sunday 12:00–5:00 PM. www .blackbirdciders.com

BLACK WILLOW WINERY, 5565 West Lake Road, Burt, 716-439-1982. www .blackwillowwinery.com

BRADDOCK BAY WILDLIFE MANAGEMENT AREA, 432 Manitour Beach Road, Hilton, 585-226-2486. Open dawn to dusk. Free admission. www.dec .ny.gov/outdoor/88339.html

BURNAP'S FARM MARKET, 7277 Maple Avenue, Sodus, 315-483-4050. www.burnapsfarm.com

BYE'S POPCORN, Route 78, Olcott, 716-751-9892 or 716-778-8218. Open March–November, hours vary seasonally.

CHARLOTTE-GENESEE LIGHTHOUSE, 70 Lighthouse Street, Rochester, 585-621-6179. Tours offered Saturday and Sunday afternoons. www .geneseelighthouse.org

CHIMNEY BLUFFS STATE PARK, 7700 Garner Road, Wolcott, 315-947-5205. Open dawn to dusk. www.nysparks.com/parks/43/details.aspx

DURAND EASTMAN PARK, 570 Lake Shore Boulevard, along Lake Ontario 7 miles north of Rochester off I-590, 585-342-9810. Open daily 10:00 AM–11:00 PM.

LAKESIDE BEACH STATE PARK, Route 18, Waterport, 585-682-4888. Open year-round dawn to dusk. www.nysparks.com/parks/161/details.aspx

LAKEVIEW VILLAGE SHOPPES, Route 78 and Ontario Street, Olcott, 716-778-8531. Open seasonally May–October; weekends only September–December.

LYNDONVILLE SHOE TREE, Lakeshore and Foss Roads, Lyndonville.

MARJIM MANOR, 7171 East Lake Road, Appleton, 716-778-7001. Open Monday–Saturday 10:00 AM–5:00 PM, Sunday 12:00–6:00 PM. www.marjim manor.com.

NIAGARA WINE TRAIL, www.niagarawinetrail.org

ONTARIO BEACH PARK CAROUSEL, ROCHESTER

OAK ORCHARD LIGHTHOUSE, 14357 Ontario Street, Kent. Open seasonally Friday 5:30–7:30 PM, Saturday and Sunday 12:00–4:00 PM. www.oakorchard lighthouse.org

OLCOTT BEACH CAROUSEL PARK, 5979 Main Street, Olcott Beach, 716-778-7066. www.olcottbeachcarouselpark.org

OLD FORT NIAGARA, Fort Niagara State Park, Route 18F at the north end of the Robert Moses Parkway, Youngstown, 716-745-7611. www.oldfortniagara .org.

ONTARIO BEACH PARK, 4800 Lake Avenue, Rochester, 585-256-4950. www.monroecounty.gov/parks-ontariobeach.php

SCHULZE WINERY, 2090 Coomer Road, Burt, 716-778-8090. www.schulze wines.com

SEABREEZE AMUSEMENT PARK, 4600 Culver Road, Rochester, 585-323-1900. www.seabreeze.com

SODUS BAY LIGHTHOUSE MUSEUM, 7606 North Ontario Street, Sodus Point, 315-483-4936. www.sodusbaylighthouse.org

THIRTY MILE POINT LIGHTHOUSE AT GOLDEN HILL STATE PARK. 9691 Lower Lake Road, Barker, 716-795-3885 or 716-795-3117. Tours Saturday and Sunday 2:00–4:00 PM, Memorial Day–Labor Day.

THORPE VINEYARDS, 8150 Chimney Heights Boulevard, Wolcott, 315-594-2502. Open April–December; days and hours vary seasonally. www .thorpevineyard.com

VICTORIANBOURG WINE ESTATE, 4402 East Lake Road, Wilson, 716-751-6576. www.victorianbourg.com

WEBSTER PARK, 1100 Lake Road, Webster, 585-872-0083.

WHISPERING PINES MINIATURE GOLF, 4383 Culver Road, Rochester, 585-323-1570. Open seasonally. www.parksidediner.com/miniature-golf

WILSON TUSCARORA STATE PARK, 3371 Lake Road, Wilson, 716-751-6361. www.parks.ny.gov/parks/69/maps.aspx

Dining

BLACK NORTH INN, Route 98 at Lake Ontario, Point Breeze, 585-682-4441. www.blacknorthinn.wordpress.com

BREEZE IN AGAIN, 928 Point Breeze Road, Kent, 585-682-6148. www .breezeinnagain.com

CAPTAIN JACK'S GOODTIME TAVERN, 8505 Greig Street, Sodus Point, 315-483-9570. www.captainjacksgoodtimetavern.com

CHARBROIL HOUSE, 1395 Island Cottage Road, Rochester, 585-750-2462.

GARDEN CAFÉ, 7277 Maple Avenue, Sodus, 315-483-4050. www.burnaps farm.com

HEDGES NINE MILE POINT, 1290 Lake Road, Webster, 585-265-3850. Open seasonally. Lunch Tuesday–Friday 11:30 AM–2:00 PM, dinner Tuesday–Saturday 5:30 PM–close. Closed Sunday and Monday. www.hedgesninemile point.com

LAKEVIEW VILLAGE SHOPPES, OLCOTT

OAK ORCHARD LIGHTHOUSE, POINT BREEZE

CAPTAIN'S GALLERY, 5885 Main Street, Olcott, 716-778-5580.

MARINER'S LANDING, 1540 Franklin Street, Olcott, 716-778-5535.

PARK PLACE RESTAURANT, 5989 East Main Street, Olcott, 716-778-5537.

PARKSIDE DINER, 4353 Culver Road, Rochester, 585-323-2710. www.parksidediner.com

SCHALLER'S DRIVE-IN, 965 Edgemere Drive, Rochester. 585-865-3319.

WILSON BOAT HOUSE RESTAURANT, 57 Harbor Street, Wilson. 716-751-6060. www.wilsonboathouse.com

WOODCOCK BROTHERS BREWERY, 638 Lake Street, Wilson, 716-333-4000. www.woodcockbrothersbrewery.com

Other Contacts

GREAT LAKES SEAWAY TRAIL, www.seawaytrail.com

NEWFANE TOWN HALL/NEWFANE TOURISM, 2896 Transit Road, Newfane, 716-778-8531. Open Monday–Friday 8:30 AM–4:30 PM. Maps, brochures, and other area information are also available at the **Red Caboose**, corner of NY 18 and NY 78 in Olcott Beach. The Red Caboose is open daily 9:00 AM–5:00 PM, end of April–beginning of November. www.olcott-newfane.com

ORLEANS COUNTY CHAMBER OF COMMERCE, 121 North Main Street, Albion, 585-589-7727. www.orleanschamber.com

ORLEANS COUNTY TOURISM, 14016 Route 31, Albion, 800-724-0314. www.orleanscountytourism.com

VILLAGE OF WILSON, 375 Lake Avenue, Wilson, 716-751-6704. www.wilsonnewyork.com

VISIT ROCHESTER, 45 East Avenue, Rochester, 800-677-7282 or 585-279-8300. www.visitrochester.com

WAYNE COUNTY TOURISM, www.waynecountytourism.com

YOUNGSTOWN, www.youngstownnewyork.us

PRIDE OF LEROY, ASHBURY ROAD, LEROY

3

BARN QUILT TRAILS OF GENESEE AND ORLEANS COUNTIES

ESTIMATED LENGTH: 50 miles each trail

ESTIMATED TIME: 1 day for each trail

HIGHLIGHTS: Rural Genesee and Orleans Counties are the perfect backdrop for these two quilt trails, both of which were started to promote their respective communities. Many of these quilt blocks, which are made of wood and measure 4 feet by 4 feet or larger, can be found on the sides of barns, businesses, garages, homes, and other locations. These two trails are only about 25 to 30 miles from each other, so it's technically possible to cover both trails in one day. However, you may want to devote a day to each trail so you can appreciate each quilt block and also have the opportunity to visit the other attractions along the way, including museums, farm markets, antiques shops, and more.

GETTING THERE: There are two barn quilt trails in the same general area. Begin the Country Barn Quilt Trail in Kendall on Route 272, which runs off Route 104 near the Orleans and Monroe County border. For the Leroy Quilt Trail, start on Main Street in the Village of Leroy, which is located just a few miles south of New York State Thruway (I-90) Exit 47.

We'll start first with the **Country Barn Quilt Trail,** since that was the first one established in the area. This trail is the brainchild of Lora Partyka, whose family owns Partyka Farms in Kendall. She was browsing through a quilting magazine one cold winter night when she spotted an article about people in a town in Iowa who started a project that put painted wooden quilt blocks on the sides of barns to draw visitors to the area. She thought that it would be great to have something like this in Kendall. She organized a group of friends to start the project, and the Country Barn Quilt Trail was born.

The first block, *The Farmer's Daughter,* was installed at Partyka Farms

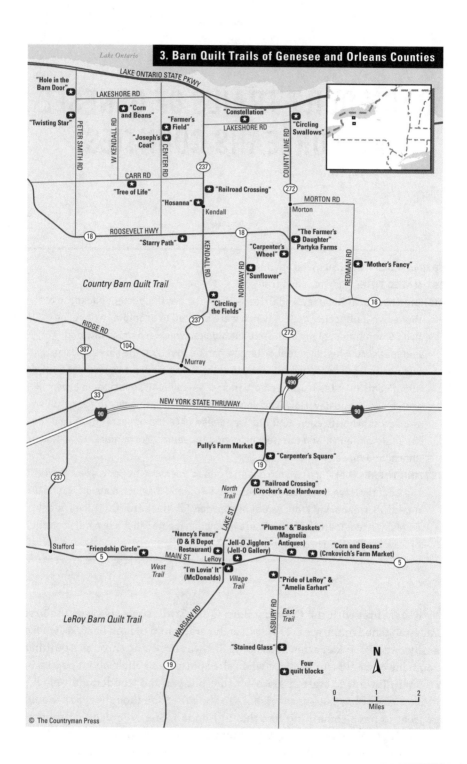

3. Barn Quilt Trails of Genesee and Orleans Counties

Lake Ontario

LAKE ONTARIO STATE PKWY

"Hole in the Barn Door"

LAKESHORE RD

"Corn and Beans"

"Farmer's Field"

"Constellation"

"Circling Swallows"

"Twisting Star"

PETER SMITH RD

W KENDALL RD

"Joseph's Coat"

CENTER RD

LAKESHORE RD

COUNTY LINE RD

CARR RD

237

"Tree of Life"

"Hosanna"

"Railroad Crossing"

272

Kendall

Morton

MORTON RD

ROOSEVELT HWY

18

18

"The Farmer's Daughter"
Partyka Farms

"Starry Path"

KENDALL RD

"Carpenter's Wheel"

REDMAN RD

"Mother's Fancy"

Country Barn Quilt Trail

NORWAY RD

"Sunflower"

18

"Circling the Fields"

237

RIDGE RD

272

387

104

Murray

490

33

NEW YORK STATE THRUWAY

90

90

Pully's Farm Market

"Carpenter's Square"

19

North Trail

"Railroad Crossing"
(Crocker's Ace Hardware)

LAKE ST

"Plumes" & "Baskets"
(Magnolia Antiques)

237

Stafford

"Friendship Circle"

5

MAIN ST

"Nancy's Fancy"
(D & R Depot
Restaurant)

"Jell-O Jigglers"
(Jell-O Gallery)

"Corn and Beans"
(Crnkovich's Farm Market)

LeRoy

5

West Trail

"I'm Lovin' It"
(McDonalds)

Village Trail

"Pride of LeRoy" &
"Amelia Earhart"

WARSAW RD

ASBURY RD

East Trail

LeRoy Barn Quilt Trail

"Stained Glass"

N

19

Four
quilt blocks

0   1   2

Miles

© The Countryman Press

FARMER'S DAUGHTER, PARTYKA FARMS, KENDALL

in 2006. Lora chose this block because that's who she is: a fifth-generation farmer on her father's side of the family. People in the community embraced this project, and soon many were participating by hanging quilt blocks on their barns and other buildings. Each participant picks his or her own colors and design, which usually have some significance to the family.

Maps of the Country Barn Quilt Trail, a self-guided tour, are available at **Partyka Farms**, which has a great selection of in-season produce, as well as a country gift shop stocked with candies, home decor items, jams, baked goods, and more. As there are now over 50 quilt blocks on the trail, it is not possible to describe each one of them in this chapter. Depending on how much time you have to spend in the area, take a look at the map and plan which ones you'd like to visit. Note that occasionally the quilt blocks are moved to different locations and removed altogether, so don't get frustrated if you can't find them.

Here is a sampling of what you can see along the trail. The majority of the barn quilts are in Kendall, near Route 237, although some are located in neighboring towns, like the quilt block in Hamlin called *Mother's Fancy* because it was created by five adult children to commemorate their mother's

JELL-O JIGGLERS, JELL-O GALLERY, LEROY

80th birthday. Another block, located on a barn on Kendall Road, is titled *Circling the Fields*, as the owners have a small airstrip on their property. *Corn and Beans*, on the side of the barn at Kludt Brothers Farm, is significant, as they are a large producer of corn, beans, and other vegetables for commercial canners.

Keep in mind that the area this quilt trail is located in is quite rural, so you won't find many amenities, such as gas stations, restaurants, and lodging along the way. Plan your trip accordingly. For the more ambitious, the Orleans County Tourism website (www.orleanscountytourism.com) has several suggested barn quilt cycling trails, where you can discover the countryside and the barn quilts while riding your bicycle.

The other quilt trail is located about 25 miles south of Kendall. **The Leroy Barn Quilt Trail** began as a bicentennial project for the town of Leroy in 2011. The first quilt, *Jell-O Jigglers*, was made and put on the outside of the Jell-O Gallery, which is part of the Leroy Historical Society. Jell-O was invented in Leroy by Peter Cooper back in 1897 and was manufactured in Leroy until the mid-1960s. The historical society hoped to have a couple dozen quilts made by the time the town's bicentennial rolled around in 2012. However, by the time that celebration took place, over 70 barn quilts had been made. There are now over 100 barn quilts on the trail.

The first place to stop is the **Jell-O Gallery/Leroy Historical Society**, where you can get a map to the barn quilt trail, which actually consists of four separate driving trails, one in the village and three in the town: the Village Trail, North Trail, East Trail, and West Trail. Take some time to visit the museum, which has exhibits on the dessert's history and lots of memorabilia, as well as a gift shop. The Leroy House, located in front of the property, has exhibits on area history.

After leaving the museum, check out the village trail, which has close

I'M LOVIN' IT, MCDONALD'S, LEROY

TOP: *CORN AND BEANS*, CRNKOVICH'S FARM MARKET, LEROY
BOTTOM: *CARPENTER'S SQUARE*, ROUTE 19, LEROY

to 20 quilt block squares sprinkled throughout the Village of Leroy, with several along Main Street. It's almost like a treasure hunt looking for them; while some are quite obvious, others are set back from the road on garages, sides of houses, or fences. Unlike the barn quilts in more rural Kendall, the ones along the Leroy Barn Quilt Trail are on busier roads, so please use caution when looking for them. One of the more interesting barn quilts is the one titled *I'm Lovin' It* located on the side of the local McDonald's. The

PULLEY'S FARM MARKET, ROUTE 19, LEROY

barn quilt, which is best viewed from the drive-thru (a good excuse to get an order of fries!), has the golden arches incorporated into the design. To view *Nancy's Fancy*, you'll have to stop for a bite to eat at **D&R Depot Restaurant**, where you can enjoy home-cooked meals in a former B&O train depot. One of their specialties is chicken pot pie. The quilt block is located inside the restaurant.

The East Trail has the largest number of quilts of the four trails: 29 at time

FRIENDSHIP CIRCLE, ROUTE 5, LEROY

of publication. Nearly a dozen are located along Ashbury Road, which runs off Main Street. Two quilt blocks of note are located on the side of the Public Works building (92 Ashbury Road). *Pride of Leroy* commemorates the 200 years of the town's existence; 200 of the town's residents were involved in painting the design. On the other end of the building, there is a quilt block titled *Amelia Earhart*, as there is a small airfield located nearby.

Some of the other quilts on Ashbury Road include *Stained Glass*, located on the second story of a barn between two windows, and four impressive quilts that are located on the side of one very large barn at 9743 Ashbury Road. Head back up to Main Street and turn right; you'll see two quilt blocks on the side of **Magnolia Antiques**; *Plumes* reminds one of a pinwheel and *Baskets* features four colorful baskets. One of the more colorful quilts on the trail, *Corn and Beans*, is located on the side of **Crnkovich's Farm Market** on Main Road.

On the North Trail there are a number of quilt blocks located on or just off North Lake Street (Route 19), including *Railroad Crossing* on the side of Crocker's Ace Hardware and *Carpenter's Square*, a simple L-shaped design on the side of a small barn.

While you're in the area be sure to stop by **Pully's Farm Market**, which is located on Route 19, just south of the New York State Thruway. This family-run farm market has a nice selection of seasonal produce, gift items, and more. In the fall they have a corn maze, children's activities, and lots of pumpkins to choose from.

The West Trail has several quilts just off Route 19 South and along Main Road, including *Friendship Circle*, a pretty blue, white, and green design on the side of a barn at 6849 West Main Road.

IN THE AREA

Attractions and Recreation

COUNTRY BARN QUILT TRAIL, www.partykafarms.com

CRNKOVICH'S FARM MARKET, 8041 East Main Road, Leroy, 585-768-7259.

JELL-O GALLERY/LEROY HISTORICAL SOCIETY, 23 East Main Street, Leroy, 585-768-7433. www.jellomuseum.com

LEROY BARN QUILT TRAIL, www.leroybarnquilt.org

MAGNOLIA ANTIQUES, 7895 East Main Street, Leroy, 585-768-6310. Open Friday and Saturday 11:00 AM–5:00 PM, Sunday 12:00–5:00 PM.

PARTYKA FARMS, 1420 County Line Road (Route 272), Kendall, 585-659-9131. Open April–November 9 AM–8 PM. daily. www.partykafarms.com

PULLY'S FARM MARKET, 8160 Lake Street Road (Route 19), Leroy, 585-768-2280. www.pullysfarmmarket.com

Dining

D&R DEPOT RESTAURANT, 63 Lake Street, Leroy, 585-768-6270. www.dandrdepot.com

Other Contacts

GENESEE COUNTY TOURISM, www.visitgeneseeny.com

ORLEANS COUNTY TOURISM, www.orleanscountytourism.com

4

HISTORIC EAST AURORA

ESTIMATED MILES: A day trip to a village about 20 miles southeast of Buffalo

ESTIMATED TIME: A day trip; can also be turned into an overnight getaway

HIGHLIGHTS: You can spend a long, leisurely day exploring the village and the surrounding countryside with an option to stay overnight. East Aurora is a quaint village rich in history, as it was once home to Millard Fillmore, the 13th president of the United States. It was also home to the Roycroft Arts and Crafts movement in the early 20th century.

Today it is better known as the headquarters for Fisher-Price Toys, as well as home to two National Historic Landmarks. In addition, it has a popular Main Street shopping district with numerous boutiques and restaurants.

GETTING THERE: From I-90 (New York State Thruway), take Exit 54 (Route 400) to either the Maple Road exit and turn right or the Route 20A exit and also turn right. Both will lead you into the village of East Aurora, which is best explored on foot. Suggested places to park include the lot behind Vidler's 5&10, between Pine and Church Streets, or the parking lot by the Roycroft Campus Visitor Center on South Grove Street. There's also another lot located between Church and Riley Streets behind Main Street businesses, along with on-street parking throughout the village.

The Town of Aurora, which includes the Village of East Aurora, as well as Marilla and Elma, was first settled in 1804, with many pioneers coming from New England. One of the town's early settlers was Millard Fillmore, who came to East Aurora in 1923 to study law and teach school. He later went on

LEFT: VIDLER'S 5&10

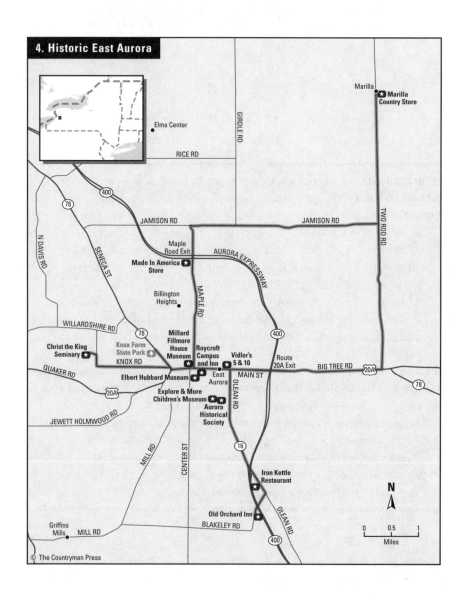

4. Historic East Aurora

Elma Center

Marilla
★ Marilla Country Store

GIRDLE RD

RICE RD

400

78

N DAVIS RD

SENECA ST

JAMISON RD

JAMISON RD

TWO ROD RD

Maple Road Exit

Made In America ★ Store

AURORA EXPRESSWAY

Billington Heights

MAPLE RD

WILLARDSHIRE RD

78

Millard Fillmore House Museum

Christ the King Seminary ★

Knox Farm State Park

KNOX RD

Roycroft Campus and Inn ★

Vidler's ★ 5 & 10

400

Route 20A Exit

BIG TREE RD

20A

QUAKER RD

Elbert Hubbard Museum ★★

East Aurora

MAIN ST

78

20A

Explore & More Children's Museum ★★

OLEAN RD

Aurora Historical Society ★

JEWETT HOLMWOOD RD

MILL RD

CENTER ST

16

Iron Kettle ★ Restaurant

N

Old Orchard Inn ★

BLAKELEY RD

OLEAN RD

400

0   0.5   1
Miles

Griffins Mills   MILL RD

© The Countryman Press

MILLARD FILLMORE HOUSE

to become the 13th U.S. president. The home he built here in 1825, which is now the **Millard Fillmore House Museum,** is a National Historic Landmark, open for tours during the summer months.

East Aurora was also home to the Roycroft Arts and Crafts movement, established by Elbert Hubbard in 1890. The Roycroft Press became well known for its beautiful books. Hubbard was an interesting and controversial character who developed a self-contained community of over 500 craftsmen that included furniture makers, metalsmiths leathersmiths, and bookbinders. Items made here were identified with the "Roycroft mark" to signify their high quality.

To Hubbard, Roycroft was not merely a place but a state of mind. Thousands of people journeyed to East Aurora to learn more about the Arts and Crafts movement, so in 1905 Hubbard opened the Roycroft Inn to accommodate visitors. Tragically, Hubbard and his wife, Alice, died in 1915 during the sinking of the *Lusitania*.

Today the 14-building **Roycroft Campus**, a designated National Historic Landmark, consists of artists' studios, museums, a gift gallery, and the **Roycroft Inn**. The inn, which was fully restored in 1995, offers modern accommodations in a historic setting. The inn's restaurant has an elegant menu and is noted for its Sunday brunch buffet. During the warmer weather, guests can dine outdoors on the peristyle.

Around the corner on Oakwood Avenue, visitors can learn more about Elbert Hubbard and the Roycroft movement at the **Elbert Hubbard Museum**. The powerhouse building (across from the inn) has been reconstructed and currently serves as the visitor center for the Roycroft Campus. Tours of the campus are available May through October, Wednesday through Sunday.

Other museums in East Aurora include the **Town of Aurora Historical Society** in the Aurora Town Hall on Gleed Avenue and the **Explore & More Children's Museum**, also on Gleed Avenue, which is designed for kids ages 1 through 10. Explore & More will move to Canalside in downtown Buffalo in late 2018.

If you want to get back to nature when visiting East Aurora, stop by **Knox Farm State Park**, a 633-acre park, formerly Ess Kay Farms, the estate of the socially prominent Knox family. The park, a mixture of grasslands, woodlands, and pastures, has numerous hiking and biking trails. The main house, which was the summer home of the Knox family, is a popular venue to rent for weddings, conferences, and special events. It is the site of spring and November art shows which are open to the public.

Adjacent to Knox Farm State Park is **Christ the King Seminary**, which is situated on 132 acres of fields and woodlands, with hiking trails on the grounds. Individuals and groups can make arrangements to have tours of the buildings on the campus; they also have an open house tour in the fall and spring. The seminary is a fully accredited graduate school of theology for candidates for the ordained priesthood and permanent diaconate in the Catholic Church, as well as for men and women who serve the church in a lay capacity.

East Aurora is a dining destination, with numerous restaurants to choose from. While it would be impossible to mention them all, here are descriptions of several of them to whet your appetite. The previously mentioned **Roycroft Inn** offers breakfast, lunch, and dinner, as well as a Sunday brunch in the main dining room. More casual fare, like wings and burgers, is offered

---

SIDE TRACKS

Wings and Weck

Chicken wings, better known as Buffalo wings in other parts of the country, and simply "wings" in western New York, have put the region on the culinary map. Created at the Anchor Bar in downtown Buffalo in 1964, chicken wings can be found on most menus throughout the area.

Beef on weck is another regional favorite. It consists of thinly sliced roast beef piled high on a salty kimmelweck roll; many people like to slather on horseradish as a condiment.

in the **Craftsman Lounge** at the Roycroft. **Rick's on Main**, which offers fresh dishes made from scratch, is located in a large older home right on Main Street. **Tony Rome's Globe Hotel**, located in a historic 1824 stagecoach stop, is noted for its barbecued ribs. It is East Aurora's oldest business operating in its original location; back in the day, it was frequented by Millard Fillmore and Grover Cleveland.

Just off Main Street is the **Riley Street Station**, which is located in a former railroad station. **Elm Street Bakery and Café** is always very busy and is popular with locals. Another restaurant popular with locals is **Charlie's**; during the warmer months, the patio is *the* place to dine.

Other local hangouts include **Wallenwein's**, a neighborhood tavern noted for wings and pizza, and **Bar Bill Tavern**, which has been voted to have the best wings and beef on weck sandwiches in the area.

You might want to take a short drive to the **Iron Kettle** restaurant, a large family-friendly establishment noted for its pies. The **Old Orchard Inn** is located on 25 acres in the East Aurora countryside in a 1901 building that

ELM STREET BAKERY

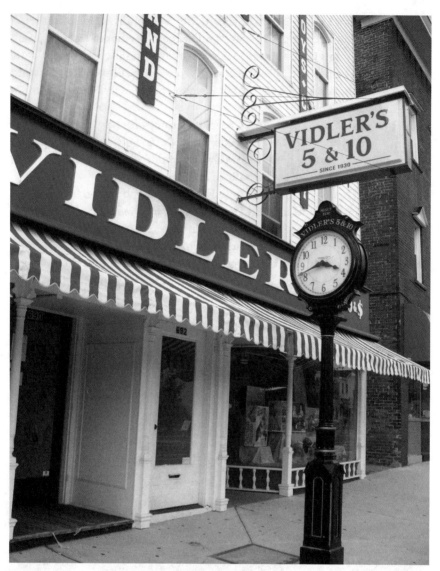

VIDLER'S 5&10

was originally a hunting lodge. It was converted into a tea room in the 1930s and is known for its home-cooked entrées.

With all the interest in craft beers and microbrewing in recent years, it's a given that East Aurora would have its own brewery. **42 North Brewery**, located on Pine Street, is named after its location on the 42nd parallel. The brewery, which has 10 beers on tap, has an indoor game room and an outdoor beer garden. Their limited food menu includes small plate offerings of locally sourced foods, including Breadhive Bakery pretzels, meatballs, bruschetta, and a Cubano sandwich.

East Aurora is also a shopper's dream, with a variety of stores and boutiques along Main Street, as well as several stores of interest outside the village. Of course, the best-known place to shop in East Aurora is the iconic **Vidler's 5&10**; just look for the distinctive red and white awning and the large "Vidler on the Roof." One of the village's most beloved landmarks, this business has been family owned since the 1930s.

Located in four connecting 1890s-era buildings, Vidler's sells many interesting and hard-to-find items. With 16,000 square feet of retail space, it is the largest 5&10 variety store in the world. You'll find toys, books, clothing, jewelry, home decor, cookware, craft items, candles, and more on two levels. The original Vidler's candy counter features old-time goodies like rock candy, Mallo Cups, and local favorites like Crystal Beach suckers.

Some of the other shops found along Main Street include **Head Over**

SIDE TRACKS

There are two other shops located outside the village that are must-sees when visiting East Aurora. The first, the **Marilla Country Store** (take route 20A east to Two Rod Road) has a little bit of everything. Originally opened in 1851, the store still has the original flooring, countertops, and gas lights. On the first floor, the store serves locals as a small grocery and dry goods store. However, climb up to the second floor and you will find the area's largest selection of country decorating items and seasonal holiday decor. They also have a small museum on the second floor, which has some of the original store fixtures and a Porter music box.

The second must-see store in the area is the **Made in America Store** in Elma, which only sells merchandise made in America. Founded in 2010 by Mark Andol, the store now has numerous locations in the Buffalo area, including its flagship store, located just off the 400 Expressway at the Maple Road exit. It has actually become a tourist destination for bus tour groups, attracted to the store's ultimate mission of preserving American jobs.

Andol owns General Welding and Fabricating across the street from the store. After losing several major welding and fabricating accounts to overseas businesses, he became passionate about saving American jobs. He created the Made in America Store as a statement. He didn't realize how much the business would strike a chord with people or how much it would grow. The store has been featured on radio and TV stations, both nationally and internationally.

ROYCROFT INN

Heels in Love with Shoes which features shoes, jewelry, clothing, accessories, and more. The connected shop, **Bella Casa**, has a variety of home decor items. **The Walk-in Closet**, a consignment shop that has the best deals in town, seems tiny when you walk in from the street. However, don't be deceived. Head down to the lower level and be amazed at room after room of clothing and household items.

If you like to read, visit **The Bookworm**, which is around the corner from the Elm Street Bakery. They carry a large selection of books as well as gift items. Cross Main Street and take a short walk down Riley Street to the **Fisher-Price Toy Store**, located at the headquarters of the Fisher-Price Toy Company, which was founded in East Aurora. This large store has a great selection of Fisher-Price and Mattel toys, some with discounted prices. A short drive down Route 16 is the **Schoolhouse Gallery and Artisan Co-op**, which features fine handmade furniture made in the Roycroft tradition, as well as handmade crafts and gifts.

There are a number of annual festivals and events that take place in East Aurora. These include several art-themed events like the Artwalk, which takes place in April, and the annual East Aurora Art Society art show and Roycroft Summer Festival, both which take place the last weekend in June. In July, enjoy the East Aurora Street Fest and Chalkwalk, as well as Racing Day Weekend and the annual East Aurora Carriage Drive and Competition, which reflects East Aurora's past as the racehorse trotting capital of the world in the late 1880s. The Toy Town Car Show takes place at the end of August, and the Carolcade along Main Street takes place the week before Christmas.

Need more than a day in East Aurora? Stay overnight at the previously mentioned **Roycroft Inn**, which offers 22 distinctive guest rooms and suites and is conveniently located just off Main Street. A designated National Historic Landmark inn built in 1905 and restored in 1995, the suites have original and reproduction furnishings along with modern amenities like Jacuzzi tubs and thick terry-cloth robes. Each room has the name of a notable personality carved into the door, including Ralph Waldo Emerson, Henry David Thoreau, and Susan B. Anthony. Alternately, the **Hampton Inn and Suites**, which has 80 deluxe guest rooms, including eight jacuzzi suites with fireplaces, is also located within walking distance of Main Street shops and restaurants. Amenities include an indoor heated pool, fitness center, and complimentary breakfast.

IN THE AREA

Accommodations

HAMPTON INN AND SUITES, 49 Olean Road, East Aurora, 716-655-3300 or 800-875-9440. www.hamptoninn3.hilton.com/en/hotels/new-york/hampton-inn-east-aurora-BUFEAHX/index.html. $$.

ROYCROFT INN, 40 South Grove Street, East Aurora, 716-652-5552. www.roycroftinn.com. $$.

Attractions and Recreation

CHRIST THE KING SEMINARY, 711 Knox Road, East Aurora, 716-652-8900. www.cks.edu

ELBERT HUBBARD MUSEUM, 363 Oakwood Avenue, East Aurora. 716-652-4735. Open June–October, Wednesday, Saturday, and Sunday 1:00–4:00 PM. $10 adult, $5 age 13–18, 12 and under free. www.aurorahistoricalsociety.com

EXPLORE & MORE CHILDREN'S MUSEUM, 300 Gleed Avenue, East Aurora, 716-655-5131. Wednesday–Saturday 10:00 AM–5:00 PM, Sunday

12:00–5:00 PM, until 8:00 PM. the first Friday of month. $7. www.exploreand
more.org

KNOX FARM STATE PARK, 437 Buffalo Road (Seneca Street), East Aurora,
716-549-1802. Open dawn to dusk. http://www.nysparks.com/parks/163/
maps.aspx or www.friendsofknoxfarm.org

MILLARD FILLMORE HOUSE MUSEUM, 24 Shearer Avenue, East Aurora,
716-652-8875. Open June–October, Wednesday, Saturday, and Sunday,
1:00–4:00 PM. www.aurorahistoricalsociety.com

ROYCROFT CAMPUS, 31 South Grove Street, East Aurora, 716-655-0261.
Visitor center open daily 10:00 AM–5:00 PM, year-round. Check website for
tours and special events. www.roycroftcampuscorp.com

TOWN OF AURORA HISTORICAL SOCIETY, Southside Municipal Center,
300 Gleed Avenue, East Aurora, 716-652-7944. Open Wednesday 1:00–4:00
PM or by appointment, free. www.aurorahistoricalsociety.com

Dining and Nightlife

42 NORTH BREWERY, 25 Pine Street, East Aurora, 716-805-7500. Open
Tuesday–Thursday 4:00–11:00 PM, Friday 1:00 PM–12:00 AM, Saturday 12:00
PM–12:00 AM, Sunday 12:00–8:00 PM. www.42northbrewing.com

BAR BILL TAVERN, 185 Main Street, East Aurora, 716-652-7959. Open
Monday–Saturday 8:00 AM–2:00 AM, Sunday 12:00 PM–2:00 AM. www.barbill
.com

CHARLIE'S, 510 Main Street, East Aurora, 716-655-0282.

CRAFTSMAN LOUNGE AT THE ROYCROFT INN, 40 South Grove Street,
East Aurora, 716-652-5552. www.roycroftinn.com

ELM STREET BAKERY AND CAFÉ, 72 Elm Street, East Aurora, 716-652-
4720. Open Tuesday–Friday 7:00 AM–9:00 PM, Saturday 8:00 AM–9:00 PM,
Sunday 9:00 AM–2:00 PM. www.elmstreetbakery.com

IRON KETTLE, 1009 Olean Road (2 miles south of the village), East Aurora,
716-652-5310. Open 6:00 AM–8:00 PM daily.

OLD ORCHARD INN

OLD ORCHARD INN, 2095 Blakeley Road, East Aurora, 716-652-4664. Lunch Wednesday–Saturday 12:00–3:00 PM. Dinner Tuesday–Thursday 4:00–8:00 PM, Friday and Saturday 4:00–9:00 PM, Sunday 12:00–8:00 PM. www.oldorchardny.com

RICK'S ON MAIN, 687 Main Street, East Aurora, 716-652-1253. Lunch Monday–Friday 11:00 AM–2:30 PM, Saturday 12:00–3:00 PM. Dinner Monday–Thursday 5:00–10:00 PM, Friday and Saturday 5:00–11:00 PM. www .ricksonmain.com

RILEY STREET STATION, 27 Riley Street, East Aurora, 716-655-4948. Open Monday–Saturday 11:00 AM–2:00 AM, Sunday 12:00 PM–2:00 AM. www.riley streetstation.com

ROYCROFT INN, 40 South Grove Street, East Aurora, 716-652-5552. www .roycroftinn.com

TONY ROME'S GLOBE HOTEL, 711 Main Street, East Aurora, 716-652-4221. Open Monday–Thursday 11:00 AM–10:00 PM, Friday and Saturday 11:00 AM– 11:00 PM, Sunday 12:00–9:00 PM. www.tonyromesea.com

WALLENWEIN'S, 641 Oakwood, East Aurora, 716-652-9801. Open Monday–Saturday 10:00 AM–1:00 AM, Sunday 12:00 PM–12:00 AM.

Shopping

THE BOOKWORM, 34 Elm Street, East Aurora, 716-652-6554. Open Monday–Thursday 10:00 AM–6:00 PM, Friday 10:00 AM–9:00 PM, Saturday 9:00 AM–4:00 PM. www.eabookworm.com

FISHER-PRICE TOY STORE, 636 Girard Avenue, East Aurora, 716-687-3300. Open Monday–Friday 10:00 AM–6:00 PM, Saturday 10:00 AM–5:00 PM. www.fisherpricetoystore.com

HEAD OVER HEELS IN LOVE WITH SHOES/BELLA CASA, 662 Main Street, East Aurora, 716-655-1811. Open Monday–Thursday 11:00 AM–6:00 PM, Friday 11:00 AM–7:00 PM, Saturday 10:00 AM –8:00 PM, Sunday 11:00 AM–5:00 PM. www.headoverheelsea.com

MADE IN AMERICA STORE, 1000 West Maple Court, Elma, 716-652-4872. Open Monday–Saturday 8:00 AM–8:00 PM, Sunday 10:00 AM–5:00 PM. www.madeinamericastore.com

MARILLA COUNTRY STORE, 1673 Two Rod Road (corner of Bullis Road), Marilla, 716-655-1031. Open Monday–Saturday 10:00 AM–7:00 PM, Sunday 10:00 AM–6:00 PM. www.marillacountrystore.com

SCHOOLHOUSE GALLERY AND ARTISAN CO-OP, 1054 Olean Road (Route 16), East Aurora, 716-655-4080. Open Monday–Saturday 10:00 AM–4:00 PM.

VIDLER'S 5&10, 680–694 Main Street, East Aurora, 716-652-0481. Open Monday–Thursday 9:00 AM–6:00 PM, Friday 9:00 AM–9:00 PM, Saturday 9:00 AM–6:00 PM, Sunday 11:00 AM–5:00 PM. www.vidlers5and10.com

THE WALK IN CLOSET CO., 650 Main Street, East Aurora, 716-652-1410. Monday–Thursday 10:00 AM–7:00 PM, Friday–Saturday 10:00 AM–8:00 PM, Sunday 11:00 AM–5:00 PM.

MARILLA COUNTRY STORE, MARILLA

Other Contacts

EAST AURORA CHAMBER OF COMMERCE, 652 Main Street, East Aurora, 716-652-8444. Open Monday–Friday 8:00 AM–4:30 PM. www.eanycc.com

5

LAKE ERIE'S WINE COUNTRY

Two Dozen Wineries in Chautauqua County and Northern Pennsylvania

ESTIMATED LENGTH: 60 miles

ESTIMATED TIME: 1–2 days

HIGHLIGHTS: This area, known as America's Grape Country, is a collaborative effort between the Chautauqua County Visitor Bureau, the Concord Grape Belt Association, and the Lake Erie Wine Trail. It is the oldest and largest grape-growing region east of the Rockies, so you know the wine has to be good. At latest count, there were 25 wineries in the region: 13 in New York State and 12 just over the border in Pennsylvania. The trail continues to grow, so there may be even more wineries added after this book's publication.

While one could drive around the region in one day, if you want to visit all or most of the wineries, allow at least a couple of days. Most of the wineries are small, family-run operations; often the owners can be found behind the tasting bar, so you'll want to allow time to enjoy the wine and chat with them. Some of the wineries have several generations working side by side. The wine trail offers several special events throughout the year, including a Wine and Chocolate Weekend in February, a Wine and Cheese Weekend in April, and a Harvest Celebration in November. The America's Grape Country Wine Festival takes place in August at the Chautauqua County Fairgrounds, and the annual Wine Country Harvest Festival in the town of North East, Pennsylvania, is in late September.

GETTING THERE: This area is easily accessible from the New York State Thruway (I-90). Starting at the northern part of this drive, take Exit 58, Silver Creek, then follow Route 20 west. Several towns and wineries can be found right on Route 20 or just a short distance away. The drive concludes just west of the town of North East, Pennsylvania, which has several wineries.

LEFT: BARCELONA LIGHTHOUSE

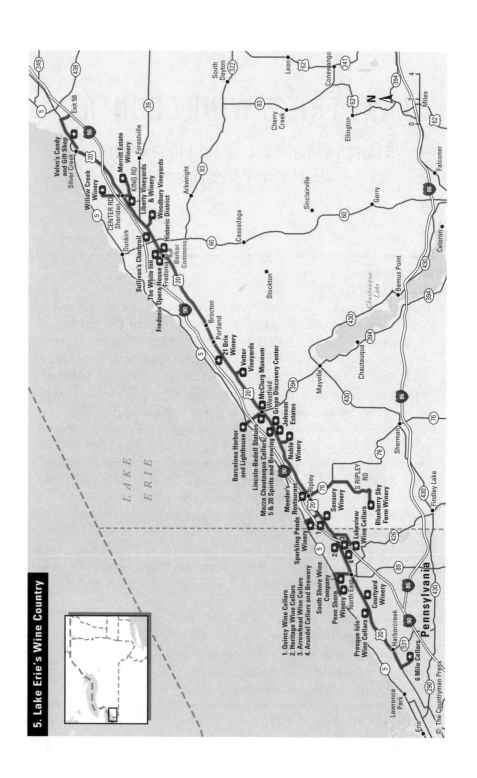

5. Lake Erie's Wine Country

1. Quincy Wine Cellars
2. Heritage Wine Cellars
3. Arrowhead Wine Cellars
4. Arundel Cellars and Brewery

© The Countryman Press

You'll start your journey by getting off the New York State Thruway at the Silver Creek exit and then heading west on Route 20, which runs parallel to the thruway. An interesting place to stop at in Silver Creek is **Valvo's Candy and Gift Shop**, which has unusual gift items, cast stone statuary for the garden, and a selection of chocolates and candies. In the town of Sheridan, turn right on Center Road and head toward Chapin Road. Your first stop will be **Willow Creek Winery**, which has a beautiful picnic grove with a pond and gazebo, along with a catering facility for receptions. Some of their signature wines include a cream sherry and Chautauqua chocolate wine.

Head back to Center Road, then south to King Road to visit **Merritt Estate Winery**, which opened in 1976. It features a large tasting room plus a gift shop stocked with wines and wine accessories. Some of their specialties include Chautauqua White and Bella Rosa. All of the wines are estate bottled and produced. The property has been in the Merritt family since the 1800s.

Head back to Route 20 to visit **Liberty Vineyards & Winery**. This winery grows its own grapes; as a matter of fact, some of its vineyards have been in the family since the 1860s. They make a variety of award-winning white, red, and rosé wines.

Nearby, **Woodbury Vineyards**, just off the beaten trail on South Roberts Road, has a number of tasty wines, including a cranberry dessert wine and a Seaport Red and Seaport White. They have a large tasting room and a nice gift shop.

WHITE INN, FREDONIA

After visiting Woodbury, head back to Route 20 and continue west. If it's time to stop to eat, check out **Sullivan's Charbroil**, which is known for home-made curly fries and milkshakes.

Soon you'll arrive in the Village of Fredonia, home to SUNY Fredonia, a top public university in the Northeast. This college town was the first village in the nation to use natural gas lighting. If you have time, take a walking tour of Fredonia's downtown historic district; a brochure can be obtained from the Fredonia Chamber of Commerce. Barker Commons, a beautifully landscaped park in the center of town, has two distinctive fountains. Of special note is the **Fredonia Opera House**, an 1891 opera house which has been restored to its original grandeur and is a year-round venue for concerts, films, and professional theater.

The White Inn, located just down the street from the park, is a great place to enjoy a meal or even stay overnight. There are 23 guest rooms decorated with Victorian-style furnishings. A full breakfast is included with the room; their dining room features American and Continental cuisine. Another place to dine in Fredonia is the **Upper Crust Bakehouse,** which, for over 20 years, has used all-natural ingredients in their homemade soups, breads, and baked goods. They even roast their own turkey for their signature roast turkey sand-wiches. If you like wings, burgers, pizza, and other casual fare served in a family-friendly atmosphere, try **Wing City Grille,** just off Route 20 on Route 60. They also have a second location in Lakewood, near Jamestown.

21 BRIX WINERY, PORTLAND

The next winery to visit is **21 Brix.** Just look for Ella, the life-sized pink elephant by the driveway; many visitors stop to take their picture with her. The winery features a 60-foot tasting bar and an indoor seating area. They have a variety of wines to sample, along with craft beers on tap. Some of their wines include Ella Red, Ella White, Ellatawba, and Thirsty Elephant.

MOORE PARK/MCCLURG MUSEUM, WESTFIELD

Take a short drive down Prospect Station Road to **Vetter Vineyards.** This small family-owned and -operated vineyard is located on a hill overlooking more vineyards.

Continue on Route 20 until you reach the **Village of Westfield**, which is filled with a number of homes built in the early 1800s.

In 1897, Dr. Thomas Welch, founder of Welch's Foods, built his first grape juice factory in Westfield; the area was known as the Grape Juice Capital of the World.

One of the best places to learn about area history is at the **McClurg Museum**, which houses the collections of the Chautauqua County Historical Society. This 16-room mansion, located in Moore Park, was built by James

MOORE PARK/MCCLURG MUSEUM, WESTFIELD

LINCOLN BEDELL STATUES, WESTFIELD

McClurg between 1818 and 1820. A wealthy man, McClurg wanted to provide his family with more stately living conditions than the other area settlers, who lived in log homes. When the last of McClurg's descendants died, the home was left to the Village of Westfield to be used as a public building.

Diagonally across the street from Moore Park you'll see the Lincoln-Bedell statues. Sculpted by Westfield native Don Sottile, they depict the meeting between 12-year-old Grace Bedell and Abraham Lincoln at the Westfield train station on February 16, 1861. Bedell had previously written Lincoln a letter suggesting he grow a beard to improve his appearance.

Some of the shops in Westfield include **Surroundings Art Gallery** and several antiques shops, including the **Westfield Village Antique Center**, which features 75 dealers of antiques and collectibles.

Back on Route 20, the **Westfield Main Diner** is a 1929 Ward and Dickinson diner decorated with antiques and Westfield memorabilia. They serve made-from-scratch classic American food like burgers, soups, and homemade pies. Across from Moore Park, **The Parkview** has been voted the best restaurant in Chautauqua County. Everything is made fresh daily. Next door, **Brazill's on Main** offers casual fine dining. Looking for pies to take home? Head around the corner to **Portage Pies**, which offers freshly baked, handmade pies. If you crave Italian, be sure to stop by **Calarco's,** which has been in business for over 80 years.

If you want to stay a little longer in Westfield, there are a few bed & breakfast inns nearby. The **Brick House B&B** has five guest rooms in an 1840 Gothic Victorian home, while the **Candlelight Lodge Bed & Breakfast** offers seven spacious suites and two rooms in an 1851 Victorian Italianate brick mansion. The **Barcelona Lakeside Bed & Breakfast**, which has four guest rooms, overlooks Lake Erie and the Barcelona Lighthouse. A short distance away on Route 394, the **William Seward Inn** offers modern amenities with Colonial charm.

Continue west along Route 20 to the **Grape Discovery Center**, which is the best place to learn about the region's grape-growing and agricultural heritage. In additional to learning all about the region's grape-growing history, visitors can sample locally produced wines from Lake Erie Wine Country as well as purchase regional food specialties and grape-themed gift items.

SIDE TRACKS

Take a short detour and head toward Lake Erie on Route 394 to Barcelona Harbor. The area has a large parking lot, a boat launch, and docking facilities, along with picnic tables and benches to sit on while viewing the lake. The Barcelona Lighthouse, a 40-foot-tall stone lighthouse, was commissioned in 1829 and decommissioned in 1859. The lighthouse was the first public building in the United States to be lit with natural gas. The adjacent lighthouse keeper's cottage now houses the Westfield-Barcelona Chamber of Commerce Visitor Center.

BARCELONA LIGHTHOUSE

If hunger strikes, there are several restaurants to choose from in this area. Just around the corner from Barcelona Harbor is **Jack's Barcelona Drive-In**, a small restaurant that has an outdoor patio. It is popular with locals for breakfast, lunch, and dinner. Across the street you can enjoy barbecue favorites at **When Pigs Fly BBQ Pit**, the only authentic west Texas–style barbecue pit on Lake Erie.

WILLIAM SEWARD INN, WESTFIELD

There are three distinct areas within the Grape Discovery Center. The front room serves as a regional welcome center, with area tourism information. A large orientation map of the region shows vineyard locations of the 30,000 acres of grapes. Also located in the front room is a gift shop which features foods made from grapes, such as jams, grape seed oil, and grape juice concentrate, as well as a number of grape-themed items like T-shirts, sweatshirts, and mugs, along with locally made gourmet food items.

The tasting room and café, located in the middle portion of the building, feature over 60 wines representing all 25 wineries in the region. One can sample a flight of four wines or just a glass. Also available are wine slushies and nonalcoholic grape juice slushies, as well as snack foods like cheese and crackers.

The center's back room features interactive exhibits and displays about grape cultivation and grape production, which is designed to teach visitors about the history of the grape production process.

The next stop is **Mazza Chautauqua Cellars** and **Five & 20 Spirits & Brewing,** New York State's first combination winery, distillery, and brewery. They are located on 80 acres of farmland, which is used to grow the grains for spirit and beer production. Mazza has been making wine in the region for over 40 years; they also own and operate South Shore Wine Company in the town of North East, Pennsylvania.

A short distance down the road, **Johnson Estates**, established in 1961, is the oldest exclusive estate winery in the state. At an estate winery, the grapes are grown and vinified and the wine bottled in the chateau tradition. Their signature wine, Liebestropfchen (Little Love Drops), a sweet white wine, was first produced in 1961.

Take a short detour off Route 20 (Creamery Road to Hardscrabble Road) to **Nobel Winery,** which has a large tasting room with a great view of Lake Erie. Ask to borrow a pair of their binoculars; on a clear day you can see across the lake to Port Dover, Ontario.

Head back to Route 20 to the village of Ripley. You may want to stop at **Meeder's Restaurant,** which is noted for home cooking and homemade pies and desserts.

The next stop is **Sensory Winery,** which produces small lots of unusual wine blends, only 45 cases per label. Their wines have names like Enthrall, Darvon, and Jaunty. They also have an art gallery which has changing exhibits, along with a retail shop featuring wine-themed and art-related items. They even offer classes in painting, photography, and more. Across the street, **Quincy Wine Cellars** is located in a 130-year-old barn, which has a stone cellar that serves as their tasting room.

Sparking Ponds Winery, on Route 5 in Ripley, is named after the ponds on their property. They make sparkling versions of traditional wines. Their wines have names like Woman Pleaser, a Niagara wine with a hint of cranberry; Fatal Attraction, made with a blend of Marechal Foch and concord wine; and a Girls-r-meaner, better known as Gewürztraminer.

You'll have to take a slight detour off Route 20 to get to **Blueberry Sky Farm Winery,** a family-owned winery located on a 70-acre blueberry farm. They specialize in sweet and dry fruit wines like blueberry and dandelion.

If you haven't had your fill of wineries, head back to Route 20 and cross over the border into Pennsylvania, where there are a dozen more wineries that are part of the trail. While this book focuses on locations in New York State, below are some wineries and other attractions found just across the state line in the town of North East, Pennsylvania.

Heritage Wine Cellars, founded in 1976, is located in a restored 18th-century barn. This winery, operated by sixth-generation farmers, features 53 varieties of wine. They make more familiar wines, like Concord, blush, Niagara, and Delaware, along with more interesting-sounding specialty and sparkling wines like elderberry, loganberry, Bubbly Niagara, and Bursting Blueberry.

The wines at **Arrowhead Wine Cellars,** a family-owned winery, include chardonnay, riesling, Niagara, and pink Catawba, along with a variety of fruit and sparkling wines. They also have the area's largest winery-themed gift shop.

Arundel Cellars and Brewery, located in a 19th-century barn that was once a cider mill, has a variety of wines, craft beers, and hard and sweet cider. Their wines have names like Young Love, Sweet Kiss, and Soulmate. During July and August they have a summer concert series, Music in the Vineyards.

HERITAGE WINE CELLARS, NORTH EAST, PA

Lakeview Wine Cellars, a small boutique winery, specializes in oak-aged wines. Some of their specialties include chardonnay, cabernet sauvignon, Niagara, and riesling. They have a view of Lake Erie and a pond on their property shaped like a wine bottle.

South Shore Wine Company, which is owned by Mazza Wines, has a tasting room located in a stone cellar that was the original home to Erie County, Pennsylvania's first commercial winery. They have a seasonal café; you can eat indoors or outside on their screened-in porch.

Courtyard Winery specializes in small-batch, handcrafted wine. They have separate sweet and dry tasting bars in their tasting room.

Penn Shore Winery Land Vineyards, established in 1969, is one of the largest and longest established wineries in Pennsylvania. They have a variety of wines to offer, from table wines like Crystal Lake White to premium wines like Seyval Blanc and Baco Noir. During the summer months they offer music in the vineyards.

Presque Isle Wine Cellars has been producing wine since 1969. They offer tastings, a café menu, and more. Some of their wines include Concord, Niagara, and pinot grigio. They also carry a large selection of wine-making supplies.

6 Mile Cellars is located in Harbourcreek, about 6 miles east of Erie. Their tasting room is in the cellar of a renovated 100+-year-old barn. White wines are their specialty; they also have several red wines to choose from.

The **Grape Country Marketplace**, in downtown North East, features locally made Welch's juice and jellies, along with other local products. They also have artwork made by local and regional artists.

There are several places to stay in this area, including the **Grape Arbor Bed & Breakfast**, located in downtown North East. This romantic inn has eight guest rooms/suites, each named after a variety of locally grown grape. They are known for their delicious breakfasts. There is also a **Holiday Inn Express** in the area, along with a number of other accommodations listed on North East's Chamber of Commerce website.

The annual Wine Country Harvest Festival takes place in North East in late September (www.nechamber.org/winefest).

SOUTH SHORE WINE COMPANY, NORTH EAST, PA

IN THE AREA

Accommodations

BARCELONA LAKESIDE BED & BREAKFAST, 8223 East Lake Road, Westfield, 716-326-3756. www.barcelonalakeside.com. $$.

BRICK HOUSE BED & BREAKFAST, 7573 East Main Road, Westfield, 716-326-6262. www.brickhousebnb.com. $$.

CANDLELIGHT LODGE BED & BREAKFAST, 143 East Main Street, Westfield, 716-326-2830. www.landmarkacres.com. $$.

GRAPE ARBOR BED & BREAKFAST, 51 East Main Street, North East, PA, 814-725-0048. www.grapearborbandb.com. $$.

HOLIDAY INN EXPRESS, 6310 Old Station Road, North East, PA, 814-725-4400. $$.

THE WHITE INN, 52 East Main Street, Fredonia, 716-672-2103. www.whiteinn.com. $$.

WILLIAM SEWARD INN, 6645 South Portage Road, Westfield, 716-326-4151. www.williamsewardinn.com. $$.

Attractions, Recreation, and Shopping

In Chautauqua County

21 BRIX WINERY, 6654 West Main Road, Portland, 716-792-2749. www.21brix.com

BLUEBERRY SKY FARM WINERY, 10243 Northeast Sherman Road, South Ripley, 716-252-6535. Open Monday–Saturday 10:00 AM-6:00 PM, Sunday 12:00–5:00 PM.

FREDONIA OPERA HOUSE, 9 Church Street, Fredonia, 716-679-1891. www.fredopera.org

GRAPE DISCOVERY CENTER, 8305 West Main Road (Route 20), Westfield, 716-326-2003. www.grapediscoverycenter.com

JOHNSON ESTATE WINERY, 8419 West Main Road, Westfield, 716-326-2191. Open daily 10:00 AM-6:00 PM. www.johnsonwinery.com

LIBERTY VINEYARDS & WINERY, 2861 Route 20, Sheridan, 716-672-2067. Open Monday–Saturday 10:00 AM-6:00 PM, Sunday 11:00 AM-5:00 PM. www.libertywinery.com

MAZZA CHAUTAUQUA CELLARS AND FIVE & 20 SPIRITS & BREWING, 8398 West Main Road (Route 20), Westfield, 716-793-9463. www.mcc.mazzawines.com or www.fiveand20.com

MCCLURG MUSEUM, Moore Park, Routes 20 and 394, Westfield, 716-326-2977. www.mcclurgmuseum.org

MERRITT ESTATE WINERY, 2265 King Road, Forestville, 716-965-4800 or 888-965-4800. Open year-round Monday–Saturday 10:00 AM-5:00 PM, Sunday 12:00–5:00 PM. www.merrittestatewinery.com

NOBLE WINERY, 8630 Hardscrabble Road, Westfield, 716-326-2600. Open daily 11:00 AM-6:00 PM. www.noblewinery.com

QUINCY WINE CELLARS, 10606 US 20, Ripley, 716-736-2021. Open Tuesday–Thursday 10:00 AM–6:00 PM, Friday–Saturday 10:00 AM–9:00 PM, Sunday 11:00 AM–5:00 PM. www.quincycellars.com

SENSORY WINERY & ART GALLERY, 10593 West Main Road, Ripley, 716-736-2444. www.sensorywinery.com

SPARKING PONDS WINERY, 10661 West Lake Road, Ripley, 716-736-4525. January 1–April 1 open Friday–Sunday 11:00 AM–5:00 PM. Rest of the year open Monday and Friday 11:00 AM–6:00 PM, Sunday, Tuesday–Thursday 11:00 AM–5:00 PM, Saturday 10:00 AM–6:00 PM.

SURROUNDINGS ART GALLERY AND FRAMING, 73 East Main Street, Westfield, 716-326-7373. www.surroundingswestfield.com

VALVO'S CANDY AND GIFT SHOP, 1277 Route 5 & 20, Silver Creek, 716-934-2535. Open daily 9:00 AM–8:00 PM. www.valvoscandy.com

VETTER VINEYARDS, 8005 Prospect Station Road (off Route 20), Westfield, 716-326-3100. Open May–November 10:00 AM–6:00 PM daily, December–April open Thursday–Monday 11:00 AM–5:00 PM.

WESTFIELD VILLAGE ANTIQUE CENTER, 58 East Main Street, Westfield, 716-232-4238. Open Monday–Thursday and Saturday 10:00 AM–5:00 PM, Friday 11:00 AM–7:00 PM, Sunday 11:30 AM–4:00 PM. www.westfieldvillage antiquecenter.com

WILLOW CREEK WINERY, 2627 Chapin Road, Sheridan, 716-934-9463. Open May–December, Monday–Friday 11:00 AM–5:00 PM, Saturday and Sunday 11:00 AM–6:00 PM. Open weekends December–April. www.willowcreek wines.net

WOODBURY VINEYARDS, 3230 South Roberts Road, Fredonia, 716-679-9463 or 888-697-9463. Open year-round, Monday–Saturday 10:00 AM–5:00 PM, Sunday 12:00–5:00 PM. www.woodburyvineyards.com

In North East, Pennsylvania

6 MILE CELLARS, 5727 Firman Road, Erie, PA, 814-580-8375, and 4753 West Lake Road, Erie, PA. www.6milecellars.com

ARROWHEAD WINE CELLARS, 12073 East Main Road, North East, PA, 814-725-5509. Open Monday–Saturday 10:00 AM–6:00 PM, Sunday 12:00–5:00 PM. www.arrowheadwine.com

ARUNDEL CELLARS AND BREWERY, 11727 East Main Road, North East, PA, 814-725-1079. www.arundelcellars.com

COURTYARD WINERY, 10021 West Main Street, North East, PA, 814-725-0236. www.courtyardwinery.com

GRAPE COUNTRY MARKETPLACE, 15 West Main Street, North East, PA. www.grapecountrymarketplace.org

HERITAGE WINE CELLARS, 12160 East Main Road (Route 20), North East, PA, 1-800-747-0083 or 814-725-8015. Open Sunday–Friday 12:00-5:00 PM, Saturday 10:00 AM–6:00 PM (Summer 10:00 AM–6:00 PM daily). www .heritagewine.biz

LAKEVIEW WINE CELLARS, 8440 Singer Road, North East, PA, 814-725-5040. Check website for hours. www.lakeviewwinecellars.com

PENN SHORE WINERY AND VINEYARDS, 10225 East Lake Road, North East, PA, 814-725-8688. Open Monday–Saturday 9:00 AM–5:30 PM, Sunday 11:00 AM–4:30 PM. www.pennshore.com

PRESQUE ISLE WINERY, 9440 West Main Road, North East, PA, 814-725-1314 or 800-488-7492. Open Monday–Saturday 8:00 AM–5:00 PM. Café open Monday–Saturday 11:00 AM–5:00 PM, Sunday 11:00 AM–4:00 PM. www.piwine .com

SOUTH SHORE WINE COMPANY, 1120 Freeport Road, North East, PA, 814-725-1585. www.ss.mazzawines.com

Dining and Nightlife

BRAZILL'S ON MAIN, 7 East Main Street, Westfield, 716-326-2203.

CALARCO'S, 15 Market Street, Westfield, 716-326-3415.

JACK'S BARCELONA DRIVE-IN, 8249 First Street, Westfield, 716-326-2277. Open Monday–Friday 7:00 AM–9:00 PM, Saturday and Sunday 7:00 AM–3:00 PM.

MEEDER'S RESTAURANT, 19 East Main Street, Ripley, 716-736-7381. www
.meedersrestaurant.com

THE PARKVIEW, 3 East Main Street, Westfield, 716-326-3600. www.park
viewcafeandcatering.com

PORTAGE PIES, 42 North Portage Street, Westfield, 716-232-4036. Open
Wednesday–Saturday 10:00 AM–6:00 PM, Sunday 11:00 AM–2:00 PM, or until
sold out. www.portagepie.com

SULLIVAN'S CHARBROIL, 3590 East Main Street, Fredonia, 716-672-6225.

UPPER CRUST BAKEHOUSE, 27 East Main Street, Fredonia, 716-672-2253.

WESTFIELD MAIN DINER, 40 East Main Street, Westfield, 716-326-4351.

WHEN PIGS FLY BBQ PIT, 8254 First Street, Westfield, 716-326-2017. www
.whenpigsflybbqpit.com

THE WHITE INN, 52 East Main Street, Fredonia, 716-672-2103. www.whiteinn
.com

WING CITY GRILLE, 10450 Bennett Road (Route 60), Fredonia, 716-679-
1116. www.wingcitygrille.com

Other Contacts

FREDONIA CHAMBER OF COMMERCE, 25 Day Street, Fredonia, 716-679-
1565. www.fredoniachamber.org

LAKE ERIE WINE COUNTRY, www.lakeeriewinecountry.org

NORTH EAST CHAMBER, 44 West Main Street, North East, PA. www.ne
chamber.org

WESTFIELD INFORMATION, visitor center in Barcelona Lighthouse
keeper's cottage on Route 5. Open Monday–Friday 10:30 AM–4:30 PM. www
.westfieldny.com; www.townofwestfield.org; www.villageofwestfield.org

AMISH FARM

6

WESTERN NEW YORK'S AMISH COMMUNITY

Cherry Creek, Leon, Conewango Valley

ESTIMATED LENGTH: Varies, round-trip from Buffalo approximately 150 miles

ESTIMATED TIME: Day trip

HIGHLIGHTS: There is a large Old Order Amish community located in the Southern Tier of western New York in Chautauqua and Cattaraugus Counties, concentrated mainly in the towns of Leon, Cherry Creek, and Conewango Valley. This particular community of Amish settled in the area in 1949 with families that came from Pennsylvania and Ohio in search of inexpensive land and a less commercial community. Today there are about 200 Amish families in this area.

The Amish are a group of Christians who revere family values, faith, and hard work. The Amish are known for their skilled craftsmanship. They make their living from farming and from selling quilts, furniture, wooden items, baked goods, and more from shops beside their homes. There are over 100 Amish shops located in this area, the majority of them in the town of Leon, where over 75 percent of the town is Amish. While most shops sell goods to both the Amish community and "the English" (everyone who's not Amish), some of these shops, such as buggy makers and blacksmiths, cater strictly to the Amish community.

GETTING THERE: From the Buffalo area, take Route 62 south to the Leon area. Once there, you will see signs pointing to various Amish businesses. From points east and west, take the Southern Tier Expressway (I-86) to Exit 16, Randolph. It's best to obtain a map to the Amish shops before traveling here; one can be downloaded from www.amishtrail.com, or call Cattaraugus County Tourism at 800-331-0543.

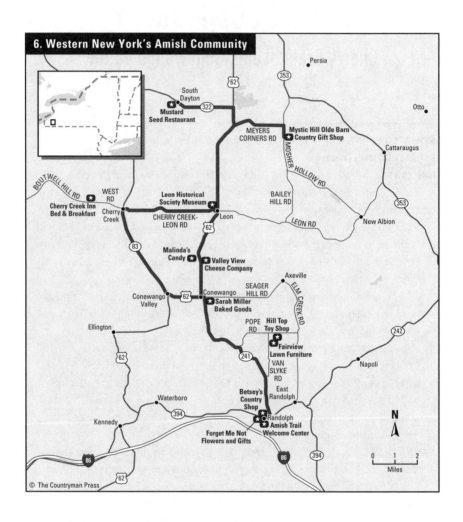

6. Western New York's Amish Community

Persia

Otto

South Dayton

★ Mustard Seed Restaurant

322

62

353

MEYERS CORNERS RD

Mystic Hill Olde Barn ★ Country Gift Shop

Cattaraugus

MOSHER HOLLOW RD

BOUTWELL HILL RD

WEST RD

★ Cherry Creek Inn Bed & Breakfast

Cherry Creek

Leon Historical ★ Society Museum

CHERRY CREEK-LEON RD

Leon

62

BAILEY HILL RD

LEON RD

353

New Albion

83

Malinda's Candy ★

★ Valley View Cheese Company

Axeville

ELM CREEK RD

Conewango Valley

62

Conewango

SEAGER HILL RD

★ Sarah Miller Baked Goods

Ellington

62

POPE RD

Hill Top Toy Shop

★
★ Fairview Lawn Furniture

241

VAN SLYKE RD

Napoli

242

Waterboro

394

Betsey's Country Shop

East Randolph

★
★ Randolph Amish Trail Welcome Center

N

Kennedy

Forget Me Not Flowers and Gifts

86

86

394

0 1 2

Miles

© The Countryman Press

62

Before we get started on our drive, here is a little background on the Amish. The religion can be traced back to the Protestant Reformation in the 16th century, when there was a split in the Roman Catholic Church. A group referred to as the Anabaptists emerged in Switzerland; they were later called Mennonites, after one of their leaders, Menno Simons. In 1693, a group of Mennonites, led by Jacob Amman, felt that the church was losing its purity, so they broke away from the Mennonites and were nicknamed "Amish."

Members of this religious group first arrived in the United States in the 1700s and settled in Pennsylvania. In the mid-1800s, there was once again a division in the church. While some sects decided to be less conservative and embrace new technology of the day, some communities, referred to as

Keep the following things in mind when visiting the area:

1. Don't take pictures of the Amish. It's against their beliefs. Photos of buildings or scenery are okay.
2. Businesses are cash only; they do not accept credit cards.
3. Amish shops are closed on Sundays and religious holidays. They also close if there is a wedding or funeral in the community.
4. The shops are in very remote areas. There are no gas stations or restaurants, so be sure to fill your tank before you go. Expect your car to get dirty on the unpaved roads.

AMISH HORSE AND BUGGY

AMISH SCHOOLHOUSE

the "Old Order Amish," live according to old traditions and continue to use mid-1800s agriculture and building methods.

They don't believe in having modern conveniences like telephones, indoor plumbing, and electricity. They travel in horse-drawn buggies; however, if an urgent need arises, they are permitted to ride in a car or use a phone—they just can't own them. Their religion is based on being humble; they all dress alike because they don't want to stand out. The three most important things to them are faith, family, and community.

If you feel uncomfortable visiting the shops on your own, especially if this is your first time here, you can make arrangements to have a personalized tour of the area. These two-hour tours are led by local historians who will join you in your vehicle and take you around to some of the shops while giving an overview of the Amish community. Contact either the **Randolph Area Community Development** or the **Leon Historical Society Museum.**

While every drive through the area will be different depending on what you are interested in, here are a few suggestions of shops to visit. There are many places that make custom furniture, both for indoors, as in bedroom sets and dining room furniture, and outdoors. If you go to any of the furniture shops with a photo of what you want, the Amish will be able to build it for you.

One shop that has really nice outdoor furniture made of maintenance-free plywood is **Fairview Lawn Furniture,** operated by Raymond and Linda

Raber. While the Amish don't use electricity, they do use gasoline-powered machines to make furniture and other items out of wood. The Rabers also have another shop on their property with woven rugs and quilted items.

If you want wooden toys or wooden kitchen items, like paper towel holders, stop by the **Hill Top Toy Shop**, operated by Dan Raber. A diesel engine located below the shop runs all the machinery.

Stop by any quilt shop and you'll be impressed with the handiwork; all the quilts are hand-pieced and hand-quilted. If you wonder how they find the time to do this, remember that since they don't have the distractions of modern life, like TVs and computers, sitting and quilting is a form of entertainment and socialization for them. Also, since Amish families are large, the children help out.

While the Amish adults speak English to visitors, among themselves they speak an old German dialect. Children younger than 6 will only speak in German; once they go to school they learn to speak English and learn to read and write in both German and English. Children attend local Amish schools until eigth grade, and then they go to work at home or in the community.

If you like sweets, you are in luck, as there are many Amish shops selling candy and baked goods. **Malinda's Candy** has a selection of homemade chocolates and fudge. Don't leave the area without getting one of the giant maple-glazed doughnuts that **Sarah Miller** has for sale, along with other yummy baked goods. The doughnuts measure about 6 inches in diameter!

Besides the Amish shops in this area, there are also a variety of other shops and businesses to visit. **Valley View Cheese Company** makes and sells cheese on-site. They also have snacks and grocery items, along with some Amish-made goods.

In the village of Randolph, shop at **Forget Me Not Flowers and Gifts** for jewelry and gift items. Across the street, **Randolph Retail Company** has clothing, jewelry, accessories, gourmet foods, and more. Down the street, **Inkley Pharmacy** also has a gift shop. **Betsey's Country Shop** has a selection of fabrics and quilting supplies; they also do sewing machine repairs.

Another shop located about a half hour north of Randolph is **Mystic Hill Olde Barn Country Gift Shop,** which specializes in the

AMISH QUILT SHOP

THE MUSTARD SEED RESTAURANT, SOUTH DAYTON

sale of local Amish wares, along with country and rustic items. Located in a 160-year-old barn, you can browse through two floors of items. They purchase items from the Amish at a slight discount, and then re-sell them at the same price you'd pay if you were buying directly from the Amish, giving people the opportunity to shop at one location rather than traveling from farm to farm.

Vern's Place, right down the street from Betsey's in Randolph, is a great place to enjoy breakfast and lunch. However, if you want a real treat, head to **The Mustard Seed Restaurant** in South Dayton, which serves sandwiches on homemade bread, soups, salads, and house-made desserts.

If you want to stay overnight in the area, the **Cherry Creek Inn Bed & Breakfast** is a popular place to stay. The 1860 Italianate-style inn features three guest rooms with private baths, plus a two-bedroom suite. There is also an inn right in downtown Randolph, the **Inn at One Bank Street**, which has four nonsmoking, pet-friendly rooms.

IN THE AREA

Accommodations

CHERRY CREEK INN BED & BREAKFAST, 1022 West Road, Cherry Creek, 716-296-5105. www.cherrycreekinn.net. $$.

THE INN AT ONE BANK STREET, 1 Bank Street, Randolph, 716-358-2022. www.theinnatonebankstreet.com. $.

Dining and Nightlife

THE MUSTARD SEED RESTAURANT, 315 Pine Street (Route 322), South Dayton, 716-988-3800. Open Thursday–Saturday 11:00 AM–8:00 PM. www .themustardseedrestaurant.com

VERN'S PLACE, 16 Jamestown Street, Randolph, 716-358-5166.

Shopping
(note that Amish shops don't have phones or websites)

BETSEY'S COUNTRY SHOP, 12 Jamestown Street, Randolph, 716-358-9704.

FAIRVIEW LAWN FURNITURE, 4789 Walker Road (off Route 241), Randolph.

FORGET ME NOT FLOWERS AND GIFTS, 144 Main Street, Randolph, 716-358-5203. www.forgetmenot-ny.com

HILL TOP TOY SHOP, 11369 Pope Road, Randolph.

INKLEY PHARMACY, 113 Main Street, Randolph, 716-358-3201.

MALINDA'S CANDY, 12656 Youngs Road, Conewango Valley.

MYSTIC HILL OLDE BARN COUNTRY GIFT SHOP, 7840 Mosher Hollow Road, Cattaraugus, 716-912-0981. Open June–October Tuesday–Saturday 10:00 AM–5:00 PM; April–May, November–December Thursday–Saturday 10:00 AM–6:00 PM.

AMISH TOY SHOP

RANDOLPH RETAIL COMPANY, 127 Main Street, Randolph, 716-358-5758. Open Tuesday–Friday 10:00 AM–5:00 PM, Saturday 10:00 AM–3:00 PM. www .randolphretail.com

SARAH MILLER BAKED GOODS, 12624 Seager Hill Road (Route 62), Cone-wango Valley.

VALLEY VIEW CHEESE COMPANY, 6028 Route 62, Conewango Valley, 716-296-5821.

Other Contacts

AMISH TRAIL, Amish Trail Welcome Center at Randolph Area Municipal Building, 72 Main Street, Randolph, 800-331-0543. www.amishtrail.com

CATTARAUGUS COUNTY TOURISM, 800-331-0543. www.enchanted mountains.info

CHAUTAUQUA COUNTY VISITOR BUREAU, 800-242-4569. www.tour chautauqua.com

LEON HISTORICAL SOCIETY MUSEUM, 716-296-5709. www.leonhistorical society.webs.com/

RANDOLPH AREA COMMUNITY DEVELOPMENT, www.enjoyrandolph .com

MOUNT MORRIS

7

THE LETCHWORTH REGION
Including Letchworth State Park, Geneseo,
Mount Morris, and Piffard

ESTIMATED LENGTH: About 60 miles

ESTIMATED TIME: Day trip; about 2 hours straight drive time, allow more time to stop and explore

HIGHLIGHTS: This drive starts out in Geneseo, a college town home to SUNY Geneseo. The Village of Geneseo was designated a National Historic District in 1991 because of all the historic buildings that line Main Street. First settled in 1790, the name *Geneseo* is a Seneca Indian name meaning "beautiful valley." You can explore a number of shops and restaurants here before heading to nearby Piffard to visit the Abbey of the Genesee, a beautiful and peaceful site. It is here where the popular Monk's Bread, sold in regional grocery stores, is made. Next, head to Mount Morris, a small town with a few antiques and gift shops, along with several restaurants. Mount Morris was the boyhood home of Frances Bellamy, who wrote the Pledge of Allegiance. Of course, the most well-known site in Mount Morris is the Mount Morris Dam, located in the Genesee River. Take a drive through the rural countryside before heading to the 17-mile-long Letchworth State Park, known as the Grand Canyon of the East. You can spend hours exploring the park, its waterfalls, and hiking trails. Stay overnight in one of their many cabins or campsites, or in the quaint Glen Iris Inn.

GETTING THERE: Access the area from Exit 8 off the I-390 expressway, which connects to the New York State Thruway (I-90) in the north and the I-86 expressway in the south. Take Route 20A west into the village of Geneseo to begin this drive.

We will start this drive in the village of Geneseo; park your car in the large municipal lot behind the Main Street shops, which can be accessed from either Chestnut Street or Center Street. Stop by the **Geneseo Welcome Center** for brochures and maps of the area, including a walking tour

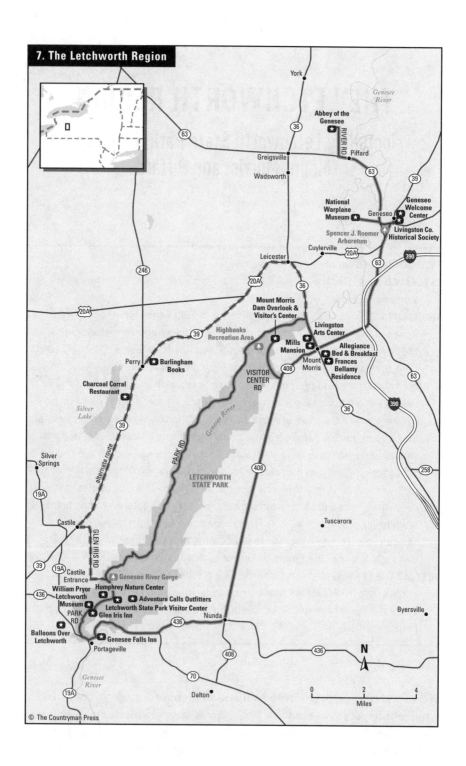

7. The Letchworth Region

York

Genesee River

Abbey of the Genesee ★

63

36

RIVER RD

Greigsville

Piffard

Wadsworth

63

39

National Warplane Museum ★

Geneseo ★

Geneseo Welcome Center ★

Spencer J. Roemer Arboretum ★

Livingston Co. Historical Society

Cuylerville

Leicester

20A

63

390

246

20A

36

20A

Mount Morris Dam Overlook & Visitor's Center

Highbanks Recreation Area

39

Livingston Arts Center ★

Mills Mansion ★

Allegiance Bed & Breakfast ★

Perry ★ Burlingham Books

Mount Morris

Frances Bellamy Residence ★

Charcoal Corral Restaurant ★

VISITOR CENTER RD

408

63

Silver Lake

Genesee River

39

36

390

PARK RD

Silver Springs

alternate route

LETCHWORTH STATE PARK

408

258

19A

Castile

GLEN IRIS RD

Tuscarora

39

19A

Castile Entrance

Genesee River Gorge

Humphrey Nature Center

William Pryor Letchworth Museum ★

★ Adventure Calls Outfitters

Letchworth State Park Visitor Center ★

Byersville

PARK RD

Glen Iris Inn ★

Nunda

436

Balloons Over Letchworth ★

408

★ Genesee Falls Inn

Portageville

436

436

N

Genesee River

70

0   2   4

Miles

19A

Dalton

© The Countryman Press

ABBEY OF THE GENESEE, PIFFARD

map of the village, which includes descriptions of the historic homes and buildings.

Some of the places to shop along Main Street include **Touch of Grayce**, which carries books, toys, clothing, jewelry, puzzles, and more. **Honey Girl Gourmet** is a specialty food and gift shop, while the **Not Dot Shop** has antiques, vintage items, gifts, and jewelry. Just a few blocks from Main Street, the **Livingston County Historical Society** is located in an 1838 cobblestone building that was once a schoolhouse. The museum has a variety of exhibits about the history of Livingston County.

There are over a dozen places to get a bite to eat in Geneseo. Some of these include **Sweet Arts Bakery**, a family-run bakery with baked goods, soups, and quiche that also has artwork by local artists for sale on its walls; **Bar Eat O**, which features Mexican fare; **Aunt Cookie's Sub Shop**, which has the best subs in town; and **Mama Mia's Restaurant**, with its pizza and pasta, popular with the locals and college crowd.

Places to stay along Main Street include the **Big Tree Inn**, which has eight renovated antiques-furnished rooms. Built in 1833, it was named after a great oak tree that once stood near Geneseo. The inn also has a restaurant that is open for lunch and dinner. **The Annabel Lee Bed & Breakfast**, also on Main Street, offers five guest rooms in an 1889 Queen Anne Victorian house. **Temple Hill Bed & Breakfast**, just four blocks from

BIG TREE INN, GENESEO

Main Street, has four large guest rooms in a brick mansion.

If you have a chance, head over to the SUNY Geneseo campus and explore the 20-acre **Spencer J. Roemer Arboretum**, which has more than 70 species of trees, shrubs, and wildflowers.

The **National Warplane Museum**, a short drive from the village off Route 63, is a warbird and military history museum dedicated to restoring and flying vintage aircraft of World War II and the Korean War era and preserving aviation history. An annual air show takes place during the summer.

Continue on Route 63, a few miles west of Geneseo, to the **Abbey of the Genesee** on River Road in Piffard. The abbey is a community of contemplative Trappist monks who have supported themselves since the 1950s by baking Monk's Bread, which is sold in area grocery stores and in their bread store at the abbey. Visitors can explore the peaceful grounds and even join the monks in prayer; there is a 6:00 AM Mass and midday prayers at 11:15 AM.

Afterward, take Route 63 west to Route 36 south to the village of Mount Morris, the birthplace of Frances Bellamy, who wrote the Pledge of Allegiance. Bellamy spent the first five years of his life here before his father, a minister, accepted a position in Rome, New York. As a young man, Bellamy was a writer for a magazine called *Youth's Companion* and wrote the pledge as part of a campaign to promote patriotism and to celebrate the 400th anniversary of Columbus's discovery of America. The house that Bellamy lived in in Mount Morris (163 Main Street) is a private residence; there is a historical marker in front of it.

You'll notice as you walk through the town that there are many signs about and references to the Pledge of Allegiance, as well of lots of flags displayed. Also, take time to look at the architecture of the buildings.

To learn more about Mount Morris history, visit the **Mills Mansion**, a 1838 Federal-style brick home, once the home of General William Mills, the founder of Mount Morris. It is now a museum operated by the Mount Morris Historical Society.

Learn about the arts in Livingston County at the **Livingston Arts Center** in Mount Morris, located on the Livingston County Campus, a former tuberculosis hospital complex. The arts center is located in the former doctors' residence building. Galleries include the New Deal Gallery, the world's only gallery dedicated to Work Progress Administration (WPA) easel art; over 200 WPA paintings from the 1930s are on display. Under

President Franklin Roosevelt's New Deal program, thousands of artists were hired to create art in public spaces in the United States. The former hospital had about 250 of these works on display; the art was stored away when the hospital closed.

The arts center's other gallery, Apartment One, has works by regional artists which are rotated every three months. The center, which has a gift shop, also offers classes and workshops, as well as a children's summer camp. Their annual holiday event takes place in November.

Some of the shops in town include **Allegiance Antiques**, which has all sorts of vintage and antique items, **Jane's Pantry**, an old-fashioned candy store that also sells gourmet foods and spices, and the adjacent **Pantry Mouse Tea House**, which has loose tea, tea accessories, and afternoon tea by reservation. **Carvings and More** is a consignment shop specializing in arts, crafts, and antiques; 35 artists and 12 antiques dealers have items for sale here.

There are also a number of restaurants in town, including **Charred Bar & Grill**, a casual restaurant featuring classic American fare and local microbrews and wines. You can get Italian fare at **Tomaso Trattoria** and **Questa Lasagna**, and hot dogs and burgers at **Regal Hots**. For dessert, stop by **Zeppo's Ice Cream Parlor**, a small shop, open seasonally, that makes its own ice cream, with unique flavors like cinnamon roll. Located just north of town,

MOUNT MORRIS

MOUNT MORRIS DAM

Brian's USA Diner is a very popular classic diner offering made-from-scratch comfort food.

If you want to stay overnight, the **Allegiance Bed & Breakfast**, which is within walking distance of shops and restaurants, has nine guest rooms in an 1838 Victorian mansion.

While the north entrance of Letchworth State Park is in Mount Morris, for the purpose of this drive we will be entering the park from the southern entrance. From Mount Morris, head south on Route 408 to the **Mount Morris Dam Overlook and Visitor Center**. Mount Morris has been named the best town by a dam site; one could say it's the best dam town in western New York!

The dam was built by the US Army Corps of Engineers between 1948 and 1952 as a result of the Flood Control Act of 1944. The purpose of the massive dam, which measures 1,028 feet across and is 245 feet tall, is to store flood waters to protect the communities downstream. After looking at the dam from the rim of the gorge, go inside the visitor center to learn more about the dam and the surrounding area. You can even take a guided tour of the inside of the dam between April and October; these are limited to 30 people, first come, first serve.

After visiting the dam, continue south on Route 408; when you get to the Village of Nunda, turn right on Route 436 toward Portageville. Located in

Portageville is the **Genesee Falls Inn**. Built in 1870, it offers comfortable rooms in a Victorian setting. It is located about a 0.5 mile from the Portageville entrance to Letchworth State Park.

Enter **Letchworth State Park** though the Portageville entrance; if that entrance is closed (open seasonally and also closed until late 2018 due to the construction of a new railroad bridge over the gorge by the Upper Falls), continue along Route 436 to Route 39 north and follow the signs to the Castile entrance.

The centerpiece of the 14,350-acre, 17-mile-long park is the 600-foot-deep Genesee River Gorge, known as the Grand Canyon of the East. The original 1,000 acres of the park were donated to the state by Buffalo businessman William Pryor Letchworth in 1859. Letchworth's former country home, now the **Glen Iris Inn**, overlooks the park's Middle Falls, one of the three major waterfalls in the park. The inn offers overnight accommodations, as well as fine dining at **Caroline's**; reservations for both are a must! The park also has almost 300 campsites and 80 cabins, some available year-round.

One of your first stops after entering the park should be the Glen Iris Inn and Middle Falls area, which is one of the most photographed areas of the park. Also in this same area is the **William Pryor Letchworth Museum**, which has displays about early settlement in the region and Native American artifacts. The park's visitor center is located between the Glen Iris Inn

GLEN IRIS INN, LETCHWORTH STATE PARK

and the Castile entrance. Here you can get park information and visit the park's gift shop.

The 5,000-square-foot **Humphrey Nature Center** opened in the park in June 2016 near the Trailside Lodge concession area. Open year-round, it includes interactive exhibits about the park, classrooms, meeting space, and an outdoor butterfly garden.

In addition to hiking the 66 miles of trails, visitors to the park can swim at the pool at the Highgate Recreation Area at the north end of the park, enjoy white-water rafting and guided canoe trips with **Adventure Calls Outfitters,** or even get a bird's-eye view of the park from a hot air balloon with **Balloons Over Letchworth.** In the winter, enjoy cross-country skiing, snowshoeing, and snowmobiling.

The most popular season to visit is the fall, when the fall foliage is at its peak. The annual **Letchworth Arts & Crafts Show,** sponsored by the Arts Council for Wyoming County, is held on Columbus Day weekend, which usually coincides with peak foliage viewing. The show features 400 vendors and draws thousands of people from all over western and central New York.

After visiting the southern portion of the park, continue driving north, following the narrow park road toward the Mount Morris entrance; be sure to stop to see the scenic views along the way. Alternately, leave the park through the Castile entrance and continue north along Route 39, which has

MIDDLE FALLS, LETCHWORTH STATE PARK

GLEN IRIS INN, LETCHWORTH STATE PARK

a nice view of the countryside and dairy farms. You may want to stop at the **Charcoal Corral Restaurant** in Perry, a seasonal, casual, family-friendly eatery which has an Old West theme. Also on the grounds is a video arcade, an 18-hole miniature golf course, and the Silver Lakes Twin Drive-In Theater.

Continue north on Route 39 through the village of Perry. **Burlingham Books**, located right on Main Street, is a good place to stop. They have a large selection of new and used books, magazines, and gifts, along with an espresso bar. The Perry Farmers' Market takes place on Saturdays, June–October, with local produce, maple products, jams, and more, along with live music and children's activities.

Continue on Route 39 until it becomes 20A, follow it east through Leicester and Cuylerville, and you will eventually return to Geneseo, where the journey began.

IN THE AREA

Accommodations

ALLEGIANCE BED & BREAKFAST, 145 Main Street, Mount Morris, 585-658-3524. www.allegiancebandb.com. $$.

THE ANNABEL LEE BED & BREAKFAST, 16 Main Street, Geneseo, 585-243-9440. www.theannabellee.com. $$.

BIG TREE INN, 46 Main Street, Geneseo, 585-243-5220. www.bigtreeinn.com. $$.

GENESEE FALLS INN, Main and Hamilton Streets, Portageville, 585-493-2484. www.geneseefallsinn.com. **.

GLEN IRIS INN, 7 Letchworth State Park, Castile, 585-493-2622. Open Good Friday to the last Saturday in October. www.glenirisinn.com. $$.

TEMPLE HILL BED & BREAKFAST, 114 Temple Hill, Geneseo, 585-243-0180. www.templehillbb.com. $$.

Attractions and Recreation

ABBEY OF THE GENESEE, 3258 River Road, Piffard, 585-243-0660. www.geneseeabbey.org

ADVENTURE CALLS OUTFITTERS, 4 Lower Falls Road, Letchworth State Park, Castile, 888-270-2410. www.adventure-calls.com/rafting_letchworth.html

BALLOONS OVER LETCHWORTH, 6773 Halvorsen Road, Portageville, 585-493-3340. www.balloonsoverletchworth.com

HUMPHREY NATURE CENTER, Trailside Lodge, Letchworth State Park, 585-493-3680. Open daily 12:00–5:00 PM. www.nysparks.com/environment/nature-centers/19/details.aspx

LETCHWORTH ARTS & CRAFTS SHOW, Arts Council of Wyoming County, 585-237-3517. www.artswyco.org

LETCHWORTH STATE PARK, 1 Letchworth State Park, Castile, 585-493-3600. www.nysparks.com/parks/79/details.aspx or www.letchworthpark.com

LIVINGSTON ARTS CENTER, 4 Murray Hill Drive, Mount Morris, 585-243-6785. Open Tuesday–Friday 12:00–4:00 PM; Saturday 11:30 AM–2:30 PM. www.livingstonarts.org

WILLIAM PRYOR LETCHWORTH MUSEUM, LETCHWORTH STATE PARK

LIVINGSTON COUNTY HISTORICAL SOCIETY, 30 Center Street, Geneseo, 585-243-9147. www.livingstoncountyhistoricalsociety.com

MILLS MANSION, 14 Main Street, Mount Morris, 585-658-3292. Open June–November, Friday–Saturday.

MOUNT MORRIS DAM OVERLOOK AND VISITOR CENTER, 6103 Visitor Center Road (off Route 408), Mount Morris, 585-658-4790.

NATIONAL WARPLANE MUSEUM, 3489 Big Tree Lane, Geneseo, 585-243-2100. www.nationalwarplane.org

SPENCER J. ROEMER ARBORETUM, 1 College Circle, Geneseo. Open dawn to dusk.

WILLIAM PRYOR LETCHWORTH MUSEUM, www.letchworthparkhistory .com/museum.html

Dining and Nightlife

AUNT COOKIE'S SUB SHOP, 96 Main Street, Geneseo, 585-243-2650.

BAR EAT O, 3 Bank Street, Geneseo, 585-243-9740. www.bar-eat-o.com

BIG TREE INN, 46 Main Street, Geneseo, 585-243-5220. www.bigtreeinn .com

BRIAN'S USA DINER, 5524 Mount Morris Road, Mount Morris, 585-658-9380.

CAROLINE'S AT THE GLEN IRIS INN, 7 Letchworth State Park, Castile, 585-493-2622. Open Good Friday to the last Saturday in October. www .glenirisinn.com

CHARCOAL CORRAL RESTAURANT, 7109 Route 39, Perry, 585-237-3372. Open March–October. www.charcoalcorral.com

CHARRED BAR & GRILL, 36 Main Street, Mount Morris, 585-658-1083. www.charredbar.com

MAMA MIA'S RESTAURANT, 87 Main Street, Geneseo, 585-243-4840. www .miasgeneseo.com

QUESTA LASAGNA, 55 Main Street, Mount Morris, 585-658-3761. www .questalasagna.com

REGAL HOTS, 39 Mill Street, Mount Morris, 585-658-2880.

SWEET ARTS BAKERY, 95 Main Street, Geneseo, 585-245-9161. www .sweetartsny.weebly.com

TOMASO TRATTORIA, 40 Main Street, Mount Morris, 585-658-1045. www .tomasostrattoria.com

ZEPPO'S ICE CREAM, 93 Main Street, Mount Morris, 585-658-3761. Open seasonally.

Shopping

ALLEGIANCE ANTIQUES, 35 Main Street, Mount Morris, 585-658-5470.

BURLINGHAM BOOKS, 2 Main Street, Perry, 585-237-3190. www.burling hambooks.com

CARVINGS AND MORE, 79 Main Street, Mount Morris, 585-658-3775.

HONEY GIRL GOURMET, 61 Main Street, Geneseo, 585-245-8368. www .honeygirlgourmet.com

JANE'S PANTRY/PANTRY MOUSE TEA HOUSE, 82-84 Main Street, Mount Morris, 585-658-9886.

NOT DOT SHOP, 127 Main Street, Geneseo, 585-243-5459. Open Wednesday–Saturday 11:00 AM–5:30 PM, Sunday 11:00 AM–4:00 PM. www.notdotshop.com

TOUCH OF GRAYCE, 65 Main Street, Geneseo, 585-243-4980.

Other Contacts

GENESEO WELCOME CENTER, 81 Main Street (Nothnagle Building), Geneseo. Open Monday–Friday 9:00 AM–5:00 PM.

LIVINGSTON COUNTY CHAMBER OF COMMERCE, 4635 Millennium Drive, Geneseo, 585-243-2222. www.livingstoncountychamber.com

LIVINGSTON COUNTY TOURISM, www.fingerlakeswest.com

MOUNT MORRIS TOURIST INFORMATION, weekends at the Mills Mansion; weekdays at the village offices, 117 Main Street, Mount Morris.

WYOMING COUNTY CHAMBER OF COMMERCE, 36 Center Street, Suite A, Warsaw, 585-786-0009. www.wycochamber.org

WYOMING COUNTY TOURISM, www.gowyomingcountyny.com

8

THE SOUTHERN TIER PART 1

Along the I-86 Corridor from Findley Lake to Angelica

ESTIMATED LENGTH: 110 miles

ESTIMATED TIME: 1–7 days

HIGHLIGHTS: The area, known as the Southern Tier of New York State, is located along the northern Pennsylvania border; it is one of the more rural areas of the state. It is a popular destination to travel to when people want to get away from the hustle and bustle of the city. The region, which has gently rolling mountains, has a variety of attractions, including skiing in the winter, golf in the summer, a number of unique museums, water activities on Chautauqua Lake, camping at Allegany State Park, plus shopping and dining galore. If you choose to fully explore each and every town described in this chapter, it would probably take almost a week; if you have less time available, just pick the places that interest you the most.

GETTING THERE: Follow the New York State Thruway (I-90) west from Buffalo, cross over the state line to Pennsylvania, and travel about 10 miles to the I-86 expressway. Although traveling on an expressway to get from town to town sounds counterintuitive in a book about backroads and byways, this is a very scenic expressway and, given the terrain of the region, it is actually the best way to travel between the many quaint small towns and villages located just off the expressway.

This drive starts in the Village of Findley Lake, on Exit 4 off the I-86 expressway, the westernmost town in New York State. Located at the north end of 3-mile-long Findley Lake, the village is a popular year-round destination, with fishing and boating in the summer and skiing in the winter at nearby Peek 'n Peak Resort, which also has golfing in the warmer months.

LEFT: ROCK CITY PARK, OLEAN

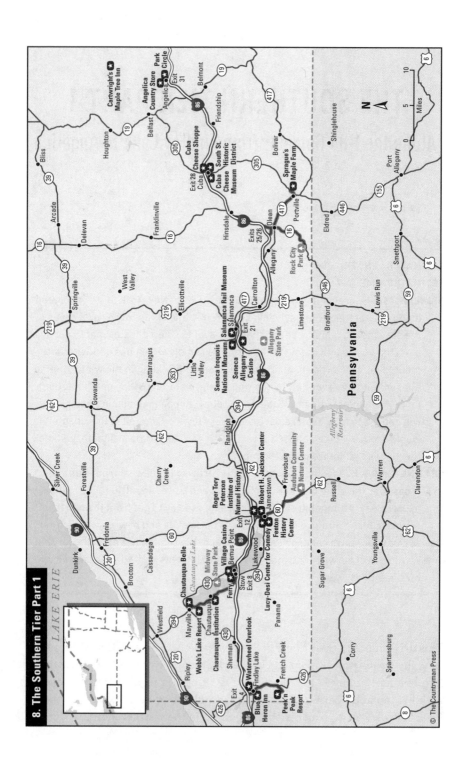

8. The Southern Tier Part 1

The area was settled in 1811 by Alexander Findley, and by the late 1800s it was a very prosperous community. However, many small towns such as Findley Lake saw a decrease in business when automobile travel became popular, as people were able to travel to farther destinations. Over the past few decades, the village has seen revitalization as a recreational and shopping destination.

Although the village is small, there are several retail shops that make the trip to Findley Lake worthwhile. If you like antiques, be sure to stop at the **Secret Cubby of Antiques**, a huge shop with nicely displayed antiques. One could easily spend hours browsing in here. Down the street, **Our Own Candle Company** has a large selection of home decor and giftware. Inside this same store, Findley Lake Fashions has reasonably priced clothing, jewelry, and accessories. Across the street they have an outlet store, **Our Own Candle Company Outlet Store**, which has bargain-priced candles and home decor items, some of which may have small imperfections that are hardly noticeable. Another place in town to find gift items is **Wonderments**, which has a selection of Victorian-inspired gifts.

If you are looking for a place to dine and/or spend the night, the **Blue Heron Inn** is the perfect place. This bed & breakfast, which overlooks Findley Lake, has three antiques-filled guest rooms, along with a dining room that's open to the public. Behind the inn, **Nostalgia at the Blue Heron Inn** is a gift shop featuring handcrafted jewelry, retro candy, Findley Lake apparel, and more.

The **Waterwheel Overlook**, located along Main Street across from the lake, is built on the same location where Alexander Findley built his waterwheel when he first settled here. The building has a meeting room used for special events, as well as rest rooms and tourism information. The adjacent gazebo is a nice place to sit and enjoy the scenery.

Several miles south of the village, **Peek 'n Peak Resort** is an all-season destination offering upscale accommodations, several dining options, and a full-service spa. Enjoy skiing in the winter and golf in the warmer months. It has both outdoor and indoor swimming pools. One can even take a guided Segway tour of the resort grounds or play mini golf.

The next stop along the I-86 corridor is the Chautauqua Lake area. Get off at Exit 8

VIEW OF FINDLEY LAKE

to explore the west side of Chautauqua Lake. The best-known destination in the area is the world-renowned **Chautauqua Institution,** a National Historic District which draws people from all over the country for a nine-week summer program of art, music, performing arts, education, and recreation. A gate fee is charged during this period, except for Sundays, when admission is free.

If you wish to stay overnight in this area, there are hundreds of small cottages, guest houses, and apartments available on and near the grounds of the institution during the summer season, as well as bed & breakfast inns. (See link at end of chapter for more information).

Of course, the most popular place to stay on the grounds is the **Athenaeum Hotel.** Built in 1881, this "grand dame," full-service hotel is on the National Register of Historic Places. It was the first hotel in the world to have electric lights, mainly due to the fact that Mina Miller, the daughter of Chautauqua founder Lewis Miller, was married to inventor Thomas Edison.

Outside the institution's grounds, the **Chautauqua Inn & Suites** in nearby Mayville has 91 guest rooms and overlooks the lake. **Webb's Lake Resort** is also located close to the lake. It has over 50 guest rooms, along with a gift shop, a specialty candy shop, and a large dining room.

CHAUTAUQUA BELLE, MAYVILLE

When in Mayville, take a ride on the *Chautauqua Belle*, a 98-foot, 18½-foot-wide stern wheel steamboat, one of only a handful of 100 percent high-pressured steam-powered vessels in North America.

There are numerous dining options in Mayville. Some of these include **The Watermark**, known for seafood, steak, and a great view of the lake; **Andriaccio's** for Italian; and **La Fleur**, a Four Diamond restaurant known for French cuisine. **The White Carrot Restaurant** offers farm-to-table fine dining; they even have their own garden out back.

Once you're done enjoying this area, head back to I-86 and head across the lake to the next exit, Bemus Point. Alternately, if you're here during the peak summer season and the **Bemus Point-Stow Ferry** is running, take the six-minute ride across the lake from the Village of Stow to Bemus Point on this motor-driven cable ferry which has been in operation since 1811. Before the I-86 bridge was built over the lake, the ferry was the only way to cross the lake at midpoint.

In Bemus Point, you'll find a lovely waterfront area, quaint shops, and several good restaurants. There are no major attractions in Bemus Point. That, in essence, is the point, as it is a place you go to when you want to relax.

Visitors can stay at the **Hotel Lenhart**, which has colorful rockers on a large veranda overlooking the lake. It has 53 guest rooms and has been operated by the same family since 1881.

One of the most popular places to dine in Bemus Point is the **Italian Fisherman**, which specializes in seafood, steak, and pasta. They have a wonderful lobster ravioli! Patrons can arrive by car or boat. Live entertainment takes place on select evenings during the summer months on the adjacent floating stage, including performances by the **Bemus Bay Pops**.

Another village landmark is the **Village Casino**, which first opened in the 1930s. Back then, big bands with headliners like Tommy Dorsey, Glenn Miller, Cab Calloway, and Al Jolson played at the casino. Today it is a casual waterfront restaurant known for sandwiches, burgers, and Buffalo-style chicken wings. Another popular restaurant is **Ellicottville Brewing**, where you can enjoy a view of the lake from a rooftop bar.

Of course, you'll want to do some shopping while in Bemus Point. There are a number of seasonal shops located along Main Street. Some of these include **Skillman's**, a three-story store that has been a household name in Bemus Point since 1908 and which carries jewelry, clothing, shoes, home decor, and more; and, across the street, **Six Main Gifts**, which has a nice selection of collectibles, toys, and other gift items.

Families with young children should check out **Midway State Park**, a few miles away in nearby Maple Springs. The park, which originally opened in 1898, has several old-time favorite rides, including a restored Allan Herschell Carousel.

The next stop along the I-86 corridor is the city of Jamestown, which has

HOTEL LENHART, BEMUS POINT

several attractions of note. If you love Lucy, as in Lucille Ball, a must-see is the **Lucy Desi Center for Comedy**. The museum has photos and artifacts documenting the careers of Lucille Ball, a Jamestown area native, and Desi Arnaz, while the Desilu Studios have complete re-creations of some of the scenes from the "I Love Lucy" show. The Comedy Center, which opened in 2017, includes items donated by the family of the late comedian George Carlin.

Other museums in Jamestown include the **Fenton History Center**, which focuses on local history, and the **Robert H. Jackson Center**, which honors the life of the Nuremberg Trial lawyer, who grew up near Jamestown. Nature lovers will want to stop by the **Audubon Community Nature Center**, located south of the city on a former farm that has 5 miles of hiking trails amid woods, wetlands, and ponds. The **Roger Tory Peterson Institute of Natural History**, located near Jamestown Community College, is named after Roger Tory Peterson, a Jamestown native considered one of the greatest naturalists of the 20th century. The 27-acre site has nature trails, a butterfly garden, and a visitors center with Peterson's life's work on display.

When you're done exploring the Jamestown area, hop back on I-86 and head toward Salamanca, the only city in the United States located entirely on a tribal reservation. There are several must-see attractions here. The **Seneca-Iroquois National Museum** houses exhibits that depict Native

American history and culture of the region. Displays depict a partial long-house and log cabin, traditional crafts, and modern art. The **Salamanca Railroad Museum** is located in a restored 1912 depot. It has many artifacts documenting the golden days of rail travel.

If you enjoy nature, plan a visit to **Allegany State Park**, the largest park in the New York State Parks system. While most of the park is made up of woodlands, there are also two beaches along the park's lake as well as numerous hiking trails. The park has 300 campsites and 300 cabins; 150 of the cabins are winterized.

Those who enjoy nightlife and casino gaming will want to stop by the **Seneca Allegany Casino**, which is open 24/7. The complex has over 68,000 feet of gaming space, along with an 11-story hotel. A 2,400-seat event center attracts national recording artists and comedians to its stage.

The next stop off I-86 is the city of Olean, a college town that is home to St. Bonaventure University. *Olean* means "oil" in Latin; in the late 19th century, the largest oil producers in the world were located in Olean. There are a couple of places to check out in this area. **Rock City Park**, located about 5 miles south of the city, is one of the largest known exposures of

ROCK CITY PARK, OLEAN

A visit to the Olean area is not complete unless you take a ride to **Sprague's Maple Farms** on Route 305 in nearby Portville. Sprague's is a popular destination year-round, but especially popular during the maple sugaring season from late February to April, when they offer tours of their sugaring house. They serve an all-day breakfast, so be sure to order pancakes to try their syrup. The restaurant also serves a variety of other choices for breakfast, lunch, and dinner, including entrees made from the free-range turkeys they raise on the farm. They also have a large retail shop that features their maple products as well as gift items.

SPRAGUE'S MAPLE FARMS, PORTVILLE

quartz conglomerate. The rock formations in this park resemble a city of rocks; the Native Americans actually used this area as a fortress. One of the more unique formations in the 23-acre park includes Balancing Rock, a huge 1,000-ton boulder balancing on another. At the park's Vista View, a popular spot for weddings, one can see 35 miles on a clear day.

Heading back to I-86, there are two more towns to include on your itinerary: Cuba and Angelica. Cuba, Exit 28, is the place to go to learn about the early cheese-making history of the area. In the late 1800s, Cuba was considered the cheese center of the world. The best place to learn about this is at the **Cuba Cheese Museum**, which has a variety of exhibits and artifacts illustrating the evolution of cheese production.

After visiting the museum, you'll probably have a craving for cheese. Luckily, the **Cuba Cheese Shoppe** is just a few blocks away. They carry 200 varieties of cheese, some locally made, along with jams, mustards, and other gourmet foods.

Before leaving Cuba, be sure to check out the four-block South Street Historic District, located just south of the cheese shop. There are numerous Victorian homes which are listed on the State and National Register of Historic Places. The most unique structure in this area is the Block Barn, which is home today to Empire City Farms. This 50-by-347-foot cement building was built in 1909 to house a famous racehorse. The Block Barn is the site of the annual Cuba Garlic Festival in September. Cuba Dairy Week takes place in June.

The last stop along this journey is Angelica, Exit 31 off I-86. Many of the buildings in Angelica, dubbed The Town Where History Lives, are listed on the National Register of Historic Places. Incorporated in 1805, Angelica, named after the mother of town founder Philip Church, is a quaint little village with a number of antiques and gift shops and restaurants.

The **Angelica Country Store** is a great place to browse, as they have something for everyone: jewelry, home decor, cookbooks, kitchen items, and more. If you like antiques, stop by **Heritage Antiques**, a multidealer shop which also has a cafe. The **Angelica Main Street Gallery** has a collection of antiques, artwork, jewelry, Amish crafts, pottery, and more, while the **Angelica Sweet Shop** has a selection of candy and ice cream.

The park circle in Angelica is one of the more picturesque areas in town. It is the site of community events and festivals, such as the Angelica Farmers Market on Saturday mornings, June to September, and the Heritage Christmas Days in December, which features caroling, a living nativity, and hundreds of luminaries lining the park circle. In early December, the Angelica Post Office has its annual angel postmark cancellation; people can bring their Christmas cards to the post office to get a special commemorative postmark. A lovely bed & breakfast inn, **Park Circle Bed & Breakfast,** overlooks the park circle.

If you happen to be visiting the area between mid-February and mid-April, the place to go is the **Cartwright Maple Tree Inn**, which is located several miles north of the village on Route 15A. This family-owned, seasonal pancake house has people from all over the area lining up for their buckwheat pancakes and house-made maple syrup. You can even purchase syrup, maple candy, pancake mix, and other items in a small gift shop inside the pancake house.

This particular journey ends in Angelica. You may continue along the I-86 corridor in the next chapter to travel from Hammondsport to Binghamton.

IN THE AREA

Accommodations

ATHENAEUM HOTEL, 716-357-4444 or 800-821-1881. www.athenaeum-hotel.com. $$$.

BLUE HERON INN, 10412 Main Street, Findley Lake, 716-769-7852. Open year-round. www.theblueheroninn.com. $$.

CHAUTAUQUA INN & SUITES, 215 West Lake Road, Mayville, 716-269-STAY (7829). www.chautauquasuites.com. $$.

CHAUTAUQUA LAKE AREA ACCOMMODATIONS, www.chautauquainns.com. **.

HOTEL LENHART, 20 Lakeshore Drive, Bemus Point, 716-386-2715. Open Memorial Day–September 15. www.hotellenhart.com. $$.

PARK CIRCLE BED & BREAKFAST, 2 East Main Street, Angelica, 585-466-3999 or 800-350-5778. www.parkcirclebedandbreakfast.com. $$.

PEEK'N PEAK RESORT, 1405 Olde Road, Clymer, 716-355-4141. www.pknpk.com. **.

WEBB'S LAKE RESORT, 115 West Lake Road, (Route 394), Mayville, 716-753-2161. www.webbsworld.com. $$.

Attractions and Recreation

ALLEGANY STATE PARK, 2373 ASP Route #1, Salamanca, 716-354-9121. Open year-round, dawn–dusk. Quaker area: www.nysparks.com/parks/1/details.aspx; Red House area: www.nysparks.com/parks/73/details.aspx

AUDUBON COMMUNITY NATURE CENTER, 1600 Riverside Road, Jamestown, 716-569-2345. www.auduboncnc.org

BEMUS BAY POPS, floating stage next to the Italian Fisherman Restaurant, 61 Lakeside Drive, Bemus Point, 716-386-7000. Season runs June–August. www.bemusbaypops.com

BEMUS POINT-STOW FERRY, Lakeside Drive, Bemus Point (by the Village Casino). In Stow, off Route 394, turn by Hogan's Hut. 716-753-2403. Operates seasonally on a sporadic basis.

CHAUTAUQUA BELLE, 15 Water Street, Mayville, 716-753-2403. www.269 belle.com

CHAUTAUQUA INSTITUTION, One Ames Avenue, Chautauqua, 1-800-836-ARTS. www.ciweb.org

CUBA CHEESE MUSEUM, 12 West Main Street, Cuba, 585-209-5312.

FENTON HISTORY CENTER, 67 Washington Street (off Route 60 just south of downtown), Jamestown, 716-664-6256. www.fentonhistorycenter .org

LUCY DESI CENTER FOR COMEDY, 2 West Third Street, Jamestown, 716-484-0800. www.lucy-desi.com

MIDWAY STATE PARK, 4859 Route 430, Maple Springs, 716-386-3165. www.nysparks.com/parks/167/details.aspx

PEEK'N PEAK RESORT, 1405 Olde Road, Clymer, 716-355-4141. www.pknpk .com

ROBERT H. JACKSON CENTER, 305 East Fourth Street, Jamestown, 716-483-6646. Open year-round Monday–Friday 8:30 AM–4:30 PM and by appointment. www.roberthjackson.org

ROCK CITY PARK, 505 Route 16 South, Olean, 716-372-7790 or 1-800-404-ROCK. Open May–October 9:00 AM–6:00 PM daily. www.rockcitypark.com

ROGER TORY PETERSON INSTITUTE OF NATURAL HISTORY, 311 Curtis Street, Jamestown, 716-665-2473. www.rtpi.org

SALAMANCA RAILROAD MUSEUM, 170 Main Street, Salamanca, 716-945-3133.

SENECA ALLEGANY CASINO, 777 Seneca Allegany Boulevard (right by I-86 Exit 20), Salamanca, 716-945-3200. www.senecaalleganycasino.com

SENECA-IROQUOIS NATIONAL MUSEUM, 814 Broad Street, Salamanca, 716-945-1760. www.senecamuseum.org

SPRAGUE'S MAPLE FARMS, 1048 Route 305, Portville (Exit 28 off I-86 to NY 305), 716-933-6637 or 800-446-2753. Open year-round. www.spragues maplefarms.com

WATERWHEEL OVERLOOK, 10400 Main Street, Findley Lake, 716-769-7610 for information, hours. Open 365 days a year.

Dining and Nightlife

AMERICAN HOUSE AND HOTEL, 128 West Main Street, Angelica, 585-466-7784 or 1-800-924-5193. Open for dinner Friday and Saturday 4:00–9:00 PM, Sunday brunch 11:00 AM–3:00 PM.

ANDRIACCIO'S, 4837 West Lake Road (Route 394) Mayville, 716-753-5200. www.andriaccios.com

BLUE HERON INN BREAKFAST, 10412 Main Street, Findley Lake, 716-769-7852. Open year-round. www.theblueheroninn.com

CARTWRIGHT MAPLE TREE INN, 4321 Route 15A, Angelica, 585-567-8181. Open seasonally mid-February–mid-April. www.cartwrightsmapletreeinn .com

ELLICOTTVILLE BREWING, 57 Lakeside Drive, Bemus Point, 716-386-1189. www.ellicottvillebrewing.com/bemus-point-ny

ITALIAN FISHERMAN, 61 Lakeside Drive, Bemus Point, 716-386-7000. www.italianfisherman.com

LA FLEUR, 5031 West Lake Road, Mayville, 716-753-3512. www.restaurant lafleur.net

PEEK'N PEAK RESORT, 1405 Olde Road, Clymer, 716-355-4141. www.pknpk .com

VILLAGE CASINO, 1 Lakeside Drive (on the lake), Bemus Point, 716-386-2333. www.bemuspointcasino.com

THE WATERMARK, 188 South Erie Street, Mayville, 716-753-2900. www .watermarkrestaurant.net

THE WHITE CARROT RESTAURANT, 4717 Chautauqua-Stedman Road, Mayville, 716-269-6000. www.whitecarrotrestaurant.com

Shopping

ANGELICA COUNTRY STORE, 50 West Main Street, Angelica, 585-466-3040. Open Tuesday–Sunday 10:00 AM–5:00 PM. www.angelicacountrystore.com

ANGELICA MAIN STREET GALLERY, 39 West Main Street, Angelica, 585-466-7658. Open Wednesday–Sunday 10:00 AM–5:00 PM.

ANGELICA SWEET SHOP, 44 West Main Street, Angelica, 585-466-7070. www.angelicasweetshop.com

CUBA CHEESE SHOPPE, 53 Genesee Street, Cuba, 800-543-4938. www.cubacheese.com

HERITAGE ANTIQUES, 42 West Main Street, Angelica, 585-466-3712. Open Wednesday–Sunday 10:00 AM–5:00 PM. www.heritageantiques.shutterfly.com.

NOSTALGIA AT THE BLUE HERON INN. Located in the red barn next to the Blue Heron Inn, Findley Lake, 716-769-7852. www.theblueheroninn.com

OUR OWN CANDLE COMPANY, 2779 North Road, Findley Lake, 716-769-5000.

OUR OWN CANDLE COMPANY OUTLET STORE, 2762 North Road, Findley Lake, 716-769-6000.

SECRET CUBBY OF ANTIQUES, 10378 Main Street, Findley Lake, 716-233-1002.

SIX MAIN GIFTS, 6 Main Street, Bemus Point, 716-386-5624.

SKILLMAN'S, 9 Main Street, Bemus Point, 716-386-3000. www.skillmansny.com

WONDERMENTS, 10365 Main Street, Findley Lake, 716-769-7190.

Other Contacts

ALLEGANY COUNTY TOURISM, 6087 Route 19, Belmont, 585-268-5500 or 1-800-836-1869. Open Monday–Friday 8:30 AM–4:00 PM. This visitor center is conveniently located just north of the I-86 Belmont exit. www .discoveralleganycounty.com

ANGELICA MERCHANTS ASSOCIATION, 585-466-3399. www.visitangelica .com

TOWN OF ANGELICA, Park Circle, Angelica, 585-466-3280. Open Tuesday–Thursday 3:30–6:30 PM. www.angelica-ny.net

VILLAGE OF ANGELICA, 21 Peacock Hill Road, Angelica, 585-466-7431. www.angelicany.com

VILLAGE OF BEMUS POINT, www.bemuspointny.org

CATTARAUGUS COUNTY TOURISM, 303 Court Street, Little Valley, 800-331-0543. www.enchantedmountains.com

ANGELICA

CHAUTAUQUA COUNTY CHAMBER OF COMMERCE, 512 Falconer Street, Jamestown, 716-484-1101. Open Monday–Friday 8:00 AM–4:30 PM. www .chautauquachamber.org

CHAUTAUQUA COUNTY VISITOR BUREAU, Chautauqua Institution Main Gate, Route 394, Box 1441, Chautauqua, 716-357-4569 or 866-908-4569. Open daily 9:00 AM–5:00 PM year-round. www.tourchautauqua.com

CUBA CHAMBER OF COMMERCE, 5 West Main Street, Cuba, 585-968-5654. Monday–Friday 10:00 AM–2:00 PM. www.cubanewyork.us

FINDLEY LAKE AREA CHAMBER OF COMMERCE, 716-769-7609, www .visitfindleylake.com

DOWNTOWN JAMESTOWN DEVELOPMENT CORPORATION, 716-664-2477. www.jamestownupclose.com

MAYVILLE/CHAUTAUQUA CHAMBER OF COMMERCE, P.O. Box 22, Mayville, 716-753-3113. www.chautauquachamber.org/community_chambers/ Mayville_Chautauqua.aspx

GREATER OLEAN AREA CHAMBER OF COMMERCE, 120 North Union Street, Olean, 716-372-4433. Open Monday–Friday 8:30 AM–4:30 PM. www .oleanny.com

SALAMANCA AREA CHAMBER OF COMMERCE, 734 Broad Street, Salamanca, 716-945-2034. www.salamancachamber.org

KEUKA LAKE, HAMMONDSPORT

9

THE SOUTHERN TIER PART 2
The I-86 Corridor from Hammondsport to Binghamton

ESTIMATED LENGTH: 100 miles

ESTIMATED TIME: 1–5 days

HIGHLIGHTS: This route, which runs through the southern part of the Finger Lakes region, allows you to explore wineries, breweries, Victorian architecture, aviation museums, glassmaking establishments, and carousels, as well as unique places to shop. While you could drive this route in a couple hours, if you want to really enjoy what this region has to offer, you may want to allow several days to fully explore the five towns described in this section.

GETTING THERE: This area is accessible from the I-390 expressway on the west (from Rochester) or the I-81 expressway on the east (from Syracuse). Although traveling on an expressway to get from town to town sounds counterintuitive in a book about backroads and byways, this is a very scenic expressway and, given the terrain of the region, it is actually the best way to travel between the many quaint small towns and villages located just off the expressway.

This journey starts in Hammondsport, a quaint village located on the southern tip of Keuka Lake. To get to Hammondsport, take Exit 38 (Bath) off I-86 and follow Route 54 north to Route 54A to Hammondsport. Besides the beautiful lakeside view, the village has a number of attractions.

Start out in the village square on Shethar Street, which is surrounded by a number of unique shops and restaurants. Stop by **Browsers**, which has two floors of merchandise, including clothing, home decor, gourmet foods, gift items, and even Keuka Lake merchandise. **The Cinnamon Stick** has all sorts of collectibles, along with gift items and gourmet foods. If you like antiques, be sure to check out **Shethar 57**; there are also a number of other shops in this area that you can browse.

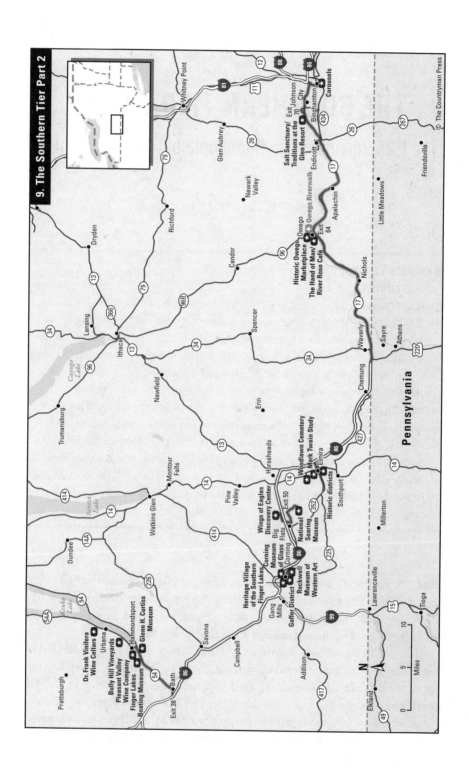

© The Countryman Press

Whitney Point

12

88

86

81

11

Carousels

434

Glen Aubrey

Salt Sanctuary/
Traditions at the
Glen Resort

Exit Johnson
70 City

Binghamton

26

26

267

Newark
Valley

79

Endicott

17

Little Meadows

Friendsville

Richford

Owego Riverwalk

Historic Owego Owego
Marketplace
The Hand of Man/
River Rose Café

Exit
64

Apalachin

96

Dryden

13

79

Candor

96B

Nichols

Lansing

366

Spencer

17

34

Ithaca

13

34

34

Waverly

Sayre

Cayuga
Lake

96

Newfield

Athens

220

Trumansburg

Erin

Pennsylvania

13

Montour
Falls

Horseheads

Chemung

414

Woodlawn Cemetery
Mark Twain Study

86

427

Seneca
Lake

Watkins Glen

14

Elmira

14

Dundee

14

Pine
Valley

Exit 50

Historic districts

144A

414

Wings of Eagles
Discovery Center

352

Southport

Millerton

14

National
Soaring
Museum

Big
Flats

Heritage Village
of the Southern
Finger Lakes

Corning
Museum
of Glass

86

225

226

Corning

Lawrenceville

Tioga

54

Rockwell
Museum of
Western Art

Keuka
Lake

Hammondsport

Gang
Mills

15

54A

Dr. Frank Vinifera
Wine Cellars

Urbana

Gaffer District

99

Bully Hill Vineyards

Glenn H. Curtiss
Museum

Addison

Pleasant Valley
Wine Company

Savona

Finger Lakes
Boating Museum

54

Bath

86

Campbell

Elkland

Prattsburgh

Exit 38

417

49

N

0   5   10

Miles

There are also several restaurants to choose from, including the **Union Block**, an Italian bistro located in the lower level of Browsers, and the **Luna Mezza Grille**, which features Mediterranean fare like baba ganoush and lamb meatballs as well as American dishes. For ice cream, be sure to stop by the **Crooked Lake Ice Cream Parlor**, a 1940s-style ice cream parlor which also serves breakfast, lunch, and dinner, in addition to ice cream treats.

Just a short walk from the village square is the Keuka Lake waterfront. The **Keuka Lakeside Inn** overlooks Keuka Lake and is within walking distance to the beach and boat docks. There are several bed & breakfast inns throughout town, all within walking distance of the village square and the lake. Some of these include the **Blushing Rose Bed & Breakfast**, located in a blush-colored 1843 Italianate home, **Lake & Vine Bed & Breakfast**, located in a newly remodeled 1868 Queen Anne–style home, and **18 Vine & Carriage House Bed & Breakfast**, located in an 1860s Colonial Revival–style home.

Hammondsport is also known as the cradle of aviation because of its most famous son, aviation pioneer **Glenn H. Curtiss**. Be sure to visit the museum which bears his name, located just outside the village on Route 54. This museum features vintage aircraft, as well as motorcycles and bicycles. Curtiss was responsible for many early aeronautical developments and was also issued the first pilot's license in the United States.

Another museum, just outside the village on Pleasant Valley Road, is the **Finger Lakes Boating Museum**, which opened its doors in 2014. Still a work in progress, this museum, located in the former Taylor Wine Company buildings, features exhibits highlighting the various boat builders once located throughout the Finger Lakes region, as well as the steamboats that traveled throughout the lakes.

There are a variety of boats in the museum's collection, including sailboats, motorboats, and canoes. There is even a boat restoration shop and a children's activity room. The lower level of the museum, the former tasting room for Taylor Wines, can be rented for private functions.

Just around the corner from the boating museum, the **Pleasant Valley Wine Company**, also known as Great Western Winery, established in 1860, was the first winery bonded in the United States. It has eight stone buildings listed on the National Register of Historic Places. Also on the same road, the **Brewery of Broken Dreams**, located in a historic stone building, offers samples of their brews currently on tap. The nearby **Black Sheep Inn Bed & Breakfast** offers five guest rooms in an 1859 octagon-shaped house. Their breakfast features organic and locally grown products.

If you want to explore some of the other wineries in the area on the **Keuka Wine Trail**, one of the more interesting ones is **Bully Hill**, which is known for its innovative wines; fun, interactive tours; and unique and artsy labels on its bottles. **Dr. Frank Vinifera Wine Cellars** produces world-class wines, which you can sample in their tasting room overlooking Keuka Lake.

When you're done visiting Hammondsport, head back to I-86 and travel about 30 miles to the city of Corning, which has a number of attractions. Note that while this area might not technically be considered the "backroads," it's a must-see when passing through this area.

Corning has been dubbed the Crystal City because of the **Corning Museum of Glass**, one of the top tourist destinations in upstate New York. This ever-expanding museum, which first opened in the 1950s, has over 45,000 objects representing 3,500 years of glass craftsmanship. It has the largest collection of glass in the world. Plan on spending at least three or four hours at minimum visiting this museum, although you could easily spend the entire day or more; your admission ticket is good for two consecutive days.

In 2015, the museum added a 26,000-square-foot contemporary arts and design wing, which has over 70 pieces of glass art on display, including a number of large-scale works. One of the most popular things to do at the museum is to see the live, narrated glass-blowing demonstrations, which take place several times each day.

Another popular section of the museum is The Studio, where visitors can

CORNING CLOCK TOWER

try their hand at glassmaking, with assistance by the museum staff. Spots fill up quickly, so be sure to sign up ahead of time, either online prior to your visit or in person when you first arrive at the museum. There is an additional fee over and above your museum admission to do this. You can choose from glass flowers, ornaments, jewelry, and more. The items need to cool overnight, so if you're not planning on staying overnight in the area, make arrangements to have the items shipped home.

CORNING MUSEUM OF GLASS

The museum also has one of the largest museum gift shops in the country, featuring pieces made by local glass artists, jewelry, and ornaments, along with everyday items for the home like glassware and Pyrex baking items. There is also a café, which offers a large selection of food to choose from.

Overnight accommodations include the **Staybridge Suites**, conveniently located right next to the museum. The **Rosewood Inn Bed & Breakfast**, located within walking distance of Corning's Market Street, has seven Victorian-themed rooms, all with private baths.

Speaking of Market Street, no visit to Corning would be complete without visiting this historic four-block area, which has many unique shops and restaurants located in 19th-century buildings. It's also referred to as the **Gaffer District**; *gaffer* is another term for a master glass blower.

A familiar landmark is the iconic Corning clock tower, located in Centerway Square in the middle of the Market Street area. Built in 1883 as a memorial to Erastus Corning, the city's founder, the clock has its original mechanisms intact and still keeps time.

Some of the shops along Market Street include **Connors Mercantile**, which can best be described as a country store within the city. They carry a variety of items; home decor, jewelry, gifts, Vera Bradley, gourmet foods, and candies. **Market Street Coffee & Tea** roasts coffee beans in-house and carries a variety of teas and gourmet chocolates.

Since this is Finger Lakes wine country, be sure to stop by **Bottles & Corks** at the far west end of Market Street. This wine and liquor store offers weekly tastings on Friday evenings and Saturday afternoons. They specialize in New York State wines and also have a large selection of wines from around the world. Corning's first distillery, **Four Fights Distilling**, which opened in 2014, is open Thursday through Sunday for tastings and sales.

There are dozens of restaurants to choose from along Market Street, from casual to fine dining. One of them is **Holmes Plate**, which has comfort food like pulled pork and chicken pot pie. The restaurant has a bar room with 54 different types of bottled beer on the menu. However, the dining room is also very family friendly. One of the unique features is that the tablecloths are actually large sheets of brown drawing paper. Big boxes of crayons are located at each table, and patrons are encouraged to draw on the tablecloth while they wait for their food. The artwork is then cut out and displayed in 8-by-10-inch frames all around the dining room.

If you crave Italian, stop by **Sorge's**, which has been serving homemade Italian foods since the 1950s. Save room for ice cream at the **Old World Café and Ice Cream,** which is located right by Centerway Square. In addition to ice cream treats, they serve paninis, soups, and sandwiches.

The **Rockwell Museum of Western Art** is located on a side street just off Market Street. The 1893 building, formerly City Hall, contains the collection of the Robert Rockwell family, which features the most comprehensive collection of western art in the United States. Works by Fredric Remington, C. M. Russell, and other artists who captured the western frontier are featured.

Another museum, the **Heritage Village of the Southern Finger Lakes** (formerly the Benjamin Patterson Inn Museum), is located just a few blocks from the Corning Museum of Glass. Explore 10 buildings that depict life in the 1800s, including the 1796 Benjamin Patterson Inn, which sits on its original site, as well as other buildings which were brought to the museum from nearby communities.

After visiting Corning, head east on I-86 to the Elmira area. If you enjoyed visiting the Glenn H. Curtiss Museum in Hammondsport, you'll also enjoy the aviation museums in this area. The **Wings of Eagles Discovery Center** is an educational institution that collects, preserves, and exhibits military aircraft and memorabilia in a 25,000-square-foot hangar.

Elmira has also been dubbed the Soaring Capital of America, so it's only fitting that the **National Soaring Museum** is located here (take Exit 51 off I-86 and follow the signs). The museum has the largest collection of gliders and sailplanes in the world. Visitors can see what soaring is like when they climb inside a soaring simulator. However, if you want to experience soaring for real, sailplane rides are offered seasonally at the adjacent **Harris Hill Soaring Company.**

After visiting these museums, head to the downtown area to experience Mark Twain's Elmira. When you stroll through Elmira's Near Westside Historic District you can almost feel the presence of author Samuel Clemens, a.k.a. Mark Twain, even though he's been gone over a century. He was a familiar figure in Elmira during the summer, when he and his wife Olivia Langdon, an Elmira native, spent time with her family.

It was here that he wrote some of his most famous works, including *The*

MARK TWAIN STUDY, ELMIRA

Adventures of Tom Sawyer, *The Adventures of Huckleberry Finn*, and *A Connecticut Yankee in King Arthur's Court*. As a matter of fact, during the summer you can actually visit the study where he wrote these works, which is now located on the campus of Elmira College. The **Mark Twain Study**, a unique octagon-shaped structure, was originally built in 1874 at his wife's family farm and moved to the college in 1952.

The 20-block Near Westside neighborhood is bound by College Avenue, Water Street, Walnut Street, and Second Street. The neighborhood, which is listed on the National Register of Historic Places, has just under 500 homes, many of them magnificently restored Victorians. In fact, the neighborhood is reputed to have the highest concentration of Victorian homes of any neighborhood east of the Mississippi.

You can stroll around the neighborhood yourself, using the map and information found on the **Near Westside Neighborhood Association's** website, www.nwnainc.com, or you can take a personalized, guided tour offered by Samuel Draper, who has been giving tours of **Historic Near Westside** for over 20 years. Tour information can be found on his website, www.historicnearwestside.com. He is knowledgeable about both the architecture and history of the area, as well as about the local folklore.

In addition to giving tours, Draper is a contractor who specializes in the restoration of historic buildings. His tours include a visit to **Park Church**, where Samuel and Olivia Clemens were married, as well as a walking tour through the historic district. Occasionally some of the homeowners in the district allow Draper to bring people inside their homes.

Next, stop at **Woodlawn Cemetery**, located at the north end of Walnut Street, to pay your respects to the Clemens family. Samuel and Olivia, along with their children, son-in-law, and granddaughter, are buried in the Langdon family plot. Note the monument near his grave. The height of the monument is the height of the measurement referred to as "mark twain," a term that was used on the Mississippi to indicate the depth of the river. This is where Clemens got his pen name.

Before leaving Elmira, head to **Eldridge Park** to ride the historic 1890 Looff carousel, which was restored in 2006. Another place to visit is **The Christmas House**, a seasonal gift shop located in an 1894 Victorian mansion, which has the largest collection of ornaments in the area, along with Christmas village figures and houses.

Next, hop back on I-86/Route 17 and head east about 30 miles to the village of Owego (Exit 64). The village, which was named "The coolest small town in America" by Budget Travel in 2009, is noted for its 19th-century architecture. Many of these vintage buildings, which have been restored, are located in the area along Front and Lake Streets known as the **Historic Owego Marketplace**. This walkable shopping district has numerous boutique shops, art galleries, and restaurants.

CHRISTMAS HOUSE, ELMIRA

MARK TWAIN GRAVE, ELMIRA

Your first glimpse of the village will be as you exit the expressway and cross over the iconic Susquehanna River Bridge. The large building directly in front of the bridge is the Tioga County Courthouse. Built in 1872, it is one of the oldest functioning courthouses in the state.

Find a place to park (space may be at a premium during the summer months) and head to some of the shops. **The Goat Boy** has a nice selection of gift items, Polish pottery, Vera Bradley items, jewelry, and more. Next door, **Carol's Coffee & Art Bar** is a great place to stop for coffee and baked goods. You can also look at artwork by local artists, which is displayed on the café's brick walls.

Across the street, **East of the Sun, West of the Moon** has a large selection of handcrafted items, including jewelry, pottery, home decor, and even kaleidoscopes. You'll spend hours browsing in **The Hand of Man**, which is packed with over 10,000 Christmas ornaments and the largest collection of Russian nesting dolls in New York State. They also have other home decor items like glassware and antiques, along with gourmet foods. Be sure to make your way to the very back of the shop, to the **River Rose Café**. You can dine inside, or, on a nice day, you can sit outside on the deck which overlooks the Susquehanna River. The menu includes salads, sandwiches, and soups; some menu items are named after notable people from Owego's past.

Book lovers will enjoy the **Riverow Bookshop** on the corner of Front and Lake Streets. They carry both new and used books, as well as gift items.

STREET SCENE, OWEGO

Head up Lake Street, where there are a number of shops and art galleries, including **Fuddy Duddy's**, which has fudge and other candies; **The Laughing Place**, an independent toy store; and the **Petal Pusher Gift Shop**, which has locally made items, jewelry, and home decor.

Be sure to allow time to browse through the **Early Owego Antique Center** at the corner of Lake and Main Streets. The center has over 90 antiques dealers with a variety of items.

Besides the previously mentioned River Rose Café, there are a number of other restaurants to choose from, including the **Calaboose Grille**, which is located in the former Tioga County Jail. You can enjoy dining while seated in a former jail cell! **The Owego Kitchen** offers freshly baked bagels each morning, along with muffins, scones, and oatmeal. Lunch features sandwiches, homemade soups, and salads with homemade dressing. They also have sweets like cookies, cakes, and brownies.

The **Owego Parkview Restaurant**, established 1867 and located about a block from the shops, looks interesting with historic murals painted on the windows. **The Cellar Restaurant**, open for dinner, offers steak, seafood, and more, while the **Old Owego Diner** has an all-day breakfast, along with homemade diner food and Greek specialties.

Take a stroll along the river on the **Owego Riverwalk**. This walking trail runs from Draper Park, goes under the Susquehanna River Bridge, passes behind the block of buildings known as Riverow on Front Street, and ends at Ahwaga Park.

To learn more about Owego's historic homes, take the free, hourlong cell phone **Owego Walking Tour**, which focuses on over 50 historic homes and buildings along Front Street. If you have a chance, look at some of the murals that are part of the **Tioga County Heritage Mural Collection**. Thirteen murals depicting historic structures in each of Tioga County's towns

PUMPELLY HOUSE ESTATE BED & BREAKFAST, OWEGO

SALT SANCTUARY, BINGHAMTON

and villages can be found on the Tioga County Office Building. There are also the murals depicting life in the early 1900s painted on the windows of the Parkview Restaurant.

Overnight accommodations in Owego include the **Pumpelly House Estate Bed & Breakfast**, located along Front Street within walking distance of the shops and restaurants. There are also several national chain hotels a short drive from the village on Route 17C.

The last stop on this drive is the city of Binghamton. There are numerous attractions in this area; however, we will focus on just a couple of the more unique places to visit.

The **Salt Sanctuary**, located in the **Traditions at the Glen Resort**, offers salt therapy, also known as halotherapy, a 100 percent natural, centuries-old European tradition that is a relaxing spa treatment said to be helpful to people with respiratory illnesses. Clients recline on chairs in the salt "cave," a large room made to look like a cave with walls and floors of salt. A machine dispenses microscopic salt particles into the air; these particles are breathed into the airway, helping to eliminate infection and promote relaxation. The spa also offers traditional spa treatments like facials, manicures, and pedicures.

The resort's main building was built in 1919 as a private residence. It was then a country club, and later a retreat facility, before being transformed into a resort with 41 hotel rooms and suites. Behind the hotel is the "glen," a 200-plus-acre mature forest which has several loop hiking trails of various lengths.

If you visit the Binghamton area during the summer months, be sure to ride the "carousel circuit." The city, dubbed the **Carousel Capital of the World,** has six antique carousels located throughout the metro area. George F. Johnson, a Binghamton shoe manufacturer, donated the carousels to local parks between 1919 and 1934 because he felt that carousels would help to contribute to a happy life. Poor as a child, Johnson stipulated that the rides on the carousels would always be free of charge, so that everyone could enjoy riding them.

The carousels are located in the following parks: C. Fred Johnson Park, George W. Johnson Park, Highland Park, Recreation Park, Ross Park (at the entrance to the zoo), and West Endicott Park. The carousels are open Memorial Day through Labor Day.

While in Binghamton, be sure to try one of their signature sandwiches, the spiedie, which consists of marinated meat (chicken, pork, lamb, beef) grilled over a charcoal pit. Some of the best-known restaurants for this specialty include the **Spiedie & Rib Pit, Lupo's S & S Char Pit,** and **Sharkey's.**

IN THE AREA

Accommodations

18 VINE & CARRIAGE HOUSE BED & BREAKFAST, 18 Vine Street, Hammondsport, 607-569-3039. www.affordablefingerlakes.com. $$$.

BLACK SHEEP INN BED & BREAKFAST, 8329 Pleasant Valley Road, Hammondsport, 607-569-3767. www.stayblacksheepinn.com. $$$.

BLUSHING ROSE BED & BREAKFAST, 11 William Street, Hammondsport, 607-569-2687. www.blushingroseinn.com. $$.

KEUKA LAKESIDE INN, 24 Water Street, Hammondsport, 607-569-2600. www.keukalakesideinn.com. $$.

LAKE & VINE BED & BREAKFAST, 61 Lake Street, Hammondsport, 607-569-3282. www.lakeandvinebb.info. $$.

PUMPELLY HOUSE ESTATE BED & BREAKFAST, 44 Front Street, Owego, 607-687-0510. www.pumpellyestate.com. $$.

ROSEWOOD INN, 134 East First Street, Corning, 607-962-3253. www.rose woodinn.com. $$.

STAYBRIDGE SUITES, 201 Townley Avenue, Corning, 607-936-7800. $$.

TRADITIONS AT THE GLEN RESORT AND THE SALT SANCTUARY, 4101 Watson Boulevard, Johnson City, 607-797-2381. www.traditionsresort.com or www.thesaltsanctuary.com. $$.

Attractions and Recreation

BREWERY OF BROKEN DREAMS, 8319 Pleasant Valley Road, Hammond-sport, 607-224-4050. www.thebreweryofbrokendreams.com

BULLY HILL WINERY, 8843 Greyton H. Taylor Memorial Drive, Hammond-sport, 607-868-3490. www.bullyhill.com

CAROUSELS OF BINGHAMTON, www.gobroomecounty.com/community/ carousels

BULLY HILL WINERY, HAMMONDSPORT

FINGER LAKES BOATING MUSEUM, HAMMONDSPORT

CORNING MUSEUM OF GLASS, 1 Museum Way, Corning, 800-732-6845. www.cmog.org

DR. FRANK VINIFERA WINE CELLARS, 9749 Middle Road, Hammondsport, 607-868-4884 or 800-320-0735. www.drfrankwines.com

ELDRIDGE PARK, 1322 College Avenue, Elmira, 607-732-8440. www.eldridgepark.org

FINGER LAKES BOATING MUSEUM, 8231 Pleasant Valley Road, Hammondsport, 607-569-2222. Open daily, 10:00 AM–6:00 PM from April–October and 10:00 AM–4:00 PM from November–March. The parking lot and entrance are located up the hill behind the museum. www.flbm.org.

FOUR FIGHTS DISTILLING, 363 East Market Street, Corning. www.fourfightsdistilling.com

GLENN H. CURTISS MUSEUM 8419 State Route 54, Hammondsport, 607-569-2160. www.glennhcurtissmuseum.org

HARRIS HILL SOARING COMPANY, 62 Soaring Hill Drive, Elmira, 607-734-0641 or 607-742-4213. www.harrishillsoaring.org

HERITAGE VILLAGE OF THE SOUTHERN FINGER LAKES, 73 West Pulteney Street, Corning, 607-937-5281. www.heritagevillagesfl.org

HISTORIC NEAR WESTSIDE, 607-732-1436. Public tours Friday and Saturday at 11:00 AM, April–October. Other times by appointment. Group and individual tours are available. www.historicnearwestside.com

KEUKA WINE TRAIL, 800-440-4898. www.keukawinetrail.com

MARK TWAIN STUDY, 1 Park Place, Elmira, 607-735-1941. Open May 1–Labor Day 9:30 AM–4:30 PM Monday–Saturday; September–mid-October Saturday 9:30 AM–4:30 PM by appointment. www.elmira.edu

NATIONAL SOARING MUSEUM, 51 Soaring Hill Drive, Elmira, 607-734-3128. www.soaringmuseum.org

NEAR WESTSIDE NEIGHBORHOOD ASSOCIATION, 353 Davis Street, Elmira, 607-733-4924. www.nwnainc.com

OWEGO CELL PHONE WALKING TOUR, 607-354-4080. Free and available daily. Call the number and follow the prompts.

PARK CHURCH, 208 Gray Street, Elmira, 607-733-9104. www.thepark church.org.

PLEASANT VALLEY WINE COMPANY, 8260 Pleasant Valley Road, Hammondsport, 607-569-6111. www.pleasantvalleywine.com

ROCKWELL MUSEUM OF WESTERN ART, 111 Cedar Street, Corning, 607-937-1430. www.rockwellmuseum.org

SALT SANCTUARY, 4101 Watson Boulevard, Johnson City, 607-797-2381. www.traditionsresort.com or www.thesaltsanctuary.com

TIOGA COUNTY HERITAGE MURAL COLLECTION, displayed on Tioga County Office Building, 56 Main Street, Owego.

WINGS OF EAGLES DISCOVERY CENTER, 339 Daniel Zenker Drive, Horseheads, 607-358-4247. www.wingsofeagles.com

WOODLAWN CEMETERY, 1200 Walnut Street, Elmira, 607-732-0151. www .friendsofwoodlawnelmira.org

Dining and Nightlife

CALABOOSE GRILLE, 176 Main Street, Owego, 607-223-4522. Open Monday–Saturday 11:00 AM–9:00 PM. www.calaboosegrille.com

CAROL'S COFFEE & ART BAR, 177 Front Street, Owego, 607-972-7532.

THE CELLAR RESTAURANT, 196 Front Street, Owego, 607-687-2016. Open Tuesday–Sunday for dinner. www.thecellarrestaurant.net

CROOKED LAKE ICE CREAM PARLOR, 35 Shethar Street, Hammond-sport, 607-569-2751.

HOLMES PLATE, 54 West Market Street, Corning, 607-377-5500. www .holmesplate.com

LUNA MEZZA GRILLE, 41 Shethar Street, Hammondsport, 607-246-4000. Open Monday–Saturday for lunch and dinner. www.lunamezzagrille.com

LUPO'S S & S CHAR PIT, 6 West State Street, Binghamton, 607-723-6106. Opens daily at 9:00 AM.

OLD OWEGO DINER, 187 Market Street, Owego, 607-223-4697.

OLD WORLD CAFÉ AND ICE CREAM, 1 West Market Street, Corning, 607-936-1953. www.oldworldcafe.com

THE OWEGO KITCHEN, 13 Lake Street, Owego, 607-223-4209. Open Monday–Saturday 7:00 AM–4:00 PM, Sunday 7:00 AM–2:00 PM. www.theowego kitchen.com

OWEGO PARKVIEW RESTAURANT, 145 Front Street, Owego, 607-687-9873. www.owegoparkviewrestaurant.com

RIVER ROSE CAFÉ (in the Hand of Man), 180 Front Street, Owego, 607-687-6643. www.handofman.com

SHARKEY'S, 56 Glenwood Avenue, Binghamton, 607-729-9201. Open Monday–Saturday 11:30 AM–1:00 AM, Sunday 12:00 PM–1:00 AM.

SORGE'S, 68 West Market Street, Corning, 607-937-5422. www.sorges.com

SPIEDIE & RIB PIT, 3908 Vestal Parkway, Binghamton, 607-729-2679, and 1268 Front Street, Binghamton, 607-722-7628. www.spiedieandribpit.com

UNION BLOCK, 31 Shethar Street, Hammondsport, 607-246-4065. www .unionblockitalian.com

Shopping

BROWSERS, 33 Shethar Street, Hammondsport, 607-569-2497. www.browsers onkeukalake.com

BOTTLES & CORKS, 130 West Market Street, 607-936-2222. www.bottles andcorks.biz

THE CHRISTMAS HOUSE, 361 Maple Avenue, Elmira, 607-734-9547. Open late June–mid-January. www.christmas-house.com

THE CINNAMON STICK, 26 Mechanic Street, Hammondsport, 607-569-2277. Hours vary seasonally. www.cinnamonstick.com

CONNORS MERCANTILE, 16 East Market Street, Corning, 607-937-4438. www.connorsmercantile.com

EARLY OWEGO ANTIQUE CENTER, 43–45 Lake Street, Owego, 607-223-4723. www.owegoantiquecenter.com

EAST OF THE SUN, WEST OF THE MOON, 206 Front Street, Owego, 607-684-6305. www.owegosunmoon.com

FUDDY DUDDY'S, 27 Lake Street, Owego, 607-687-3834. www.fuddyduddys .com

THE GOAT BOY, 175 Front Street, Owego, 607-687-2042. Open daily 10:00 AM–6:00 PM.

HAND OF MAN, 180 Front Street, Owego, 888-842-0388. www.handofman .com

HISTORIC OWEGO MARKETPLACE, located along Front Street, Lake Street, and Main Street. www.owegolovesshoppers.com

THE LAUGHING PLACE, 19 Lake Street, Owego, 607-687-3294.

MARKET STREET COFFEE & TEA, 61 East Market Street, Corning, 607-936-3351. www.marketstreetcoffeeandtea.com

THE PETAL PUSHER GIFT SHOP, 39 Lake Street, Owego, 607-760-5745. Open Monday–Saturday 11:00 AM–5:00 PM. www.thepetalpushergiftshop .com

RIVEROW BOOKSHOP, 187 Front Street, Owego, 607-687-4094. www .riverow.com

SHETHAR 57, 57 Shethar Street, Hammondsport, 607-569-3399. Open daily 10:00 AM–5:00 PM.

Other Contacts

CHEMUNG COUNTY CHAMBER OF COMMERCE, 1-800-MARK TWAIN. www.marktwaincountry.com

CORNING'S GAFFER DISTRICT, www.gafferdistrict.com

GREATER BINGHAMTON CONVENTION & VISITOR BUREAU, 800-836-6740. www.visitbinghamton.org

HAMMONDSPORT CHAMBER OF COMMERCE, 47 Shethar Street, Hammondsport, 607-569-2989. www.hammondsport.org

TIOGA COUNTY TOURISM, 80 North Avenue, Owego, 800-671-7772. www .visittioga.com

10

MURAL MANIA IN WAYNE COUNTY

ESTIMATED LENGTH: 50 miles for murals along Erie Canal. Add an additional 50 miles if you want to explore murals in northern Wayne County.

ESTIMATED TIME: Drive time is about an hour, but allow a full day to stop and explore the sights along the way.

HIGHLIGHTS: While there are over 85 murals (a number which is growing) in various communities between Rochester and Syracuse, this drive will focus on murals in a half-dozen communities in Wayne County, located along the Erie Canal. Also mentioned will be murals in several communities in northern Wayne County. Keep in mind that most of these murals are painted on mural boards, so there is the possibility that they could be moved to a different location or removed at some point in the future, just in case you don't find them at the location described.

A little background on how Mural Mania came about. Mark DeCracker had the idea back in 2007 to have a few murals painted in the village of Lyons to help revitalize the downtown area and to tell the history of the area through public art. Along with mural artist James Zeger and the late Noel Dobbins, the idea of Mural Mania spread from a few murals in Lyons to more than 50 miles of murals in other communities along the Erie Canal and vicinity. In fact, the Global Mural Conference was held outside Rochester in 2016.

GETTING THERE: From the New York State Thruway (I-90), take Exit 45 to I-490 north, toward Rochester. Exit at Route 250 to Route 31 east toward Macedon.

The first stop along this drive will be the village and town of Macedon; the town was incorporated in 1823, the village in 1856. There are two murals here. The first mural is on a building at 105 West Main Street; pull into Old Erie Square Municipal Parking (free) to view the mural titled *They Walked*

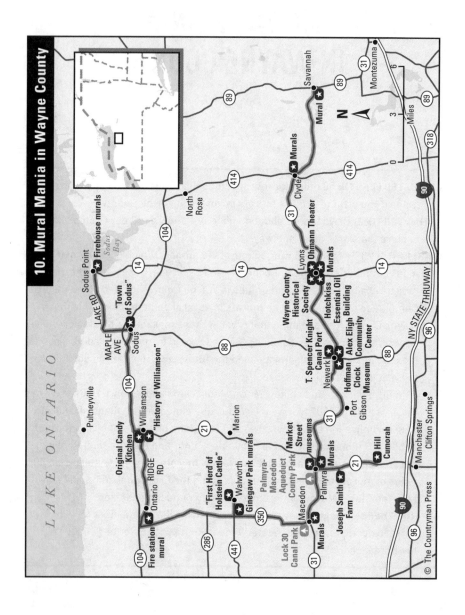

10. Mural Mania in Wayne County

LAKE ONTARIO

Montezuma

31

89

89

Savannah

Mural

N

89

89

Miles

318

6

3

0

414

Clyde

Murals

90

Firehouse murals

Sodus Bay

North Rose

104

31

Ohmann Theater

414

14

LAKE RD

Sodus Point

MAPLE AVE

"Town of Sodus"

Sodus

14

Lyons

Murals

Wayne County Historical Society

14

Pultneyville

Williamson

"History of Williamson"

104

Original Candy Kitchen

88

Hotchkiss Essential Oil Building

Alex Eligh Community Center

88

96

NY STATE THRUWAY

Marion

21

T. Spencer Knight Canal Port

Newark

Hoffman Clock Museum

Port Gibson

RIDGE RD

Ontario

Market Street museums

31

Fire station mural

104

"First Herd of Holstein Cattle"

Walworth

Ginegaw Park murals

Palmyra-Macedon Aqueduct County Park

Murals

Palmyra

Joseph Smith Farm

21

Hill Cumorah

Manchester

Clifton Springs

286

441

350

Macedon

Lock 30 Canal Park

31

Murals

96

90

© The Countryman Press

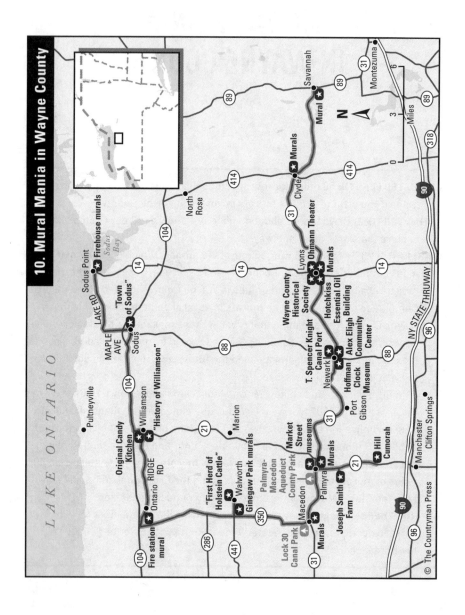

Before Us, which shows a 1910 view of Macedon's Main Street. This mural was painted by Michael Buell and volunteers.

The second mural in Macedon is in **Lock 30 Canal Park**; head east on Route 31, left on Route 350, then head about a block north to the park's entrance. This mural, painted by Dawn Jordan, is on the side of the Elmer Clark Pavilion. The mural, titled *Historical Presence in the Village*, depicts "Old Betsy," an 1864 fire pumper restored by the Macedon Volunteer Fire Department in 1983. Also shown in the mural is Elmer Clark, the longtime fire chief for whom the picnic pavilion is named. The mural also shows a canal boat moving through the canal. Located in the park is Lock 30 on the Erie Canal; you can watch boats "locking through." (Note that the canal season runs from late April through early November, so if you want to see boats on the canal, visit during these times.)

You can also view the remnants of Lock 60, also called the Lower Macedon Lock, a mile east of the village on the north side of the canal, off Quaker Road. This lock, in use until 1914, was built in 1841 to replace the original 1822 lock when the canal was enlarged.

Head back to Route 31 and drive east toward Palmyra. Before you get into the downtown area you may want to stop at the **Palmyra-Macedon Aqueduct County Park**, where Erie Canal Lock 29 is located. In addition to this being a picturesque park, there are a couple of historic structures of

HISTORICAL PRESENCE IN THE VILLAGE, MACEDON

note here. The remnants of the Mud Creek Aqueduct can be viewed from the park as well as from the walking trail along the park. Before the canal was rerouted, it crossed Ganargua Creek over the top of the aqueduct.

Also in this park is the Aldrich Change Bridge No. 35. A change bridge allowed the towpath to switch from side to side of the canal. It was originally erected in 1858 in Rochester and later moved to downtown Palmyra. It was sold to a farmer in 1915 and used as a farm bridge until 1970, when it was abandoned. It was salvaged, restored, and erected in this park in 2004.

Head into the village of Palmyra, which is referred to as the Queen of the Erie Canal Towns. Besides the two large murals, there are a number of other attractions here. You could spend quite a bit of time here if you wanted to.

First, let's look at the murals. The first mural is a very large mural located on the wall of a parking lot at 133 Market Street. It was painted by Macedon High School art students and their teacher in 2006. This mural, *Palmyra's History*, depicts significant people and places in the village's history, including General John Swift, the founder of Palmyra; William Sampson, a Spanish-American War hero who was a resident of Palmyra; and Moroni, the angel who gave Joseph Smith, the founder of the Mormon church, ancient records on Hill Cumorah (more about Mormon sites later).

Places depicted in the mural include the four churches on the corner of Main and Church Streets, which you may have noticed as you drove along

Main Street. Palmyra is the only city or village in the United States to have four churches at a four-corner intersection facing each other.

Garlock Sealing is shown in the mural. The company, founded in Palmyra in 1887, played an important role in the village's economy. The previously mentioned Aldrich Change Bridge is also depicted in the mural, as are trolleys, an important means of transportation which served Palmyra between 1906 and 1931.

There are several historic museum sites located across the street from the mural. **The Palmyra History Museum** (132 Market Street) has 23 rooms of displays about local history; **The Erie Canal Depot** (136 Market Street) is an old canal passenger and commercial depot; The **William Phelps General Store Museum** (140 Market Street) is a 19th-century general store that has original items; and **The Print Shop** (140½ Market Street) has printing equipment made in Palmyra. These museums are open year-round. Around the corner, **The Alling Coverlet Museum** (122 William Street) has the largest collection of handwoven coverlets in the United States. The coverlet museum is open from June to September.

Head down Market Street toward the Erie Canal to see Palmyra's second

PALMYRA MAIN STREET

PALMYRA HISTORY

mural, *Palmyra Main Street*, which is painted on a fence by the parking lot of the Port of Palmyra Marina. Main Street, past and present, is depicted in the mural, which was painted by Palmyra Middle School students in 2010.

After looking at the mural, you can stop by **Muddy Waters Café**, across the parking lot, to get a bite to eat. They offer home-cooked food for breakfast and lunch and a great view of the canal. Be sure to walk down to the marina to see boats traveling in the Erie Canal.

Palmyra is the birthplace of the Church of Jesus Christ of Latter Day Saints, better known as the Mormon Church. There are several historic sites that are open to the public, including the **Book of Mormon Historic Publication Site**, where the Book of Mormon was first printed in 1829.

Other Mormon historic sites include **Hill Cumorah**, which is located 5 miles south of town. The visitor center is open for tours, and an annual outdoor pageant is held in July. The **Joseph Smith Farm**, home of the church's founder, is also open daily for tours.

Places to eat, shop, and stay in Palmyra include **Lock 29 Tavern**, which has a variety of pub foods like burgers, wings, and tacos; and **Athenia Restaurant**, a casual family restaurant with a huge selection of items on the menu. Places to shop include **Mackenzie's**, a boutique shop with home decor and jewelry; and **Mulberry Hollow**, which has home decor, candles, furniture, and more. If you want to stay overnight in Palmyra, the **Palmyra Inn**, located south of town, is within walking distance of the Mormon historic sites. Right in town, the **Liberty House Bed & Breakfast** offers three guest rooms in a Victorian Italianate–style home.

Annual events taking place in Palmyra include a pirate weekend in early August; **Canaltown Days** in September, which features a parade, music, walking tours of the canal, and more; and, in mid-October, Palmyra's famous cemetery walk, sponsored by **Historic Palmyra**.

The next stop in the drive along Route 31 is the village of Newark. Before viewing the murals, stop to check out the **Hoffman Clock Museum**, which is located in the Newark Public Library on High Street. This museum, which opened in 1954, is the collection of watchmaker and jeweler Augustus Hoffman (1858–1945). It is one of the largest collections of New York State–made clocks in the country, along with a collection of clocks and watches from all over the world. Included in the collection is an ornate fretwork clock made in the 1890s by a local craftsman and an organ clock made in the Black Forest of Germany in the 1840s which plays eight different folk tunes. The museum also has an extensive collection of ceramic clocks and grandfather clocks.

From the clock museum, head east on High Street, then cut over to Church Street to East Avenue to the **Alex Eligh Community Center**. A large

HOFFMAN CLOCK MUSEUM, NEWARK

mural is on the side of this 1917 building, which was the first official school gymnasium in the area. It is currently a community center named after Alex Eligh, who was director of the center from 1948 to 1974. The mural, painted by Corky Goss and Chip Miller, depicts young people participating in sporting activities.

Next, head north on East Avenue and cross over the Erie Canal, turn left on Van Buren Street, and park your car by the **T. Spencer Knight Canal Port**. You have to get out of your car to see the large murals, as they are painted on the walls facing the canal. These murals depict scenes in Erie Canal history. Be sure to walk all the way to the bridge, as there is a canal boat scene painted on the wall right under it. On Friday evenings in July and August, you can enjoy Music on the Canal. The Newark Chamber of Commerce, located in the white building here, has maps and other area information.

Head east on Route 31 toward Lyons, which has the most murals out of any town on this drive. It was in Lyons that the first murals on this mural

MURAL OF CANAL BOAT, NEWARK

HOTCHKISS ESSENTIAL OIL BUILDING, LYONS

trail were painted. From Route 31, turn left on Leach Road and cross over the canal; look to your left as you cross the bridge and you will see *Winston's Dream*, the first of the murals to be painted. Formerly a garbage pit, this area was transformed into a park and the mural was painted by many community volunteers.

On the corner of Leach Road and Water Street is the **H. G. Hotchkiss Essential Oil Building,** which is now a museum operated by the Lyons Heritage Society. Lyons is referred to as the peppermint village because of the peppermint oil industry founded here in 1841 by Hiram Hotchkiss, who bottled and sold peppermint oil both nationally and internationally. The company was one of the world's largest producers of peppermint oil, as well as its leading distributor.

Outside the building, a mural titled *Hotchkiss*, painted by artist Dawn Jordan, has scenes that depict the peppermint oil business in Lyons. In mid-July, Lyons holds its annual Peppermint Days festival.

A short distance away on Butternut Street, visit the **Wayne County Historical Society,** located in the former 1856 Wayne County Jail and sheriff's residence. There are three floors of exhibits focusing on local history, the Erie Canal, and Lyons's peppermint industry.

Head to Montezuma Street and park in the large parking lot behind Dobbins Drugs. From the parking lot you will see a very large mural located in

TOP: *HOTCHKISS*, LYONS
BOTTOM: *BELIEVE ALL THAT YOU CAN ACHIEVE*, LYONS

an alleyway on the side of a building at 28 Canal Street. Titled *Believe All That You Can Achieve*, the mural reflects the goals of the youths participating in the Goal Chaserz program who helped paint the mural.

Across the street, *Steamer Hose No. 2*, at 2 Montezuma Street, painted by Maria Hoover, features a 1936 pumper from the Lyons Fire Department. On the other side of the street (1 Montezuma Street), *Street of Dreams*, painted by James Zeger, portrays downtown Lyons in 1915.

Head down William Street toward **The Old Pharmacy Gift Shop & Dobbins Drugs.** The mural on the front of the store, commissioned by Sean Dobbins, is called *Generations*. It shows an old-fashioned apothecary with three generations of the Dobbins family depicted. Be sure to go inside the store to look around. There is a large gift shop with locally themed merchandise, jewelry, candy, home decor, and more, along with a full-service drug store. Another shop to check out on William Street is **Evolve for the Home**, which carries antiques, primitives, and home decor.

GENERATIONS, LYONS

OHMANN THEATRE, LYONS

In an alleyway directly across the street, *Generations of Smiles*, commissioned by dentist Randy Mitchell, memorializes another dentist, Dr. Arthur Santelli, who had his office in this area. Both of these murals were done by Corky Goss and Chip Miller.

One of the more unique places in Lyons is the **Ohmann Theatre**, also on William Street. It is the oldest movie and live stage show theater in the United States. It opened in 1915 and was in operation until 1993, when it closed for a few years before being restored by the third generation of the Ohmann family in 2004. Today the theater is used for multiple purposes, including meetings, conferences, fundraisers, live productions, and movies. Note that there is a display about the history of the Ohmann Theater at the previously mentioned Hotchkiss Peppermint Museum.

There is one more mural in Lyons, located on the side of a building at 16 Forgham Street. It's actually best viewed from the McDonald's parking lot next door. Titled *Canal Town*, this mural depicts scenes from the 1800s, including a canal packet boat, the Lyons United Methodist Church, and the Lyons Aqueduct, which was part of the canal from 1841–1950.

Before leaving Lyons you might want to check out the **Trail of Hope**, which is located by the Lyons Community Center. This quarter-mile, fully accessible nature trail was built through the efforts of many community volunteers.

Want to stay overnight in Lyons? **Peppermint Cottage B&B**, located several miles south of town, is a good choice. They have a private cottage available, along with a guest room in the main house.

The next town along Route 31 is Clyde, which is named after the Clyde River in Scotland. The town has several murals. Turn left when you get to Glasgow Street and drive a few blocks to the Clyde-Savannah Library (204 Glasgow Street). The trolley mural on the front of the building depicts the Clyde Trolley Station in the early 1900s. It was painted by students from Clyde-Savannah High School.

Head back to the downtown area, where there are several murals. The Clyde Hardware murals are located on the side of the Clyde Hardware Store (87 Glasgow Street). These murals, painted by Stacy Kirby, offer windows into the past, suggesting what one might have bought at the hardware store in the late 1800s.

LINCOLN'S VISIT TO CLYDE

FIRST HOLSTEIN CATTLE, WALWORTH

Around the corner, *Citizen's Bank*, (81 Glasgow Street) painted by Chip Miller and Corky Goss, is on the former Citizen's Bank which operated here from 1920 to 1943. The mural shows the interior of the bank as it appeared in the 1930s.

On the side of the car wash at 17 Sodus Street, *Lincoln's Visit to Clyde*, painted by Robert Gillespie, depicts the stop by Lincoln's Inaugural Train in Clyde on February 18, 1861. It was the only stop the train made between Rochester and Syracuse.

The final mural, also painted by Robert Gillespie, is located on the side of the Clyde Grange Building (16 East Genesee Street/Route 31). It shows a number of scenes from Clyde's history, including rural mail delivery, equal opportunity for men and women, the grange library, and school busing.

There are several more towns with murals located throughout the county between the Erie Canal and Lake Ontario. Most of these towns are much smaller than the ones we just visited, so you won't find too many attractions to speak of besides the murals. However, if you want to add another hour or two to your drive, you may want to check them out.

In Savannah, about 6 miles east of Clyde on Route 31, there is a large 7-by-32-foot mural at 1565 North Main Street that depicts Savannah history and area wildlife. The other murals in the county are best reached by traveling back to Macedon on Route 31 and then heading north on Route 350 toward the town of Ontario.

However, you might want to make a slight detour when you get to Walworth. Turn right on Walworth Penfield Road, then right on Lorraine Drive into Ginegaw Park, where there are two murals. One, *Festival in the Park*, depicts the annual festival held in the park. A newer mural, at the location of the farmers' market which takes place on Tuesdays, June through October, shows a large basket of fresh vegetables. A few miles down the street, on the side of the Walworth Post Office, *First Holstein Cattle*, depicts the first herd of cattle imported to the area in 1885.

When you get to Ridge Road (Route 103), turn right and look for Walter Cone Drive; there is a mural of an 1861 hand pumper on the side of the Ontario Fire Department.

Also located in Ontario is the **L. W. Emporium**, a huge barn filled with antiques, collectibles, and crafts from over 60 vendors. Also in the same area are the **Whistle Stop Antique Center** and the **Feathered Nest Gift Shop**, which has a nice selection of jewelry, accessories, and more.

Head east on Ridge Road (Route 103), toward Williamson to view the *History of Williamson*, (4090 Ridge Road), which depicts scenes from

WALWORTH FARMERS' MARKET

TOWN OF SODUS

Williamson's history. Next, stop by the **Original Candy Kitchen,** which, under four generations of the same family, has been making handmade chocolates and other candies since 1890. Within the candy store, they also operate a diner-like restaurant that serves a variety of comfort foods. While in town, shop at the **Apple Crate Gifts Shop** and the **Country Attic,** inside Williamson Hardware Store. Other places of interest in Williamson include the **Apple Town Farm Market** on Route 104, which has locally grown produce, cider, and more. Down the street, **Orbaker's Drive-In** has been serving burgers, sandwiches, and ice cream since 1932.

Head east on Route 104 about 7 miles to the Town of Sodus to view the mural titled *Town of Sodus,* which has eight images representing the hamlets and villages in the town. It is on the side of Laundry Junction (31 State Street). There are also three murals located in nearby Sodus Point on the walls of the Sodus Point firehouse, which were described in Chapter 2, Travel Along Lake Ontario's Shore.

As mentioned earlier, murals continue to be added, and in some instances are removed or moved to different locations. Check www.muralmania.org for more information.

IN THE AREA

Accommodations

LIBERTY HOUSE BED & BREAKFAST, 131 West Main Street, Palmyra, 315-592-0011. www.libertyhousebb.com. $.

PALMYRA INN, 955 Canandaigua Street, Palmyra, 315-597-8888. www.palmyrainn.com. $$.

THE PEPPERMINT COTTAGE B&B, 336 Pleasant Valley Road, Lyons, 315-946-4811. www.peppermintcottage.com. $$.

Attractions and Recreation

ALEX ELIGH COMMUNITY CENTER, 303 East Avenue, Newark, 315-331-2532. www.alexeligh.com

ALLING COVERLET MUSEUM, 122 William Street, Palmyra, 315-597-6981. www.historicpalmyrany.com.

BOOK OF MORMON HISTORIC PUBLICATION SITE, 217 East Main Street, Palmyra, 315-597-5982. Open 9:00 AM–6:00 PM for tours. www.mormon.org.

CANALTOWN DAYS, Palmyra, www.palmyracanaltowndays.org

ERIE CANAL DEPOT, 136 Market Street, Palmyra, 315-597-6981. Open June–September Tuesday–Saturday 11:00 AM–4:00 PM; October–May Tuesday–Thursday 1:00–4:00 PM. www.historicpalmyrany.com

HOTCHKISS PEPPERMINT MUSEUM/H. G. HOTCHKISS ESSENTIAL OIL BUILDING, 95 Water Street, Lyons. Open Friday and Saturday 10:00 AM–3:00 PM. www.lyonshs.angelfire.com

HILL CUMORAH, 603 Route 21, Palmyra, 315-597-5851. www.hillcumorah.org

HISTORIC PALMYRA, 315-597-6981. www.historicpalmyrany.com

HOFFMAN CLOCK MUSEUM, 121 High Street, Newark. www.hoffman clockmuseum.org

JOSEPH SMITH FARM 843 Stafford Street, Palmyra, 315-597-5851. www .hillcumorah.org

LOCK 30 CANAL PARK, 1 Canal Park, Macedon, 315-986-3976.

OHMANN THEATRE, 65 William Street, Lyons, 315-946-4604. www.ohmann theatre.com

PALMYRA HISTORY MUSEUM, 132 Market Street, Palmyra, 315-597-6981. Open June–September Tuesday–Saturday 11:00 AM–4:00 PM; October–May Tuesday–Thursday 1:00–4:00 PM. www.historicpalmyrany.com

PALMYRA-MACEDON AQUEDUCT COUNTY PARK, 2685 Route 31, Palmyra.

THE PRINT SHOP, 140½ Market Street, Palmyra, 315-597-6981. Open June– September Tuesday–Saturday 11:00 AM–4:00 PM; October–May Tuesday– Thursday 1:00–4:00 PM. www.historicpalmyrany.com

TRAIL OF HOPE, 9 Manhattan Street, Lyons. www.trailofhope.org

T. SPENCER KNIGHT CANAL PORT, 199 Van Buren Street, Newark.

WAYNE COUNTY HISTORICAL SOCIETY, 21 Butternut Street, Lyons, 315-946-4943. Open April–November Thursday–Friday 10:00 AM–4:00 PM, Saturday 10:00 AM–1:00 PM. www.waynehistory.org

WILLIAM PHELPS GENERAL STORE MUSEUM, 140 Market Street, Palmyra, 315-597-6981. Open June–September Tuesday–Saturday 11:00 AM–4:00 PM; October–May Tuesday–Thursday 1:00–4:00 PM. www.historic palmyrany.com

Dining and Nightlife

ATHENIA RESTAURANT, 6069 Main Street, Palmyra, 315-597-4287.

LOCK 29 TAVERN, 222 East Main Street, Palmyra, 315-597-0286.

MUDDY WATERS CAFÉ, 100 Division Street, Palmyra, 315-502-4197. Open Tuesday–Friday 7:00 AM–2:00 PM, Saturday 8:30 AM–2:00 PM.

ORBAKER'S DRIVE-IN, 4793 Route 104, Williamson, 315-589-9701. Open year-round, 11:00 AM–8:00 PM. daily. www.orbakers.com

ORIGINAL CANDY KITCHEN, 4069 West Main Street, Williamson, 315-589-9085. Open Monday–Thursday 6:00 AM–3:00 PM, Friday 6:00 AM–8:00 PM, Saturday 7:00 AM–2:00 PM, Sunday 8:00 AM–2:00 PM.

Shopping

APPLE CRATE GIFTS SHOP, 4091 Main Street, Williamson, 315-589-9788. www.applecrategiftsshop.com

APPLE TOWN FARM MARKET, 4734 Route 104, Williamson, 315-589-9102.

COUNTRY ATTIC, at Williamson Hardware, 4101 Main Street, Williamson, 315-589-4011.

L. W. EMPORIUM, ONTARIO

ORIGINAL CANDY KITCHEN, WILLIAMSON

EVOLVE FOR THE HOME, 59 William Street, Lyons, 315-946-4623. Open Monday–Friday 10:00 AM–5:30 PM, Saturday 8:00 AM–4:00 PM.

FEATHERED NEST GIFT SHOP, 6355 Knickerbocker Road, Ontario, 315-524-3343. Open Tuesday–Sunday 10:00 AM–5:00 PM.

L. W. EMPORIUM, 6355 Knickerbocker Road, Ontario, 315-534-8841. Open Tuesday–Sunday 10:00 AM–5:00 PM. www.lwemporium.com

MACKENZIE'S, 138 East Main Street, Palmyra, 315-597-5986. Open Tuesday–Saturday 10:00 AM–4:00 PM, Friday until 5:00 PM. www.mymackenzies.com

MULBERRY HOLLOW, 235 West Main Street, Palmyra, 315-502-4025.

THE OLD PHARMACY GIFT SHOP & DOBBINS DRUGS, 52 William Street, Lyons, 315-946-6691. www.dobbinsdrugs.com

ORIGINAL CANDY KITCHEN, 4069 West Main Street, Williamson, 315-589-9085. Open Monday–Thursday 6:00 AM–3:00 PM, Friday 6:00 AM–8:00 PM, Saturday 7:00 AM–2:00 PM, Sunday 8:00 AM–2:00 PM.

WHISTLE STOP ANTIQUE CENTER, 6363 Knickerbocker Road, Ontario, 315-524-3965.

Other Contacts

LYONS CHAMBER OF COMMERCE, 315-573-8170. www.lyonsny.com

NEWARK CHAMBER OF COMMERCE, 199 Van Buren Street, Newark, 315-331-2705. www.newarknychamber.org

ONTARIO CHAMBER OF COMMERCE, 315-524-5886. www.ontariony chamber.org

SODUS CHAMBER OF COMMERCE, 315-576-3818. www.sodusny.org

WAYNE COUNTY TOURISM, 9 Pearl Street, Lyons. Open Monday–Friday 9:00 AM–5:00 PM. www.waynecountytourism.com

WILLIAMSON CHAMBER OF COMMERCE, www.williamsonchamberof commerce.com

TRINITY EPISCOPAL CHURCH ON VAN CLEEF LAKE, SENECA FALLS

11

AN AUTHENTIC AMERICAN ROAD
Route 5 & 20 from Avon to Skaneateles

ESTIMATED LENGTH: 80 miles

ESTIMATED TIME: 2 hours to just drive; 3–4 days to fully explore all the sights

HIGHLIGHTS: Leave the expressway behind and enjoy a drive along a route that's been dubbed "An Authentic American Road." You can explore quaint towns and villages and visit antiques shops, unique restaurants, wineries, wildlife, museums, and more. This route began thousands of years ago as a Native American foot trail. Later, the early pioneers used it as the main east-west route across the state. It remained a major route until the 1950s, when the New York State Thruway was built and Route 5 & 20 became the road less traveled. However, it remains popular with those seeking to discover the backroads of New York State.

GETTING THERE: This route, which takes you from Avon to Skaneateles, runs parallel to the New York State Thruway (I-90). It is accessible from either the New York State Thruway Exit 47 (Route 19 south to Route 5 east to Avon) or New York State Thruway Exit 46 (take I-390 south to Avon exit and head west a few miles to begin in Avon). If you just wish to take a drive, this route can be covered in about two hours, but if you want to stop to enjoy everything along the way, allow several days.

This drive begins in Avon, which was once a tourist mecca for those seeking the healing waters of sulphur spring spas in the 19th century. Today it is a small, quaint village best known for the annual Avon Corn Fest, which takes place the second Saturday in August and draws thousands of people from all over the region. Those who enjoy hiking will be glad to hear that the **Genesee Valley Greenway** hiking trail passes through this area just west of the village near River Road (www.fogvg.org for trail map).

The village is also home to the original **Tom Wahl's**, a popular burger

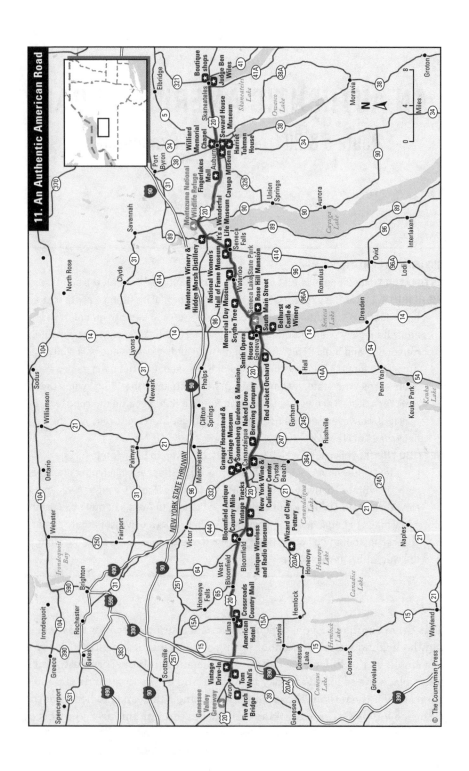

11. An Authentic American Road

Boutique shops
Judge Ben Wiles
Skaneateles
Elbridge
Groton
Moravia
Williard Memorial Chapel
Seward House Museum
Auburn
Harriet Tubman House
Port Byron
Fingerlakes Mall
Cayuga Museum
Union Springs
Aurora
Montezuma National Wildlife Refuge
It's a Wonderful Life Museum
Seneca Falls
Savannah
North Rose
Montezuma Winery & Hidden Marsh Distillery
National Women's Hall of Fame Museum
Waterloo
Seneca Lake State Park
Rose Hill Mansion
Interlaken
Ovid
Lodi
Clyde
Memorial Day Museum
Scythe Tree
Geneva
South Main Street
Belhurst Castle & Winery
Dresden
Lyons
Smith Opera House
Red Jacket Orchard
Hall
Penn Yan
Keuka Park
Newark
Clifton Springs
Phelps
Granger Homestead & Carriage Museum
Sonnenberg Gardens & Mansion
Canandaigua Naked Dove Brewing Company
Gorham
Rushville
Palmyra
Manchester
Bloomfield Antique Country Mile
Vintage Tracks
New York Wine & Culinary Center
Crystal Beach
Naples
Victor
Bloomfield
Antique Wireless and Radio Museum
Wizard of Clay Pottery
Honeoye
Fairport
Webster
Ontario
Williamson
Sodus
Honeoye Falls
West Bloomfield
American Crossroads Country Mall
Hemlock
Livonia
Brighton
Rochester
Lima
Conesus Lake
Conesus
Irondequoit
Greece
Gates
Scottsville
Vintage Drive-In
Tom Wahl's
Avon
Geneseo
Groveland
Wayland
Five Arch Bridge
Genessee Valley Greenway
Spencerport

© The Countryman Press

N

0   4   8
Miles

and hot dog restaurant which has a 1950s theme and old-time photos on the walls. Their special root beer, which can be ordered in a frosted glass mug, is worth the trip alone. (There are several other Tom Wahl's locations in the region.)

Take a short detour south on Route 39 to see the remains of the Five-Arch Bridge, which was built in 1856–57 by the Genesee Valley Railroad. The structure is 200 feet long and 12 feet wide. This section of the rail line was abandoned in the 1940s; the tracks were removed, but the bridge, which is listed on the National Register of Historic Places, remains. A small park with picnic tables is located along the bridge. If you like drive-in movies, be sure to check out the **Vintage Drive-in**, located just north of Route 5 & 20 on Route 15.

TOM WAHL'S, AVON

Continue east on Route 5 & 20 to Lima, which is referred to as The Crossroads of Western New York. It was founded in 1788 near the crossing of two major Indian trails. A place of note in town is the **American Hotel**, a 150-year-old Lima landmark that has been run by the same family since the 1920s. The dining room is noted for the large variety of homemade soups served there. The hotel also offers overnight accommodations; however, note that most of the rooms have shared baths.

Just down the street, the **Crossroads Antiques of Lima** features over 50 dealers on two floors in a former church. Items for sale include furniture, glassware, jewelry, primitives, books, toys, and vintage clothing.

Further down the road, in the village of Bloomfield, there are a number of antiques shops; the area has been dubbed the **Bloomfield Antique Country Mile**, although it's actually about a 3-mile area. You can find everything from Early American antiques and primitives to retro items. Some of the shops include **One Potato Two** and **Peddlers Antiques**.

If time permits, there are a number of lovely historic homes in Bloomfield that are described on a walking tour map found on www.bloomfieldbuzz .com. The village is also home to the country's largest **Antique Wireless and Radio Museum**. A vintage tractor museum, **Vintage Tracks**, is also located a short distance from Route 5 & 20.

Before leaving Bloomfield, dine at the **Holloway House** on Route 5 & 20, located across from Elton Park, the village square of Bloomfield. The restaurant, listed on the National Register of Historic Places, was built in 1808 by

SIDE TRACKS

If you like pottery, take a side trip to the **Wizard of Clay Pottery** on Route 20A, about 10 minutes from Route 5 & 20. Inside the geodesic dome the "wizards" go through 100,000 pounds of clay each year, creating all sorts of pottery, including their trademark Bristoleaf pottery, which is decorated with impressions of real leaves.

Peter Holloway as a stagecoach tavern. Specialties include comfort food like roast turkey and Sally Lunn bread.

The next stop along the way is the city of Canandaigua. Although definitely not the "backroads," it is a good spot to stop along the way. Canandaigua—the name means "chosen place"—is located on the north shore of Canandaigua Lake. As a matter of fact, the main attraction in Canandaigua is its beautiful waterfront. One can take a stroll along the Canandaigua City Pier to view the picturesque circa 1903 boathouses located at the end of the pier. They are often the subject of photos and paintings by local photographers and artists.

Another way to discover the waterfront is to take a sight-seeing cruise on the *Canandaigua Lady*, the only replica 19th-century paddle-wheel steamboat in the Finger Lakes region.

Learn more about the region's history at the **Ontario County Historical**

CANANDAIGUA LADY, CANANDAIGUA

GRANGER HOMESTEAD, CANANDAIGUA

Society or the **Granger Homestead & Carriage Museum**, a restored 1816 Federal-style mansion built by Gideon Granger, the first US Postmaster General. Over seventy 19th-century horse-drawn vehicles are on display in the barns behind the home.

Another picturesque place to spend time is **Sonnenberg Gardens and Mansion State Historic Park**, which is just a short drive from Main Street. This site features 50 acres of manicured gardens and an 1897 Queen Anne–style mansion which is open for tours. The estate was once the summer home of Frederick and Mary Clark Thompson; Frederick was one of the founders of the bank now known as Citibank.

Located next to Sonnenberg's parking lot is the **Finger Lakes Wine Center**, where one can sample wine from a number of Finger Lakes wineries. The wine center is part of the **Canandaigua Wine Trail**.

Shoppers will love strolling down Canandaigua's Main Street, which is actually the widest Main Street in the country. There are numerous shops to choose from, including **Unique Toy Shop**, which has educational toys and games; **The Goodie II Shop**, which has gift and home decor items; and **American Made**, which only sells products made in the United States. For reasonably priced handcrafted jewelry, stop by **Adorn Jewelry and Accessories.**

There are many restaurants to choose from in Canandaigua, from casual to upscale. **Simply Crêpes** is a good choice; its welcoming country chic

TOP: SONNENBERG GARDENS AND MANSION STATE PARK, CANANDAIGUA
BOTTOM: INN ON THE MAIN, CANANDAIGUA

decor will make you feel at home the minute you walk in. Choose from a variety of tasty and innovative crêpes and other dishes.

Other dining choices include **Nolan's on the Lake**, the **Shore Restaurant** at the Inn on the Lake, and **Nick's Chophouse, Wine and Martini Bar. Schooners,** a nautical-themed restaurant not far from the lake, features specialties like prime rib, seafood, and pasta, as well as burgers, sandwiches, soups, and salads for lunch.

The **Upstairs Bistro** at the **New York Wine & Culinary Center** features locally sourced food and beverages. Downstairs, enjoy tasting New York State wines and craft beers. There is also a hands-on kitchen where one can take cooking classes, and a culinary boutique gift shop.

There are a number of overnight accommodations in Canandaigua, including the **Inn on the Lake**, which is right on the shore of Canandaigua Lake. There are also numerous bed & breakfast inns in the region, including several right on Main Street like the **1840 Inn on the Main, Bed & Breakfast at Oliver Phelps**, and the **Bella Rose Bed & Breakfast**.

Back on the road, head east toward Geneva, which is located on the north shore of Seneca Lake. Before you get into the downtown Geneva area you'll see the **Naked Dove Brewing Company**, as well as the **Red Jacket Orchards**, which has locally grown produce, local products, and gift items. The large cobblestone home at the corner of Route 6 is the **Cobblestone Restaurant,** which specializes in northern Italian cuisine, as well as steaks and chops.

Geneva is noted for its elegant architecture, especially in the **South Main Street Historic District** along Route 14, just north of Route 5 & 20. Included in this area are many early 1800s homes and colorful row houses built in the 1820s. The **Geneva Historical Society** is located here.

There are a couple of upscale resorts of note on Route 14 South. **Geneva on the Lake** is a Four Diamond luxury hotel in an Italian Renaissance–style

BELHURST CASTLE, GENEVA

GENEVA WATERFRONT

villa. It was originally built as a private residence in 1914, then later served as a monastery before being converted into a resort hotel in 1981. Nearby, **Belhurst Castle** has been voted one of the most romantic places in New York State. Built in the 1880s as a private residence, it is now an elegant country inn, restaurant, and winery. The main building is a Richardson Romanesque–style castle which overlooks Seneca Lake. Their restaurants, which are open to the public, include **Edgar's Steakhouse**, which offers fine dining for breakfast, lunch, and dinner, along with the **Stonecutters Tavern**, which serves more casual fare for lunch and dinner. Their winery, **Belhurst Estate Winery**, is part of the **Seneca Lake Wine Trail**, which consists of almost three dozen wineries around Seneca Lake.

In the downtown area, the **Smith Opera House**, built in 1894, has been fully restored and is listed on the National Register of Historic Places. It is the site of many performances and special events in Geneva. There are a couple shops located right by the opera house, including **Don's Own Flower Shop; Earthly Possessions**, which has jewelry, accessories, handmade gifts, and more; and **Finger Lakes Gifts & Lounge**, which has a variety of gifts and cards, along with pizza, salad, sandwiches, wine, beer, and coffee.

Check out Geneva's beautiful lakefront. Park at the visitors center located in **Lakefront Park**, overlooking Seneca Lake. The park has a walking trail, gazebo, and picnic facilities. Adjacent to Lakefront Park is **Seneca Lake**

State Park, which has a hike and bike path, marina, boat launch, picnic facilities, a playground, swimming beach, and even a "sprayground," the perfect spot for kids to cool off on a hot day. The **Ramada Geneva Lakefront**, which also overlooks the lake, is located nearby. This 148-room inn, which also has several suites, includes amenities such as an indoor pool, workout room, and the popular lakefront Pier House Restaurant.

Often large extended families like to rent vacation properties in the Finger Lakes region for reunions and family vacations. **Finger Lakes Premier Properties** is one company that specializes in renting vacation homes that accommodate groups of four to 24 or more.

Another must-see in the Geneva area is **Rose Hill Mansion**, a designated National Historic Landmark. This 1839 manor house is one of the finest examples of Greek Revival architecture in the country. Docents in period costumes take visitors through the two-room mansion, which is furnished with antiques and reproductions.

The next place along the drive is the Village of Waterloo, which is considered the birthplace of Memorial Day. However, the first stop in the area will be the **Scythe Tree**, a local landmark and roadside attraction located about 2 miles west of Waterloo, on the north side of the road by the State Police station.

According to the plaque on the tree, in 1861, James Wyman Johnson hung his scythe in the tree and told his family to leave it there until he returned

ROSE HILL MANSION, GENEVA

from fighting in the Civil War. Unfortunately, he died in the war, and his parents, not accepting his death, left the scythe in the tree. Later, during World War I, the Schaffe brothers also left their scythes in the same tree. They returned home from the war, however, they did not retrieve the scythes from the tree. As the tree grew, the handles fell off but the metal blades remained embedded in the tree.

Continue on to the **Memorial Day Museum** and take a guided tour of the museum, which has artifacts, photos, and other items that document the history of Memorial Day, which actually was first celebrated in the 1860s. Included among the artifacts is the pen used by President Lyndon Johnson to sign the proclamation making Memorial Day a national holiday on May 26, 1966.

The next stop is the town of Seneca Falls, but first you may want to stop at **Abigail's Restaurant**, which has been popular in this area for over 30 years. Of special note on the menu are their award-winning Bleu Bayou chicken wings.

One could easily spend the entire day in Seneca Falls, which is the home of women's rights as well as the inspiration for the movie *It's a Wonderful Life*. Park in the free parking lot on Water Street and plan on walking around town, as it isn't very big. You can get an overview of the town by looking at the large map, which also has historical information, located in the park-

NATIONAL MEMORIAL DAY MUSEUM, WATERLOO

SENECA FALLS CANAL HARBOR

ing lot. People's Park, adjacent to the parking lot, is where the **Seneca Falls Farmers Market** is held Wednesdays during the summer and early fall.

You may want to start by walking along the harbor promenade along the Cayuga-Seneca Canal. From the promenade you can see the Bridge Street Bridge, also known as the George Bailey Bridge. It is locally believed to be the inspiration for the bridge in the movie *It's a Wonderful Life*. The fact that the film's director, Frank Capra, had visited Seneca Falls on his way to see his aunt in Auburn just before the film was made adds credibility to the widely held belief that the movie setting was based on Seneca Falls.

To get an overview of the town, stop by the **Seneca Falls Visitor Center and Museum,** which has three floors of exhibits about the history of Seneca Falls and the various industries that have flourished in the area. Of special prominence was the Seneca Knitting Mill, which operated from 1844 to 1999 in the large stone building on the opposite side of the canal from the parking lot. That building is in the process of being renovated and will be the new home of the **National Women's Hall of Fame Museum and Research Center,** which is currently located on Fall Street.

Another women's rights site is the **National Women's Rights Historical Park**, operated by the National Park Service. This site tells the story of the first women's rights convention, which was held in Seneca Falls in 1848 in the adjacent Wesleyan chapel.

At the other end of Fall Street, the **It's a Wonderful Life Museum** is

TOP: IT'S A WONDERFUL LIFE MUSEUM, SENECA FALLS
BOTTOM: *WHEN ANTHONY MET STANTON*, SENECA FALLS

located in a 1913 building that was formerly
the Seneca Theater, the town's first movie theater. The museum is full of all sorts of memorabilia from the movie, including over 200
items from the personal collection of Karolyn
Grimes, who played Zuzu Bailey in the film.
Grimes was instrumental in founding the
museum in 2010. The town hosts an annual It's
a Wonderful Life celebration the second weekend in December.

Be sure to cross over the Ovid Street Bridge
to the other side of the canal to see the sculpture *When Anthony Met Stanton*, which depicts
women's rights activist Amelia Bloomer intro-
ducing Susan B. Anthony to Elizabeth Cady
Stanton. It makes a great photo, especially
with Trinity Episcopal Church in the background across Van Cleef Lake. The church is
one of the most photographed churches in the

GOULD HOTEL, SENECA FALLS

state and is featured in many New York State
tourism ads. There are also more sculptures along the Ludovico Sculpture
Trail, which has sculptures inspired by the women's rights movement. The
trail starts at the southern end of the Bridge Street Bridge.

When hunger strikes, try **Parker's Grille & Tap House**, which serves
burgers, steaks, and more, including their famous lobster roll. **Downtown Deli** serves giant New York–style sandwiches, homemade soups,
and bagels.

The **Gould Hotel**, a boutique hotel that overlooks Seneca Falls' Main
Street, has 48 modern rooms with flat-screen TVs, iPod docking stations,
Keurig coffeemakers, and WiFi. The hotel's dining room is open for lunch
and dinner, featuring American cuisine, local products, Finger Lakes wines,
and craft beers.

Continue the journey by heading east toward Auburn. You may want to
stop at the **Montezuma Winery/Hidden Marsh Distillery** or the **Montezuma National Wildlife Refuge**; both of these attractions are described in
detail in Chapter 12.

There are a number of attractions to see in Auburn. If you're a fan of
the outdoors, stop at the **Bass Pro Shop** located at the Fingerlakes Mall
just before you get to the downtown area. There are several historical sites
in Auburn, including the South Street Historic District, a 2-mile stretch
of South Street (Route 34) lined with mansions of various styles of 19th-
century architecture. A walking tour brochure of the area can be obtained
from the Cayuga County Office of Tourism.

SEWARD HOUSE MUSEUM, AUBURN

Of special note is the **Seward House Museum**, which was home to William H. Seward, who served as a New York senator and governor, as well as the Secretary of State under Presidents Abraham Lincoln and Andrew Johnson. The home, a designated National Historic Landmark, can be viewed by guided tour.

WILLARD MEMORIAL
CHAPEL, AUBURN

Located a few miles south of the Seward House Museum is another National Historic Landmark, the **Harriet Tubman House**, which is also open for tours. Tubman, a former slave, was a conductor on the Underground Railroad; she helped many slaves escape to freedom. Another interesting museum in Auburn is the **Cayuga Museum and Case Research Lab**. The Cayuga Museum has exhibits on area history, while the Case Research Lab is where Theodore Case invented the first successful system of recording sound on film in 1924.

Visit the National Historic Landmark **Willard Memorial Chapel**, which was once part of the Auburn Theological Seminary. The interior of the chapel was designed by Louis Comfort Tiffany and built between 1892 and 1894 as a memorial to Dr. Sylvester Willard and his wife Jane by their

DOUG'S FISH FRY, SKANEATELES

daughters. It is the only complete and unaltered Tiffany chapel in existence. It has 14 opalescent stained-glass windows and a large rose window, plus many more details that Tiffany is noted for.

While Route 5 & 20 part ways in Auburn, we will make one more stop on this drive, following Route 20 for about 7 miles to the quaint little village of Skaneateles on the northern shore of Skaneateles Lake. You can enjoy the beautiful waterfront and take a scenic boat cruise on the *Judge Ben Wiles.*

There are all sorts of boutique shops that line the main streets in the village. Some of these include **First National Gifts,** "Home of Retail Therapy," which is located in a historic former bank building and has lots of jewelry, accessories, and unique gift and home decor items; and the **Skaneateles Artisans Gallery,** located in the lower level of a stone mill, which has a nice selection of photos, paintings, jewelry, glassware, and other items for the home, handcrafted by local artisans. There's even a **White Birch Vineyards** tasting room, right in town.

One of the most popular places to eat in town is **Doug's Fish Fry,** which has been serving fresh seafood since 1982. Down the street, **Johnny Angel's** is known for its burgers, while the **Blue Water Grill** has dining overlooking the lake.

There are a number of places to stay overnight in town, including the **Sherwood Inn,** which overlooks the lake, or the **Mirbeau Inn and Spa,** voted

SHERWOOD INN, SKANEATELES

one of the top 10 resorts in New York State by *Conde Nast Traveler*. Even if you don't stay at the inn, you can still enjoy a meal in their dining room, which overlooks a lily pond. The inn also operates the less pricey **Finger Lakes Lodging**, a cute and cozy Adirondack-style motel located just across the street.

Annual events in Skaneateles include their classic boat show in late July and their Dickens Christmas, which takes place weekends from Thanksgiving until Christmas.

IN THE AREA

Accommodations

1840 INN ON THE MAIN, 176 North Main Street, Canandaigua, 585-394-0139 or 877-659-1643. www.innonthemain.com. $$.

AMERICAN HOTEL, 7304 Main Street, Lima, 585-624-9464. www.american hoteloflima.com. $.

BED & BREAKFAST AT OLIVER PHELPS, 252 North Main Street, Canandaigua, 585-396-1650 or 800-926-1830. www.oliverphelps.com. $$.

BELHURST CASTLE, 4069 Route 14 South, Geneva, 315-781-0201. Open year-round. www.belhurstcastle.com. $$$.

BELLA ROSE BED & BREAKFAST, 290 North Main Street, Canandaigua, 585-393-9937. www.bellarosebb.com. $$.

FINGER LAKES LODGING, 834 West Genesee Street, Skaneateles, 315-217-0222. www.fingerlakeslodging.com. $$.

FINGER LAKES PREMIER PROPERTIES, 142 Lake Street, Penn Yan, 888-414-5253. www.fingerlakespremierproperties.com. **.

GENEVA ON THE LAKE, 1001 Lochland Road (Route 14), Geneva, 315-789-7190 or 800-3-GENEVA. Open year-round. www.genevaonthelake.com. $$$$.

GOULD HOTEL, 108 Fall Street, Seneca Falls, 877-788-4010. www.thegould hotel.com. $$.

THE INN ON THE LAKE, 770 South Main Street, Canandaigua, 585-394-7800. www.theinnonthelake.com. $$$.

MIRBEAU INN AND SPA, 851 West Genesee Street, Skaneateles, 877-647-2328. www.mirbeau.com. $$$.

MIRBEAU INN AND SPA, SKANEATELES

RAMADA GENEVA LAKEFRONT, 41 Lakefront Drive (Route 5 & 20), Geneva, 315-789-0400 or 800-990-0907. Open year round. www.geneva ramada.com. $$.

SHERWOOD INN, 26 West Genesee Street, Skaneateles, 315-685-3405. www.thesherwoodinn.com. $$$.

Attractions and Recreation

Avon, Bloomfield, and Canandaigua

ANTIQUE WIRELESS AND RADIO MUSEUM, 6925 Route 5 & 20, Bloomfield, 585-257-5119. Open Tuesday 10:00 AM–3:00 PM, Saturday 1:00–5:00 PM. www.antiquewireless.org

CANANDAIGUA LADY, 205 Lakeshore Drive, Canandaigua, 585-396-7350. www.cdgaboatcruises.com

CANANDAIGUA WINE TRAIL, www.canandaiguawinetrail.com

FINGER LAKES WINE CENTER, www.sonnenberg.org/wine-center

GENESEE VALLEY GREENWAY, www.fogvg.org

GRANGER HOMESTEAD & CARRIAGE MUSEUM, 294 North Main Street, Canandaigua, 585-394-1472. Open mid-May–mid-October Tuesday–Friday 1:00–5:00 PM; also open Saturday and Sunday 1:00–5:00 PM June–August. www.grangerhomestead.org

NAKED DOVE BREWING COMPANY, 4048 Route 5 & 20, Canandaigua, 585-396-2537. www.nakeddovebrewing.com

NEW YORK WINE & CULINARY CENTER, 800 South Main Street, Canandaigua, 585-394-7070. www.nywcc.com

ONTARIO COUNTY HISTORICAL SOCIETY, 55 North Main Street, Canandaigua, 585-394-4975. Open Tuesday–Friday 10:00 AM–4:30 PM, Saturday 11:00 AM–3:00 PM. www.ochs.org

SONNENBERG GARDENS AND MANSION STATE HISTORIC PARK, 151 Charlotte Street, Canandaigua, 585-394-4922. Open May–Columbus Day daily 9:30 AM–4:30 PM, until 5:30 PM July and August. www.sonnenberg.org

VINTAGE DRIVE-IN, 1520 West Henrietta Road (Route 15) Avon, 585-226-9290. www.vintagedrivein.com

VINTAGE TRACKS, 3170 Wheeler Station Road, Bloomfield, 585-657-6608. www.huffequipment.com/vintage.htm

WIZARD OF CLAY POTTERY, 7851 Route 20A, Honeoye, 585-229-2980. Open daily 9:00 AM–5:00 PM. year-round. www.wizardofclay.com

Geneva

BELHURST ESTATE WINERY, 4069 Route 14 South, Geneva, 315-781-0201. Open year-round. www.belhurstcastle.com

GENEVA HISTORICAL SOCIETY, 543 South Main Street, Geneva, 315-789-5151. www.genevahistoricalsociety.com

LAKEFRONT PARK, Route 5 & 20, Geneva, 315-789-1776. Open dawn to dusk.

ROSE HILL MANSION, Route 96A (1 mile south of Route 5 & 20), Geneva, 315-789-3848. Open May–October Monday–Saturday 10:00 AM–4:00 PM, Sunday 1:00–5:00 PM. www.genevahistoricalsociety.com

SENECA LAKE STATE PARK, 1 Lakefront Drive, Geneva, 315-789-2331 or 607-387-7041. www.nysparks.com/parks/125/details.aspx

SENECA LAKE WINE TRAIL, www.senecalakewine.com

SMITH CENTER FOR ARTS/SMITH OPERA HOUSE, 82 Seneca Street, Geneva, 315-781-5483 or 866-355-5483. www.thesmith.org

SOUTH MAIN STREET HISTORIC DISTRICT, Route 14, just north of Route 5 & 20, near the Geneva Historical Society.

Waterloo, Seneca Falls, Auburn, and Skaneateles

CAYUGA MUSEUM AND CASE RESEARCH LAB, 203 Genesee Street, Auburn, 315-253-8051. Open Tuesday–Sunday 12:00–5:00 PM. Free admission. www.cayugamuseum.org

HARRIET TUBMAN HOUSE, 180 South Street, Auburn, 315-252-2081. Open Tuesday–Friday 10:00 AM–4:00 PM, Saturday 10:00 AM–3:00 PM. www.harriet house.org

IT'S A WONDERFUL LIFE MUSEUM, 32 Fall Street, Seneca Falls, 315-568-5838. Open Tuesday–Saturday 11:00 AM–4:00 PM. www.therealbedfordfalls .com

JUDGE BEN WILES, 11 Jordan Street, Skaneateles, 315-685-8500 or 800-545-4318. www.midlakesnav.com

MEMORIAL DAY MUSEUM, 35 Main Street, Waterloo, 315-539-9611. www .waterloony.com

MONTEZUMA NATIONAL WILDLIFE REFUGE, 3395 Route 5 & 20, Seneca Falls, 315-568-5987. www.fws.gov/refuge/montezuma

MONTEZUMA WINERY/HIDDEN MARSH DISTILLERY, 2981 Auburn Road, Seneca Falls, 315-568-8190. www.montezumawinery.com

NATIONAL WOMEN'S HALL OF FAME MUSEUM AND RESEARCH CENTER, 76 Fall Street, Seneca Falls, 315-568-8060. www.womenofthehall.org

NATIONAL WOMEN'S RIGHTS HISTORICAL PARK, 136 Fall Street, Seneca Falls, 315-568-0024. Free admission. www.nps.gov/wori

SCYTHE TREE, Route 20, 2 miles west of Waterloo.

SENECA FALLS FARMERS MARKET, People's Park, Water Street, Seneca Falls. Open Wednesdays 9:00 AM–1:30 PM, early June–mid-October. www .senecamarket.com

SEWARD HOUSE MUSEUM, 33 South Street, Auburn, 315-252-1283. Open Tuesday–Saturday 10:00 AM–5:00 PM, Sunday 1:00–5:00 PM. www.sewardhouse .org

WHITE BIRCH VINEYARDS TASTING ROOM, 18 West Genesee Street, Skaneateles, 315-685-9463. www.whitebirchvineyards.com

WILLARD MEMORIAL CHAPEL, 17 Nelson Street, Auburn, 315-252-0339. Open Tuesday–Friday 10:00 AM–4:00 PM. www.willard-chapel.org

SKANEATELES SHOPS

Dining and Nightlife

Avon, Lima, Bloomfield, and Canandaigua

AMERICAN HOTEL, 7304 Main Street, Lima, 585-624-9464. Open Monday–Friday 11:30 AM–3:00 PM and 5:00–9:00 PM; Saturday 11:30 AM–9:00 PM Sunday 12:00–8:00 PM. www.americanhoteloflima.com

HOLLOWAY HOUSE, corner Route 5 & 20 and South Avenue, Bloomfield, 585-657-7120. www.thehollowayhouse.com

NICK'S CHOPHOUSE, WINE AND MARTINI BAR, 5 Beeman Street, Canandaigua, 585-393-0303. Open Monday–Thursday 11:30 AM–3:00 PM and 4:30–8:30 PM, Friday and Saturday 11:30 AM–3:00 PM and 4:30–10:00 PM. www.nickschophouseandbar.com

NOLAN'S ON THE LAKE, 726 South Main Street, Canandaigua, 585-905-0201. Open Monday–Thursday 1:30–8:30 PM, Friday and Saturday 11:30 AM–9:00 PM. www.nolansonthelake.com

SCHOONERS, corner of East Lake Road and Lakeshore Drive, Canandaigua, 585-396-3360. Open Monday–Thursday 11:00 AM–9:00 PM, Friday–Saturday 11:00 AM–10:00 PM.

SHORE RESTAURANT AT INN ON THE LAKE, 770 South Main Street, Canandaigua, 585-394-7800. www.theinnonthelake.com

SIMPLY CRÊPES, 101 South Main Street, Canandaigua, 585-394-9090. www.simplycrepes.com

STONECUTTERS TAVERN AT BELHURST CASTLE, 4069 NY 14 South, Geneva, 315-781-0201. Open year-round. www.belhurstcastle.com

TOM WAHL'S, 283 East Main Street, Avon, 585-226-2420. www.tomwahls.com

UPSTAIRS BISTRO AT NEW YORK WINE & CULINARY CENTER, 800 South Main Street, Canandaigua, 585-394-7070. www.nywcc.com

Geneva

COBBLESTONE RESTAURANT, 3610 Pre Emption Road, Geneva, 315-789-8498. Open for lunch Tuesday–Friday 11:30 AM–2:00 PM, dinner daily 5:00–9:00 PM. www.cobblestonegeneva.com

EDGAR'S STEAKHOUSE, 4069 Route 14 South, Geneva, 315-781-0201. Open year-round. www.belhurstcastle.com

FINGER LAKES GIFTS & LOUNGE, 60 Seneca Street, Geneva, 315-759-5247. Open Monday–Thursday 9:00 AM–5:00 PM, Friday and Saturday 9:00 AM–6:00 PM.

Waterloo, Seneca Falls, Skaneateles

ABIGAIL'S RESTAURANT, 1978 Route 20, Waterloo, 315-539-9300. Open Monday–Friday 11:00 AM–2:00 PM for lunch, Monday–Saturday 5:00 PM–close for dinner, Sunday 4:00–8:00 PM.

BLUE WATER GRILL, 11 West Genesee Street, Skaneateles, 315-685-6600. www.bluewaterskaneateles.com

DOWNTOWN DELI, 53 Fall Street, 315-568-9943. Open Monday–Friday 7:30 AM–8:00 PM, Saturday 10:00 AM–8:00 PM. www.sfdowntowndeli.com

DOUG'S FISH FRY, 8 Jordan Street, Skaneateles, 315-685-3288. www.dougs fishfry.com

JOHNNY ANGEL'S, 23 Jordan Street, Skaneateles, 315-685-0100. www .johnnyangels.biz

PARKER'S GRILLE & TAP HOUSE, 86 Fall Street, Seneca Falls, 315-712-4152. www.parkersgrille.com

Shopping

ADORN JEWELRY AND ACCESSORIES, 36 South Main Street, Canandaigua, 585-393-1520. www.adornjewelryandaccessories.com

AMERICAN MADE, 143 South Main Street, Canandaigua, 585-919-2828.

BASS PRO SHOP, 1579 Clark Street, Auburn, 315-258-2700. www.basspro .com/auburn

BLOOMFIELD ANTIQUE COUNTRY MILE, numerous antique shops can be found in Bloomfield, located 6 miles west of Canandaigua on Route 5 & 20. Please note that 5 & 20 is a very busy highway with a 55 mph speed limit in many places. Plan on driving from store to store, as it would not be safe to walk along or cross this road. You can visit the shops virtually at www .bloomfieldantiquemile.com.

CROSSROADS ANTIQUES OF LIMA, 7348 East Main Street, Lima, 585-624-1993. www.crossroadsantiquesmall.com

DON'S OWN FLOWER SHOP, 40 Seneca Street, Geneva, 315-789-2554. Open Monday–Friday 8:30 AM–5:30 PM, Saturday 9:00 AM–4:00 PM. www .donsownflowershop.com

EARTHLY POSSESSIONS, 70 Seneca Street, Geneva, 315-781-1078. Open Tuesday–Thursday 10:30 AM–5:30 PM, Friday 10:30 AM–7:30 PM, Saturday 11:00 AM–5:00 PM. www.agirlstore.com

FIRST NATIONAL GIFTS, 2 East Genesee Street, Skaneateles, 855-810-9076. Open Monday–Saturday 10:00 AM–5:00 PM, Sunday 11:00 AM–5:00 PM. www.firstnationalgifts.com

THE GOODIE II SHOP, 56 South Main Street, Canandaigua, 585-394-6528. Open Monday–Wednesday and Friday 9:30 AM–6:00 PM, Thursday 9:30 AM–8:00 PM, Saturday 9:30 AM–5:30 PM.

ONE POTATO TWO, 6900 Route 5 & 20, Bloomfield, 585-657-7446. www .onepotatotwo.com

PEDDLERS ANTIQUES, 6980 Route 5 & 20, Bloomfield, 585-657-4869.

RED JACKET ORCHARDS, 957 Route 5 & 20, Geneva, 315-781-2749 or 800-828-9410. Open daily 8:00 AM–7:00 PM, until 6:00 PM in winter. www .redjacketorchards.com

SKANEATELES ARTISANS GALLERY, 3 Fennell Street #2, Skaneateles, 315-685-8580. Open Monday–Saturday 11:00 AM–7:00 PM, Sunday 11:00 AM–6:00 PM. www.skaneatelesartisans.com

UNIQUE TOY SHOP, 120 South Main Street, Canandaigua, 585-394-2319. Open Monday–Friday 9:30 AM–8:00 PM, Saturday 9:30 AM–5:30 PM, Sunday 12:00–4:00 PM. www.uniquetoyshop.com

Other Contacts

AUBURN, www.auburnny.gov

CANANDAIGUA CHAMBER OF COMMERCE, 113 South Main Street, Canandaigua, 585-394-4400. Open Monday–Friday 9:00 AM–5:00 PM; also open Saturday, Sunday, and holidays 10:00 AM–4:00 PM. from Memorial Day–Columbus Day. www.canandaiguachamber.com

DOWNTOWN GENEVA, www.downtowngeneva.com

GENEVA CHAMBER OF COMMERCE, 35 Lakefront (Route 5 & 20) Geneva, 315-789-1776 or 877-5-GENEVA. Open year-round Monday–Friday 9:00 AM–5:00 PM; Memorial Day–Columbus Day also open Saturday–Sunday 10:00 AM–4:00 PM. www.visitgenevany.com

SENECA FALLS VISITOR CENTER AND SENECA MUSEUM OF WATER-WAYS AND INDUSTRY, 89 Fall Street, Seneca Falls, 315-568-1510. www.senecafalls.com

SKANEATELES CHAMBER OF COMMERCE, 22 Jordan Street, Skaneateles, 315-685-0552. www.skaneateles.com

VILLAGE OF BLOOMFIELD, 12 Main Street, Bloomfield, 585-657-7554. Open Monday–Thursday 9:00 AM–12:30 PM and 1:00–4:00 PM. www.bloomfieldny.org

12

CAYUGA LAKE SCENIC BYWAY
A Road Trip around Cayuga Lake

ESTIMATED LENGTH: 90 miles

ESTIMATED TIME: 3 hours to several days

HIGHLIGHTS: The Cayuga Lake Scenic Byway has been voted one of the 10 Great All-American Road Trips by Yahoo Travel. This 87-mile-long loop trail takes you to a variety of diverse locations, from the Montezuma National Wildlife Refuge, where you can discover nature and wildlife, to luxurious accommodations overlooking the lake. You'll be able to sample wine at over a dozen wineries on or near the byway, and you can see how the whimsical MacKenzie-Childs pottery is handmade at their studios in the village of Aurora. In Ithaca you can explore several museums and discover a number of waterfalls, some of them right in the city. All along the trail you can enjoy beautiful scenery and views of the lake.

GETTING THERE: While you can pick up the byway at any point along the route, just look for the Cayuga Lake Scenic Byway signs. For the purposes of this book we will begin the journey at the north end of Cayuga Lake. To get there, take the New York State Thruway (I-90) to Exit 41, Waterloo. Head south on Route 414, east on Route 318, and then east on Route 5 & 20. We will stop at the Montezuma National Wildlife Refuge before heading south on Route 90 down the east side of the lake toward Ithaca, then back up the west side of the lake on Route 89.

Our journey begins at the 10,000-acre **Montezuma National Wildlife Refuge,** which is a major resting spot for migrating waterfowl. Start at the visitors center to view displays about the wildlife found at the refuge; the deck on the roof of the visitors center has a great view of the area. Take a short walk to the observation tower and climb to the top get an even better view.

LEFT: TAUGHANNOCK FALLS, TRUMANSBURG

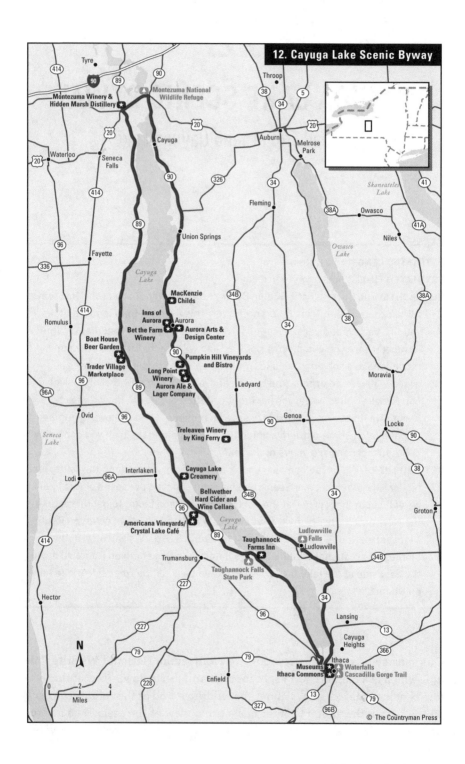

12. Cayuga Lake Scenic Byway

Tyre

414
90
89
90
Throop
38
5
34

Montezuma Winery & Hidden Marsh Distillery
Montezuma National Wildlife Refuge

20
20
Cayuga
Auburn
Melrose Park
20

Waterloo
20
Seneca Falls
90
326
34
Skaneateles Lake
41

414
Fleming
38A
Owasco

89
Union Springs
Niles
41A

96
Fayette
Owasco Lake

336
Cayuga Lake

414
MacKenzie Childs
34B
38A

Romulus
Inns of Aurora
Aurora
38

Bet the Farm Winery
Aurora Arts & Design Center
34

Boat House Beer Garden
Pumpkin Hill Vineyards and Bistro

Trader Village Marketplace
90

96
Long Point Winery
Moravia

96A
89
Aurora Ale & Lager Company
Ledyard

Ovid
96
90
Genoa
Locke
90

Seneca Lake
Treleaven Winery by King Ferry
90
38

Lodi
96A
Interlaken
Cayuga Lake Creamery

Bellwether Hard Cider and Wine Cellars
34B
34
Groton

96
Cayuga Lake

Americana Vineyards/ Crystal Lake Café

414
89
Ludlowville Falls
Ludlowville
34B

Trumansburg
Taughannock Farms Inn

227
Taughannock Falls State Park

Hector
34

96
Lansing
13

227
Cayuga Heights
366

N
79
79
Ithaca
Museums
Waterfalls
Ithaca Commons
Cascadilla Gorge Trail

0   2   4
Miles
228
Enfield
13
79
327
96B

© The Countryman Press

To really get up close and personal with the wildlife, get back in your car and take the 3.5-mile wildlife drive, which circles the main pool of the preserve. You have to stay in your car for the majority of the drive, so as not to disturb the wildlife; however, there are a few designated spots where you are permitted to get out for a better view and photo opportunities.

Continue the journey along the byway by following Route 90 south down the east side of Cayuga Lake. The first stop will be the headquarters of **MacKenzie-Childs** in Aurora, makers of hand-decorated tableware and home furnishings that are sold in exclusive shops around the world. Pull into the parking lot and enjoy the breathtaking view of Cayuga Lake and the surrounding countryside before heading inside the retail shop. Be warned, most items are rather pricey, although you will be able to find some moderately priced items that won't break the bank.

You can see how their products are made by watching a 15-minute video in a room adjacent to the retail shop. In that same room is a huge dollhouse decorated with miniature MacKenzie-Childs items. Be sure to check out the bathrooms in the visitor center, even if you don't need to use the facilities, as they are uniquely decorated in MacKenzie-Childs style.

If time permits, sign up to take the free one-hour tour of the circa 1840 farmhouse, which showcases their designs and furnishings. You can also enjoy the beautiful gardens on the grounds.

A few miles south of MacKenzie-Childs is the charming village of Aurora,

MONTEZUMA NATIONAL WILDLIFE REFUGE, SENECA FALLS

MACKENZIE-CHILDS, AURORA

which is listed on the National Register of Historic Places. During the 19th century it was a bustling village and a major stop on the transportation route that was part of the Erie Canal corridor. Henry Wells, of Wells Fargo Stagecoach, established Wells College here in 1868. However, over the years it became a sleepy, nondescript village. Fortunately for the village, a philanthropic alumna of the college, who made her fortune by designing the American Girl dolls, stepped in and gave funds to renovate the Aurora Inn, one of the centerpieces of the village, along with the entire downtown business district.

There are now four properties that are part of the **Inns of Aurora**. The *Aurora Inn,* a circa 1833 Federal-style brick inn, which was built by E. B. Morgan, a good friend of Henry Wells, offers 10 luxurious guest rooms, including some with balconies overlooking the lake. The inn's cozy dining room is open to the public; during nicer weather you can dine outdoors on the patio. Other properties include the *E. B Morgan House,* built in 1858 as Mor-

POND AT MACKENZIE CHILDS, AURORA

FARMHOUSE AT MACKENZIE-CHILDS, AURORA

gan's residence, which has seven guest rooms, including a ground-floor handicapped-accessible suite. *The Roland House*, a 10,000–square-foot Queen Anne mansion, has 10 suites and is often rented out for small weddings and retreats. The newest addition, *Wallcourt Hall*, a modern boutique hotel with 17 guest rooms, is located in an early 1900s building that once served as a dormitory for the college.

Even if you don't plan on staying overnight at one of the inns, park your car and explore some of the village businesses and restaurants. Sample locally produced wine at **Bet the Farm Winery**, just down the street from the Aurora Inn. The **Aurora Arts & Design Center** has a collection of fine art, crafts, antiques, and gifts, with many items made by local artisans. Across the street, **Fargo Bar & Grill** is a popular spot to enjoy burgers, crab rolls, and more.

Take a 10-minute walk down the street, which is lined with lovely Victorian homes, to **Dorie's**, a casual eatery that has baked goods, sandwiches, and ice cream on the menu.

It will be hard to leave Aurora. However, if you want to continue your drive along the byway, you must bid goodbye to the village. Some of the places to stop along the way include **Pumpkin Hill Vineyard**, a seasonal restaurant in a country farmhouse setting which features locally grown produce in its menu items. Also in this area is **Long Point Winery**, located on

AURORA INN

72 acres overlooking Cayuga Lake. They are known for their dry red and white wines.

Down the road, **Aurora Ale & Lager Company** is a nanobrewery that makes small batches of unique beers; their most popular is The Ruckus IPA. Nearby is **Treleaven Winery by King Ferry,** which opened in 1988 and is the oldest established winery on the east side of Cayuga Lake. They are especially known for their chardonnays and rieslings.

The byway continues south toward Ithaca along Route 34B. Make a stop at Ludlowville Falls, which can be viewed from Ludlowville Park on Ludlowville Road. Note: The waterfalls in the Ithaca area are best viewed in the spring or after a heavy rain. During dry summers the waterfalls are sometimes reduced to just a trickle.

Follow Route 34 into the city of Ithaca. There are a lot of things to see and do here; however, this book will not go into great detail about those things, as Ithaca is not really "backroads." Below is a brief overview; for more detailed information contact the **Ithaca/Thompson County Convention and Visitor Bureau.**

There are several museums, including the **Science Center, Museum of the Earth, Johnson Museum of Art**, and the **Cornell Lab of Ornithology**, just to name a few. You can also explore some of the area's many waterfalls, some located right in the city, including Ithaca Falls, off Lake Street, which is one of the more powerful falls in the city; Triphammer Falls, on the Cornell

University campus; and Cascadilla Falls, which is near Cornell's Schwartz Center for the Arts.

Enjoy a hike along the 1.3-mile **Cascadilla Gorge Trail**, which goes from Cornell to downtown Ithaca; there are six larger waterfalls along the trail. Downtown you'll want to explore the **Ithaca Commons**, an area of restored buildings that has over 100 specialty shops and restaurants and is home to many festivals and events. Just a short distance from the Commons is the iconic **Moosewood Restaurant**, which has been known for vegetarian and vegan cuisine for over 40 years. They have even published their own cookbook.

Following Route 89, head north up the west side of the lake. The next stop is **Taughannock Falls State Park**. There are a couple options for viewing the falls. You can park in the lower paid parking lot and hike the 0.75-mile trail through the gorge to the base of the falls. However, if you want to just stop for a quick view of the falls from above, with no hiking involved, turn left onto Taughannock Falls Road and drive to the overlook parking area, where parking is free. There are restrooms and a tourist information booth there. Take a short walk to the overlook area to view the falls, which, at 215 feet, are the highest single-drop waterfalls in the United States. Taughannock Falls is 33 feet higher than Niagara Falls.

The **The Inn at Taughannock**, adjacent to the park, is a Victorian mansion

BET THE FARM WINERY, AURORA

originally built as a private residence in 1873. In addition to overnight accommodations, they also have a fine dining restaurant with a view of the lake.

As you continue north on Route 89, you'll see a number of wineries, cideries, and breweries which are part of the **Cayuga Wine Trail.** Some of these include **Americana Vineyards**, which is home to the **Crystal Lake Café**, where you can enjoy house-made breakfasts and lunches, as well as live music on Friday evenings and Sunday afternoons. **Bellwether Hard Cider**, established in 1999, was the first cider producer in the Finger Lakes Region. They produce 10 varieties of hard cider, from dry to semisweet, some with carbonation. For a complete list of all the wineries and other places on the Cayuga Wine Trail, visit their website, www .cayugawinetrail.com.

Of course, not every business is a winery, cidery, or brewery. Stop at the **Cayuga Lake Creamery** in Interlaken to sample some homemade ice cream or soft-serve custard. They also serve burgers, hot dogs, and locally roasted coffee. Kids can enjoy a small playground that features a wooden train.

If you like craft brews, be sure to stop at the **Boathouse Beer Garden,** a large facility where people can enjoy the view of Cayuga Lake while drinking local craft beers. Adjacent to the beer garden, the 16,000-square-foot **Shops at Traders Village** is open on Saturdays, with vendors selling antiques, home decor, jewelry, and items produced at local farms.

This drive concludes at the corner of Route 89 and Route 5 & 20; be sure to stop at **Montezuma Winery/Hidden Marsh Distillery.** They have a wine-themed gift shop, a tasting bar, and a large selection of wines and distilled spirits. Particularly tasty is the Cranberry Bog wine and the maple liqueur, which is made with maple syrup and vodka.

IN THE AREA

Accommodations

INNS OF AURORA, 391 Main Street, Aurora, 315-364-8888. www.innsof aurora.com. $$$$.

THE INN AT TAUGHANNOCK, 2030 Gorge Road, Trumansburg, 607-387-7711. www.t-farms.com. $$$$.

Attractions and Recreation

AMERICANA VINEYARDS, 4367 Covert Road, Interlaken, 888-600-8067. www.americanavineyards.com

AURORA ALE & LAGER COMPANY, 1891 Route 90, King Ferry. Friday 4:00–7:00 PM, Saturday 12:00–6:00 PM, Sunday 1:00–5:00 PM. www.brew aurora.com

BELLWETHER HARD CIDER, 9070 Route 89, Trumansburg, 607-387-9464. www.cidery.com

BET THE FARM WINERY, 381 Main Street, Aurora, 315-294-5643. www .betthefarmny.com

BOATHOUSE BEER GARDEN/SHOPS AT TRADERS VILLAGE, 6128 Route 89, Romulus, 607-280-0064. www.boathousebeergarden.com

CASCADILLA GORGE TRAIL, trailheads are off Linn Street and behind Schwartz Performing Arts Center, Ithaca. Open from spring to fall. www .cornellbotanicgardens.org/our-gardens/natural-areas/cascadilla-gorge

CAYUGA WINE TRAIL, 800-684-5217. www.cayugawinetrail.com

CORNELL LAB OF ORNITHOLOGY, 159 Sapsucker Woods Road, Ithaca, 800-843-2473. www.birds.cornell.edu

JOHNSON MUSEUM OF ART, 114 Central Avenue, Cornell University campus, 607-255-6464. www.museum.cornell.edu

LONG POINT WINERY, 1485 Lake Road, Aurora, 315-364-6990. Open Sunday–Thursday 10:00 AM–5:00 PM, Friday and Saturday 10:00 AM–6:00 PM. www.longpointwinery.com

MACKENZIE-CHILDS, 3260 Route 90, Aurora, 888-665-1999. www.macken ziechilds.com

MONTEZUMA NATIONAL WILDLIFE REFUGE, 3395 Route 5 & 20, Seneca Falls, 315-568-5987. www.fws.gov/refuge/montezuma/

MONTEZUMA WINERY/HIDDEN MARSH DISTILLERY, 2981 Auburn Road, Seneca Falls, 315-568-8190. www.montezumawinery.com

MUSEUM OF THE EARTH, 1259 Trumansburg Road, Ithaca, 607-273-6623. Open Thursday–Monday 10:00 AM–5:00 PM, Labor Day to Memorial Day; daily in summer. www.priweb.org

SCIENCE CENTER, 601 First Street, Ithaca, 607-272-0600. Open Tuesday–Saturday 10:00 AM–5:00 PM, Sunday 12:00–5:00 PM. www.sciencecenter.org

TAUGHANNOCK FALLS STATE PARK, 2221 Taughannock Park Road, Trumansburg, 607-387-6739. www.nysparks.com/parks/62/details.aspx

TRELEAVEN WINERY BY KING FERRY, 658 Lake Road, King Ferry, 315-364-5100. www.treleavenwines.com

Dining and Nightlife

AURORA INN DINING ROOM, 391 Main Street, Aurora, 866-364-8888. www.aurora-inn.com

CAYUGA LAKE CREAMERY, 8421 Route 89, Interlaken, 607-532-9492. www.cayugalakecreamery.com

CRYSTAL LAKE CAFÉ, at Americana Vineyards, 4367 Covert Road, Interlaken, 888-600-8067. Café phone 607-387-6804. www.americanavineyards.com

DORIE'S, 283 Main Street, Aurora, 315-364-8818.

FARGO BAR & GRILL, 384 Main Street, Aurora, 315-364-8006.

MOOSEWOOD RESTAURANT, Seneca and Cayuga Streets, Ithaca, 607-273-9610. www.moosewoodcooks.com

PUMPKIN HILL VINEYARD, 2051 Route 90, Aurora, 315-364-7091. www.pumpkinhillbistroaurora.com

TAUGHANNOCK FARMS INN, 2030 Gorge Road, Trumansburg, 607-387-7711. www.t-farms.com

Shopping

AURORA ARTS & DESIGN CENTER, 371 Main Street, Aurora, 315-364-8005. www.auroraartsanddesign.com

ITHACA COMMONS, www.downtownithaca.com

LUDLOWVILLE FALLS, REDUCED WATER FLOW IN SUMMER

MACKENZIE-CHILDS, 3260 Route 90, Aurora, 888-665-1999. www.mac kenziechilds.com

Other Contacts

CAYUGA COUNTY, 131 Genesee Street, Auburn, 315-255-1658 or 800-499-9615. www.tourcayuga.com

CAYUGA LAKE SCENIC BYWAY, www.cayugalake.com

ITHACA/THOMPSON COUNTY CONVENTION AND VISITOR BUREAU, 904 East Shore Drive, Ithaca, 800-284-8422. www.visitithaca.com

SENECA COUNTY, 2020 Route 5 & 20, Seneca Falls, 315-568-2903 or 800-732-1848. www.fingerlakesgateway.com

UNCLE SAM BOAT TOURS, ALEXANDRIA BAY

13

1000 ISLANDS REGION
Boating, Castles, Wineries, and More

ESTIMATED LENGTH: 30 miles

ESTIMATED TIME: 3–4 days if you want to explore all the area has to offer

HIGHLIGHTS: While this area is known as the 1000 Islands, there are actually more than 1,000 islands: 1,864 to be exact! The islands were formed about 12,000 years ago during the last Ice Age. The region became a popular summer resort area beginning in the late 19th and early 20th centuries, when wealthy families from New York, Chicago, Cleveland, and Pittsburgh visited the numerous grand hotels which dotted the region during that era. Many of these people also built opulent summer homes on private islands.

While the area still has its share of wealthy people with homes on private islands, the region is also popular with fishermen, boaters, and people who just enjoy beautiful scenery and the outdoors.

GETTING THERE: Most people will travel to the 1000 Islands region via I-81 north to Exit 50. Once in the area, Route 12, which is part of the 518-mile-long Great Lakes Seaway Trail, which runs from the Ohio-Pennsylvania state line to Massena, New York, will be the road you'll follow. We will begin this drive in Alexandria Bay and later travel to Clayton and Cape Vincent. While one could drive this route from end to end in about an hour, if you wish to explore all the area has to offer, allow at least three or four days.

We will start our journey in Alexandria Bay, which has more lodging, restaurants, shops, and nightlife than the other two towns on this route. If you wish to stay here, there are a number of accommodations, from full-service resorts to small, locally owned hotels. Many people enjoy staying in accommodations overlooking the Saint Lawrence River and Boldt Castle, one of the major attractions in the region (which will be discussed later in this chapter).

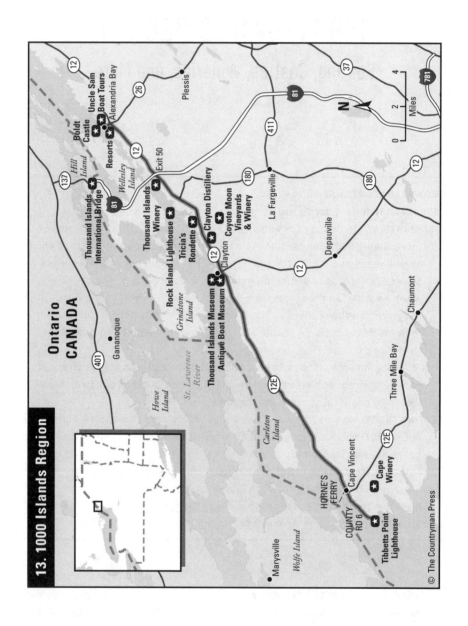

13. 1000 Islands Region

Ontario
CANADA

Gananoque

St. Lawrence
River

Howe
Island

Marysville

Wolfe Island

Carleton
Island

Grindstone
Island

Hill
Island

Wellesley
Island

Thousand Islands
International Bridge

Thousand Islands
Winery

Rock Island Lighthouse

Tricia's
Rondette

Thousand Islands Museum
Antique Boat Museum

Clayton Distillery

Coyote Moon
Vineyards
& Winery

Clayton

La Fargeville

Uncle Sam
Boat Tours

Boldt
Castle

Resorts

Alexandria Bay

Plessis

Depauville

HORNE'S
FERRY

Cape Vincent

COUNTY
RD 6

Cape
Winery

Tibbetts Point
Lighthouse

Three Mile Bay

Chaumont

Exit 50

N

0 2 4
Miles

© The Countryman Press

RIVEREDGE RESORT, ALEXANDRIA BAY

Because the river is part of the Saint Lawrence Seaway, you will often see huge freighters passing by throughout the day. The **Riveredge Resort** and **Bonnie Castle Resort** have the best view of Boldt Castle and are just a short walk to shops and restaurants in the village. The **Edgewood Resort**, just on the edge of town, is a bit more rustic but also has a nice view of Boldt Castle. With any accommodations, please make sure to make reservations months in advance, especially to book a room with a view during the summer months.

The village of Alexandria Bay is very touristy, with a number of gift shops selling T-shirts and other tchotchkes. There are also a few shops that have nicer home decor items, jewelry, and items handcrafted by local artisans. For fine dining, the upscale **Jacques Cartier** restaurant on the top floor of the Riveredge Resort has a great view along with a gourmet menu. It is rather pricey, but worth it if you want to splurge. In the village, **Cavallario's Steak House** is noted for their steak and seafood, as is the **Admirals' Inn**. For more casual fare, try **Riley's by the River**. There are also a number of very casual bars throughout the downtown area which also serve food and often have live entertainment during the summer season.

One of the more popular things to do while in the 1000 Islands is to explore the region by boat. If you don't have your own boat, take the two-hour, two-nation tour offered by **Uncle Sam Boat Tours**, which has been offering tours since 1926. Part of this tour takes you past "Millionaire's Row," with exquisite mansions built on some of the islands. The tour makes a stop

UNCLE SAM BOAT TOURS, ALEXANDRIA BAY

at Boldt Castle on Heart Island, which, as mentioned earlier, is one of the region's main attractions.

Boldt Castle has a beautiful yet tragic love story behind it. George Boldt, who achieved his wealth as manager of the Waldorf Astoria Hotel in New York City, commissioned architects to build a castle as a symbol of his love for his wife, Louise. The castle was 90 percent completed when Louise died suddenly in 1904. George ordered work on the structure to be halted immediately, and it remained unfinished, exposed to the elements, and vandalized until 1977, when the 1000 Islands Bridge Authority acquired the property and began restoration. Today it is beautifully restored, although it will never be fully restored, as it was stipulated by the family that it could only achieve 90 percent completion. You should plan on at least spending two to three hours touring the castle, the grounds, and the Boldt yacht house; that's in addition to the two hours on the boat tour. So, in other words, plan on spending almost the entire day doing this.

There is also another castle in the region that is open to the public. **Singer Castle**, located about 10 miles east of Alexandria Bay, was constructed on Dark Island in 1905 by the Bourne family. Members of the family resided in it until the 1960s. Mr. Bourne made his fortune as president of the Singer Sewing Machine Company. Boat tours to the castle are offered by local tour boat companies, like Uncle Sam Boat Tours, until mid-October.

Visit Alexandria Bay in mid-August and you'll get to experience **Bill**

Johnston's Pirate Days, a 10-day annual event that commemorates some of the exploits of Bill Johnston, a renegade in the 1830s who hid in the 1000 Islands while on the run from both American and Canadian authorities.

Head west on Route 12 toward Clayton; there are several places to stop along the 10-mile drive. The **Thousand Islands Winery,** which is located off Route 12 just past I-81, offers wine tastings, tours, and retail sales. Their VIP Tasting and Tour, which takes place Monday–Friday at 2:00 PM, is very popular and highly recommended. Reservations are a must. Participants are escorted upstairs in the winery's vintage barn and seated at tables covered with grape-themed tablecloths. You get to choose nine of their wines to taste, and you even get a keepsake souvenir glass. A tour of their production facility is included in the experience. Afterward, browse in their gift shop, which has a selection of wine-themed and 1000 Islands–related items, as well as bottles of their wines.

From the grounds of the winery, view the Thousand Islands International Bridge over Saint Lawrence River. The winery also has three cottages available on the grounds that can be rented by the week or day (minimum two-night stay).

For additional information about the area, stop by the New York State Welcome Center operated by the 1000 Islands International Tourism Council; the driveway to the welcome center is almost right across from the winery. The center is open year-round and, in addition to maps and

BOLDT CASTLE, ALEXANDRIA BAY

ENJOY COMFORT FOOD AT TRICIA'S RONDETTE

other information, they offer WiFi, restrooms, and outdoor picnic tables.

Continue west down Route 12 and stop for a bite to eat at **Tricia's Rondette**, a very cute diner with nautical and lighthouse decor. You can eat at the counter or in the dining room. The staff is very friendly and a lot of locals seem to eat here. Everything coming out of the kitchen looks good, and menu items are reasonably priced.

A little farther down the road, the **Clayton Distillery** offers samples of a variety of adult beverages, including whiskey, various liquors, and even moonshine, all which are made on-site. By law, they can only let you sample a quarter ounce of three different products for free, which doesn't sound like much. However, their products are rather potent, so that's more than enough for most people! If you feel the need to sober up after your tasting, walk across the parking lot and play a round of mini golf at **River Golf Adventures**. Let's just say that, after whiskey tasting, the water hazards can be quite challenging. Fortunately, golf balls float!

Another place to sample adult beverages is the **Coyote Moon Vineyards**,

CLAYTON DISTILLERY

located on Route 3, which runs parallel to Route 12. They offer a fun atmosphere for tasting over 18 varieties of wine. They also have a tasting room and retail store in downtown Clayton.

The main attraction in the Village of Clayton is the **Antique Boating Museum**, a large complex with six buildings to tour at your own pace, along with a houseboat that was once owned by the Boldt family. The museum has the largest collection of antique and classic boats in North America. One building has exhibits focusing on powerboat racing, while another has a large exhibit with a variety of wooden boats, including two cruisers you can climb aboard and explore. There is also a boat restoration building where visitors can watch volunteers and staff at work restoring vintage boats. Another building has a theater and rotating exhibits, as well as a gift shop. Canoes and skiffs are displayed in a building near the water; their in-house fleet, composed of vintage boats that they take out on the river, is in the yacht house. The highlight of the museum's collection is *La Duchesse,* a 106-foot houseboat built for George Boldt in 1903 and later owned by the McNally family. The houseboat is open by guided tour only.

COYOTE MOON VINEYARDS, CLAYTON

From the museum, walk a few blocks to downtown Clayton, which has a number of art galleries, gift shops, and restaurants concentrated along James Street and Riverside Drive. Businesses here tend to be a bit more upscale than the ones found in Alexandria Bay. Find out more about the history of life along the Saint Lawrence River at the **Thousand Islands Museum** or take a walking tour of the downtown area, which has a large number of 19th and early 20th century buildings. Walking tour maps are available at the Antique Boating Museum. Take a boat tour with **Clayton Island Tours** to see Boldt Castle or the **Rock Island Lighthouse**, a New York State Park, accessible only by boat, which has a 50-foot lighthouse open seasonally for tours.

A great place to sit and relax and watch the boats along the river is the pavilion at **Frink Park**, which is the site of summer concerts and other events in town. The Riverwalk Trail begins west of the pavilion and goes to the transient boat docks just beyond the nearby 1000 Islands Harbor Hotel.

There are a number of restaurants in town, including fine dining at **Bella's**, which has an outdoor patio overlooking the Saint Lawrence River; and the **Johnston House**, which is located in an Italianate-style 1880s home. More casual fare can be found at **Lyric Coffee House and Bistro** or at **Koffee**

TOP: THOUSAND ISLANDS WINERY, ALEXANDRIA BAY
BOTTOM: FRINK PARK, CLAYTON

1000 ISLANDS HARBOR HOTEL, CLAYTON

Kove Restaurant. Get subs and ice cream to go at **The Scoop** and eat them while sitting on one of the colorful Adirondack chairs facing the water at Frink Park. If you enjoy craft beers, stop by the **Wood Boat Brewery,** located across from the Antique Boating Museum. Besides craft brews, they serve brick-oven pizza, sandwiches, salads, and more. Their outdoor deck, which has a view of the Saint Lawrence River, is popular in warmer months.

The newest place to stay while visiting Clayton is the **1000 Islands Harbor Hotel**, which opened in 2014. The hotel, located on 4 acres overlooking the Saint Lawrence River, was awarded the AAA Four Diamond status, one of only 24 hotels in upstate New York to have that designation. You can enjoy fine dining at the hotel's Seaway Grille. If you have a boat, there is a 44-slip marina adjacent to the hotel.

After visiting Clayton, head west on Route 12E toward Cape Vincent, which is referred to as Where Lake and River Meet. This is where Lake Ontario flows into the Saint Lawrence River. The must-see destination in Cape Vincent is the **Tibbetts Point Lighthouse**. After passing through the Village of Cape Vincent, take the 2-mile drive to the lighthouse, which winds down a narrow residential road overlooking the river. The lighthouse is located at the end of the road.

The present 59-foot-tall lighthouse tower was built in 1854 and features the only working Fresnel lens on Lake Ontario; it is visible to sailors 16

TIBBETTS POINT LIGHTHOUSE, CAPE VINCENT

miles distant. While the tower is not open to the public due to insurance regulations, you can get a nice view of the area using a telescope located on the grounds. A small museum, a gift shop, and restrooms are located in the visitors center. The keeper's house and assistant keeper's house are currently used together as a youth hostel.

Another place in Cape Vincent to visit is the **Cape Winery**, which has a number of award-winning wines and offers a variety of special wine pairings and tasting events throughout the year.

One of the larger festivals taking place in Cape Vincent is the annual French Festival, held the second Saturday in July, which is close to Bastille Day. The event was started by local residents in 1968, reflecting the heritage of many of the area's early settlers.

IN THE AREA

Accommodations

1000 ISLANDS HARBOR HOTEL, 200 Riverside Drive, Clayton, 315-686-1100. www.1000islandsharborhotel.com. $$$$.

BONNIE CASTLE RESORT, 31 Holland Street, Alexandria Bay, 800-955-4511. www.bonniecastle.com. $$$.

SIDE TRACKS

Cape Vincent has the distinction of having the only auto/passenger ferry, **Horne's Ferry,** which crosses the Saint Lawrence River; it connects Cape Vincent with Wolfe Island, Ontario, Canada (315-283-0638, www.hferry.com). The ferry runs May 1 to mid-October. Visitors entering Canada are required to have proper identification, such as a US or Canadian passport, enhanced driver's license, or NEXUS card, to cross the border. Children are required to have a birth certificate with a raised seal. The other point of entry into Canada in the region is the Thousand Island International Bridge, which crosses the river near Alexandria Bay.

EDGEWOOD RESORT, 22467 Edgewood Road, Alexandria Bay, 315-482-9923. www.theedgewoodresort.com. $$.

RIVEREDGE RESORT, 17 Holland Street, Alexandria Bay, 800-365-6987. www.riveredge.com. $$$.

Attractions and Recreation

ANTIQUE BOATING MUSEUM, 750 Mary Street, Clayton, 315-686-4104. Open seasonally, May–October. www.abm.org

BILL JOHNSTON'S PIRATE DAYS, this festival takes place in mid-August. www.visitalexbay.org/index.php/thousand-islands-events/bill-johnstons -pirate-days/

BOLDT CASTLE, 315-482-9724. www.boldtcastle.com

CAPE WINERY, 2066 Deerlick Road, Cape Vincent, 315-654-3218. Open seasonally April–December. www.thecapewinery.com

CLAYTON DISTILLERY, 40164 Route 12, Clayton, 315-285-5004. www.clay tondistillery.com

CLAYTON ISLAND TOURS, 39621 Chateau Lane, Clayton, 315-686-4820. www.claytonislandtours.com

COYOTE MOON VINEYARDS, 17371 East Line Road (Route 3), Clayton, 315-686-5600. They also have a second location at 524 Riverside Drive, Clayton, 315-686-4030. www.coyotemoonwinery.com

FRINK PARK, 300 Riverside Drive, Clayton, 315-686-5552.

RIVER GOLF ADVENTURES, 40168 Route 12, Clayton, 315-777-0225. www .rivergolfadventures.com

ROCK ISLAND LIGHTHOUSE, 315-775-6886. www.rockislandlighthouse .org

SINGER CASTLE, 1-877-327-5475. www.singercastle.com

THOUSAND ISLANDS MUSEUM, 312 James Street, Clayton, 315-686-5794. www.timuseum.org

RIVER VIEWS AT THE ANTIQUE BOATING MUSEUM, CLAYTON

THOUSAND ISLANDS WINERY, 43298 Seaway Avenue, Alexandria Bay, 315-482-9306. www.thousandislandswinery.com

TIBBETTS POINT LIGHTHOUSE, 33435 County Road 6, Cape Vincent, 315-654-2700. www.capevincent.org/lighthouse

UNCLE SAM BOAT TOURS, www.usboattours.com

Dining and Nightlife

ADMIRALS' INN, corner of James and Market Streets, Alexandria Bay, 315-482-2781.

BELLA'S, 602 Riverside Drive, Clayton, 315-686-2341. www.bellasonlinenow .com

CAVALLARIO'S STEAK HOUSE, 26 Church Street, Alexandria Bay, 315-482-9867. Open seasonally. www.cavallarios.net

JACQUES CARTIER, in the Riveredge Resort, 17 Holland Street, Alexandria Bay, 800-365-6987. www.riveredge.com

JOHNSTON HOUSE, 507 Riverside Drive, Clayton, 315-686-3663. www
.johnstonhouserestaurant.com

KOFFEE KOVE RESTAURANT, 220 James Street, Clayton, 315-686-2472.

LYRIC COFFEE HOUSE AND BISTRO, 246 James Street, Clayton, 315-686-
4700. www.lyriccoffeehouse.com

RILEY'S BY THE RIVER, 48 James Street, Alexandria Bay, 315-482-7777.
Open seasonally May–mid-October. www.rileysbytheriver.com

THE SCOOP, 421 Riverside Drive, Clayton, 315-686-3676. www.thescoop
clayton.com

TRICIA'S RONDETTE, 40685 Route 12, Clayton, 315-686-4760.

WOOD BOAT BREWERY, 625 Mary Street, Clayton, 315-686-3233. Open
Monday–Saturday 11:00 AM–11:00 PM, Sunday 12:00–11:00 PM. www.wood
boatbreweryny.com

Other Contacts

1000 ISLANDS INTERNATIONAL TOURISM COUNCIL, 800-847-5263.
www.visit1000islands.com

ALEXANDRIA BAY CHAMBER OF COMMERCE, 7 Market Street, Alexandria Bay, 315-482-9531. www.visitalexbay.org

CAPE VINCENT CHAMBER OF COMMERCE, 315-654-2481. www.cape
vincent.org

CLAYTON CHAMBER OF COMMERCE, 517 Riverside Drive, Clayton, 315-
686-3771 or 800-252-9806. www.1000islands-clayton.com

HYDE HALL COVERED BRIDGE, GLIMMERGLASS STATE PARK, COOPERSTOWN

14

CENTRAL NEW YORK
Brews, Baseball, BBQ, Butterflies, Books, and More

ESTIMATED LENGTH: 150 miles

ESTIMATED TIME: Drive time about 4 hours, but allow 4–5 days to see all the sites in the area

HIGHLIGHTS: This drive explores several villages, towns, and cities in central New York. You can enjoy brewery tours and sample craft beer in Utica and along the Cooperstown Beverage Trail, visit the Baseball Hall of Fame, sample really good barbecue in Oneonta, and visit a butterfly garden. You will visit Hobart, a book village, and if you want, you can take a side trip to Norwich to tour the Northeast Car Museum.

GETTING THERE: This drive will begin in Utica, Exit 31 off the New York State Thruway (I-90). Alternately, you can get to this area from the I-88 expressway (Exits 13, 14, or 15 in Oneonta); however, if that's the case, you may want to follow the route in reverse order.

While the city of Utica is definitely not backroads, it's a great starting point for this particular trip. The main place you want to check out in Utica is the **FX Matt Brewing Company/Saranac Brewery** on Varick Street, makers of Saranac and Utica Club beer; a family-owned business which has been brewing beer since 1888. While one can just stop by to shop in their beer shop, you really should try to take one of their brewery tours, which lasts about an hour. The tour takes visitors through the entire brewery and covers everything from how the company was founded to how the beer is brewed and bottled. The tour ends in their tasting room, where you can sample some of their beers, or sodas for those under 21.

Down the street from the brewery, enjoy lunch at the **Nail Creek Pub & Brewery**, known for their burgers and daily specials. Plus, they only have craft beer on tap. A few doors down is the **Mohawk Valley Winery**, Utica's

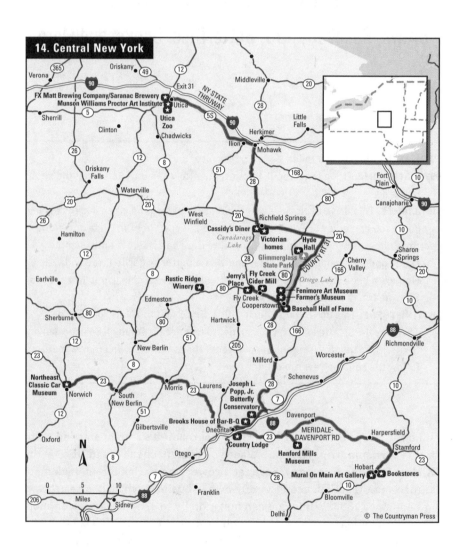

14. Central New York

365 · Verona · Oriskany · 49 · 12

90

Exit 31 · NY STATE THRUWAY · Middleville · 20

FX Matt Brewing Company/Saranac Brewery ★
Munson Williams Proctor Art Institute ★ Utica · 28

5 · 5S · 90

Sherrill · Little Falls

Utica Zoo · Herkimer

Clinton · Chadwicks · Ilion · Mohawk

26 · 12 · 8

Oriskany Falls · 51 · 168 · Fort Plain · 10

28

Waterville · 80 · Canajoharie · 90

20 · 20

West Winfield · 20 · Richfield Springs · 10

26

Hamilton · Cassidy's Diner ★ · Victorian homes ★ · Hyde Hall ★ · 20

Canadarago Lake · Sharon Springs

12 · Glimmerglass State Park · COUNTY RT 31 · Cherry Valley · 166 · 20

28

8 · Rustic Ridge Winery ★ · Jerry's Place ★ · Fly Creek Cider Mill ★ · 80 · Otsego Lake

Earlville · 80

Edmeston · Fly Creek · Fenimore Art Museum ★ · Farmer's Museum · 10

Cooperstown · Baseball Hall of Fame ★

Sherburne · 80 · 80 · Hartwick · 28 · 166

12 · 88 · Richmondville

23 · New Berlin · 51 · 205 · Worcester · 10

8 · Milford · Schenevus

Northeast Classic Car Museum ★ · 23 · Morris · 23 · Laurens · Joseph L. Popp, Jr. Butterfly Conservatory ★ · 28 · 10

Norwich · South New Berlin · 7

12 · 51 · Davenport · MERIDALE-DAVENPORT RD

Gilbertsville · Brooks House of Bar-B-Q ★ · Oneonta · 88 · Harpersfield

Oxford · Country Lodge ★ · 23

N · Otego · Hanford Mills Museum ★ · Hobart · Stamford · 23

0 · 5 · 10 · 7 · 28 · Mural On Main Art Gallery ★ ★ Bookstores

206 · Miles · 88 · Franklin · 10 · Bloomville

Sidney · Delhi · © The Countryman Press

SAMPLE BEER AT SARANAC BREWERY, UTICA

first winery located in the brewery district. They serve a selection of appetizers and desserts in their tasting room. There is also a distillery in this same district, **The Adirondack Distilling Company**, which produces handcrafted spirits, including vodka, gin, white whiskey, and bourbon from locally sourced ingredients. Tours of the distillery are available by appointment.

Other points of interest in Utica include the **Utica Zoo**, which has over 200 animals. The zoo celebrated 100 years in 2015. Art lovers will want to stop by the **Munson Williams Proctor Art Institute**, a regional arts center which features a permanent collection of internationally recognized works, as well as changing exhibits, performances, classes, and more.

There are several restaurants of note in Utica that you may want to check out, including **The Tailor & The Cook**, which is known for farm-to-table cuisine; the upscale **Ocean Blue Restaurant and Oyster Bar**, which is Utica's premier rooftop restaurant; **Bella Regina**, noted for chicken riggies, a popular Utica dish; or **O'Scugnizzo's**, established in 1914, the oldest pizza shop in upstate New York!

Don't leave Utica without sampling its signature half-moon cookies, either from the **Gingerbread Bake Shop** or the **Holland Farms Deli & Bakery**. If you want to try more Utica signature foods, stop by **Sammy and Annie Foods** for local specialties, including pastaciotti, pusties, half-moon cookies, and more.

After visiting Utica, head east on Route 5S to Route 28 south. You'll notice the scenery quickly becomes very rural, with many farms dotting the countryside. Turn left on Route 20 and drive through a number of small villages, including Richfield Springs, which has many lovely Victorian homes. If you're hungry, check out **Cassidy's Diner,** which serves huge portions of homemade food for breakfast and lunch.

When you reach Route 31, head south toward Cooperstown. Be sure to make a stop at **Glimmerglass State Park** on the shores of Otsego Lake. Author James Fenimore Cooper, a Cooperstown native, called the lake "Glimmerglass" in his book, *The Leatherstocking Tales*, because the surface reflects the surroundings like a mirror.

The 600-acre park was originally part of the estate of George Clarke (1768–1835). Today the Clarke family owns about 90 percent of the land along Otsego Lake. The family wishes for the lakeshore to remain natural and undeveloped; that's the reason there is so little development along the shore.

Located within the park is **Hyde Hall**, which was built by George Clarke between 1817 and 1834. This National Historic Landmark is considered one of the finest examples of a Neoclassical country house in the country. It is open for guided tours from May to October. Because it is purported to be haunted, evening ghost tours are offered during the summer and in October.

Also located in the park is the **Hyde Hall Covered Bridge**, which can be

GLIMMERGLASS STATE PARK, COOPERSTOWN

HYDE HALL COVERED BRIDGE, GLIMMERGLASS STATE PARK, COOPERSTOWN

found on the right side of the park road, a short distance past the entrance. Built in 1825, it is the oldest existing covered bridge in the United States; it was restored by New York State in 1967. Park your car in the small lot; it's just a short stroll to the bridge. You can actually walk through the 53-foot-long single-span bridge, which uses the Burr Arch design. Other amenities in the park include a large beach, fishing access, and hiking trails, as well as overnight camping from mid-May to mid-October.

Continue south on the narrow, tree-lined Route 31 toward Cooperstown; you'll see an occasional glimpse of the lake through the trees. You'll want to spend at least a couple days in Cooperstown, as there are several interesting museums and other things to see and do.

Of course, the best-known attraction in Cooperstown is the **National Baseball Hall of Fame and Museum**, which has three floors of exhibits that highlight the history of baseball and honor the players of the game. The museum has many interactive displays, videos, photos, and artifacts; plan on spending three hours or more here. The Hall of Fame Plaque Gallery houses over 300 bronze plaques of those players inducted into the Baseball Hall of Fame. If you want to attend the annual inductions in July, make hotel reservations well in advance; if you don't like crowds, avoid coming during that week!

Another well-known attraction is **Doubleday Field**, just down the street from the Baseball Hall of Fame. It is named after Abner Doubleday, consid-

NATIONAL BASEBALL HALL OF FAME AND MUSEUM, COOPERSTOWN

ered the "Father of Baseball." The grounds have been used since the 1920s; the stadium was built in 1939 and is used for the annual Hall of Fame exhibition game, as well as amateur games the rest of the year.

Other museums in the Cooperstown area include **The Farmers' Museum**, which features a re-creation of 19th-century village life in buildings that have been moved to this location from other communities in the state. Be sure to visit the museum's Empire State Carousel, which has been described as "a museum you can ride." The carousel, which opened in 2006, has 25 hard-carved animals representing the resources found in New York State. Murals represent moments in state history, and the frames around the murals depict the different regions of the state.

Across the street, the **Fenimore Art Museum** houses the collection of the New York Historical Association, which includes a large collection of folk art and American Indian art. The museum also has a number of artifacts associated with James Fenimore Cooper, Cooperstown's most famous son.

Cooperstown was developed in 1786 by William Cooper, the father of James Fenimore Cooper, who penned *The Leatherstocking Tales*, a series of novels which included *The Last of the Mohicans*. The village was originally incorporated as Otsego, but the name was later changed to Cooperstown in 1812, after the elder Cooper was appointed a judge.

While in Cooperstown, take a relaxing cruise on the *Glimmerglass*

Queen, where you can view lovely scenery along the lake and get an up-close view of Kingfisher Tower, which can only be viewed from the lake. This 60-foot-tall tower, modeled after a 14th-century castle on the Rhine River in Germany, was built in 1876 by Edward Clarke to beautify the lake. It has stained-glass windows and once had a drawbridge.

You can spend a lot of time browsing through shops along Cooperstown's Main Street; many of them are baseball-themed, like the **Cooperstown Bat Company**. There is even a **Heroes of Baseball Wax Museum** featuring over 30 wax figures depicting some of baseball's most famous players.

Folks over 21 may want to sample some adult beverages at the **Cooperstown Beverage Exchange**; be sure to sample the Spitball Cinnamon Whiskey. A café in the rear of the business is open evenings only.

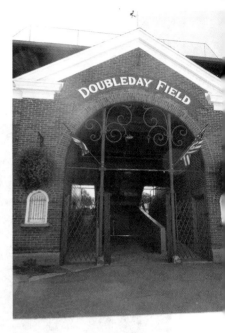

DOUBLEDAY FIELD, COOPERSTOWN

When hunger strikes, there are numerous restaurants to choose from in Cooperstown, from tiny casual diners to upscale fine-dining establishments.

THE FARMERS' MUSEUM, COOPERSTOWN

TOP: FENIMORE ART MUSEUM, COOPERSTOWN
BOTTOM: STATUE OF JAMES FENIMORE COOPER, COOPERSTOWN

For a delicious, reasonably priced breakfast, try the very tiny **Cooperstown Diner**, which has been in business since 1921. How tiny is it? It's so tiny it only has half an address! Commonly found in older downtown areas, a smaller business establishment with a separate entrance is located in part of a larger building, so it is given a half address. There are four tables and 12 seats at the counter. Another popular breakfast spot is the **Doubleday Café**; be sure to get there early to beat the crowds. Try their crab cakes eggs Benedict, a new twist on an old favorite.

Mel's at 22 is popular for fine dining, as is **The Lake Front Restaurant**, which has a menu heavy on seafood. For baked goods, check out **Schneider's Bakery**; they bake their items without preservatives or chemicals.

Another spot in the Cooperstown area to enjoy a great meal and sample craft beers is **Brewery Ommegang**; established in 1997, they make Belgian-style brews. Tours and tastings are offered year-round, and their café is open daily for lunch and also for dinner on Friday and Saturday evenings. In addition, they have a summer concert series and host an annual beer festival each summer.

There are a variety of accommodations to choose from in the area, from motels and bed & breakfast inns to resort hotels. If you're looking for something reasonably priced, the **Mohican Motel**, a 10-minute walk to the village along Chestnut Street, has simple, clean accommodations, including several two-room family suites. There are also a number of lovely bed & breakfast

GLIMMERGLASS QUEEN, COOPERSTOWN

COOPERSTOWN DINER, COOPERSTOWN

inns along Chestnut Street, including the **White House Inn Bed & Breakfast, Baseball Bed & Breakfast**, and **Landmark Inn Bed & Breakfast**. The **Lakefront Hotel** overlooks the waterfront.

For a bit more upscale accommodations, the **Cooper Inn** is a Federal-style manor house turned boutique hotel. It has 15 guest rooms with 19th-century decor and modern amenities. If you want to go all out, book a stay at the **Otesaga Resort Hotel**, which first opened its doors in 1909. This luxury inn offers fine dining, a spa, and even its own golf course.

After exploring Cooperstown, head south on Route 28 toward Oneonta, where there are several places to visit. If you like butterflies, be sure to stop at the **Joseph L. Popp Jr. Butterfly Conservatory**, a 3,000-square-foot indoor butterfly garden which has free-flying butterflies and birds, along with tortoises, lizards, and frogs. Note that from the parking lot, the main building is hidden from sight; however, just follow the path and you'll see it.

There are several places to eat in Oneonta, the most well-known being **Brooks' House of Bar-B-Q**, which has been an Oneonta mainstay since 1951. This casual, family-friendly restaurant is famous for its barbecued chicken and ribs. They have the largest indoor charcoal pit east of the Mississippi! In 2016 they won the prestigious James Beard Foundation America's Classic Award, the highest honor in the restaurant business.

They make all their own sauces, which are gluten-free and contain no high-fructose corn syrup. You can buy the sauces at the restaurant or online. A seasonal ice cream and gift shop is located behind the restaurant.

Another well-known Oneonta restaurant is **The Farmhouse at Emmons,** which has been voted the best fine dining restaurant in the area; reservations are recommended. The menu includes steak, seafood, and poultry, as well as an extensive wine list and house-made desserts.

If you want to stay overnight in Oneonta, try **Christopher's Country**

SIDE TRACKS

There are also several places of note a short drive from Cooperstown, including **Jerry's Place** in nearby Fly Creek. You can enjoy a variety of grilled items like burgers and hot dogs, as well as 18 flavors of milkshakes and homemade ice cream. However, their claim to fame is their collection of over 100 vintage metal lunch boxes from the 1950s and 1960s, as well as model cars; all are displayed on long shelves around the restaurant. They have a small arcade and host car cruises during the summer months.

Another unique and fun spot, also in Fly Creek, is the **Fly Creek Cider Mill & Orchards,** which originally opened in 1856. Plan on spending several hours here, as they have a lot of things to see. Enjoy food from their snack bar and bakersy before heading inside to their marketplace, which has all sorts of gourmet foods, sauces, dips, jams, baked goods, candy, and more, including their apple cider, made on-site in the fall on their 1889 water-powered hydraulic press. Because they also sell hard cider and apple wine, they are a part of the **Cooperstown Beverage Trail,** which counts a number of local breweries and wineries as members, including the nearby **Pail Shop Vineyards** and **Rustic Ridge Winery**.

FLY CREEK CIDER MILL, FLY CREEK

NORTHEAST CLASSIC CAR MUSEUM, NORWICH

Lodge, which is decorated in a cozy, rustic Adirondack style, complete with antler chandeliers and log-paneled walls.

From Oneonta we will be heading east on Route 23 toward Hobart. However, before or after heading there, if you like classic cars you may want to take an optional side trip to Norwich to the **Northeast Classic Car Museum** (see Side Tracks).

On your way to Hobart, take a slight detour down Meridale-Davenport Road to the **Hanford Mills Museum**, which is listed on the New York State and National Registers of Historic Places. It is one of only a few operating water-powered mills in the country. You can take tours of the sawmill and several other buildings, and there are also hiking trails on the 70-acre site.

Head back to Route 23 and then east to Route 10 and south to the tiny village of Hobart, which is known as "The Book Village of the Catskills." The village has several bookstores selling a variety of books. The stores are open daily during the warmer months and weekends only in the winter. Almost all of the shops have a cat or dog acting as a "greeter." Be careful not to let Big Red the cat escape when you go to **Mysteries & More,** which specializes in mystery, suspense, and science fiction books.

Liberty Rock Books is located in a 5,000-square-foot building. In addition to books, they also have vintage postcards and an art gallery. Across the street, **Creative Corners Books** specializes in cookbooks and craft and hobby books. **WM. H. Adams Antiquarian Book Shop** has three floors of books, most of them very reasonably priced. **Blenheim Hill Books** also features reasonably priced books.

SIDE TRACKS

The **Northeast Classic Car Museum** in Norwich, which opened in 1997, features over 170 cars and other vehicles, from 1901 to the early 1980s, displayed in nine exhibits in five connecting buildings. The majority of the cars are from the collection of the late George Staley. The museum features the largest collection of Franklin automobiles in the world. The Franklin, unlike other automobiles, does not have a radiator; it has an air-cooled engine. It was manufactured in Syracuse between 1902 and 1934.

Almost all the cars in the museum are in running condition, and while some have been restored, most are in their original condition. Besides the Franklin, other makes of cars on display include Lincoln, Studebaker, Cadillac, Cord, Packard, and Pierce Arrow, just to name a few. One exhibit features cars made in New York State; over 200 makes of cars have been made in the state.

NORTHEAST CLASSIC CAR MUSEUM, NORWICH

While most of the cars in the museum are behind ropes and strictly hands-off, there are a couple cars that visitors can actually touch and sit in for photos: a 1926 Ford Model T Roadster in the lobby and a Franklin Olympic in the Franklin display building.

If you are in Hobart on a weekend, stop in at the **Mural on Main Art Gallery**, which is operated by the Mount Utsayantha Regional Arts League. Stop for breakfast or lunch at the **Coffee Pot Restaurant**, located right next to the municipal parking lot. The **Dinner Plate Restaurant**, located in the historic Hobart Inn, serves American fare for lunch and dinner.

If you haven't already visited the Northeast Classic Car Museum in Norwich, you may want to head there next; otherwise, this concludes this drive.

IN THE AREA

Accommodations

Cooperstown

BASEBALL BED & BREAKFAST, 54 Chestnut Street, Cooperstown. www.baseballbandb.com. **.

COOPER INN, 15 Chestnut Street, Cooperstown, 800-348-6222. www.cooperinn.com. $$$.

LAKEFRONT HOTEL, 10 Fair Street, Cooperstown, 607-547-9511. www.cooperstownlakefronthotel.com. $$.

LANDMARK INN BED & BREAKFAST, 64 Chestnut Street, Cooperstown, 607-547-7225. www.landmarkinncooperstown.com. $$$.

MOHICAN MOTEL, 90 Chestnut Street, Cooperstown, 607-547-5101. www.mohican-motel.com. $$.

OTESAGA RESORT HOTEL, 60 Lake Street, Cooperstown, 607-547-9931. www.otesaga.com. $$$$.

WHITE HOUSE INN BED & BREAKFAST, 46 Chestnut Street, Cooperstown, 607-547-5054. www.thewhitehouseinn.com. $$.

Oneonta

CHRISTOPHER'S COUNTRY LODGE, 739 Route 28, Oneonta, 607-432-2444. www.christopherslodging.com. **.

Attractions and Recreation

Utica

THE ADIRONDACK DISTILLING COMPANY, 601 Varick Street, Utica, 315-316-0387. www.adirondackdistilling.com

FX MATT BREWING COMPANY/SARANAC BREWERY, 830 Varick Street, Utica, 315-624-2490. www.saranac.com

MOHAWK VALLEY WINERY, 706 Varick Street, Utica, 315-790-7659. www.mohawkvalleywinery.com

MUNSON WILLIAMS PROCTOR ART INSTITUTE, 310 Genesee Street, Utica, 315-797-0000. www.mwpai.org

UTICA ZOO, 1 Utica Zoo Way, Utica, 315-738-0472. www.uticazoo.org

Cooperstown

BASEBALL HALL OF FAME, 25 Main Street, Cooperstown. www.baseballhall.org

BREWERY OMMEGANG, 656 Route 33, Cooperstown, 607-544-1800. www.ommegang.com

DOUBLEDAY FIELD, 1 Doubleday Court, Cooperstown, 607-547-2270. www.doubledayfield.com

THE FARMERS' MUSEUM, 5775 Route 80, Cooperstown, 607-547-1450. www.farmersmuseum.org

FENIMORE ART MUSEUM, 5798 Route 80, 607-547-1400 or 888-547-1450. www.fenimoreartmuseum.org

GLIMMERGLASS QUEEN, 10 Fair Street, Cooperstown, 607-547-9511. www.cooperstownlakefronthotel.com

GLIMMERGLASS STATE PARK/HYDE HALL COVERED BRIDGE, 1527 Route 31, Cooperstown, 607-547-8662. www.nysparks.com/parks/28/details.aspx

HEROES OF BASEBALL WAX MUSEUM, 99 Main Street, Cooperstown, 607-547-1273

HYDE HALL, 1527 Route 31, Cooperstown, 607-547-5098. www.hydehall .org

Oneonta and Norwich

HANFORD MILLS MUSEUM, 73 Route 12, East Meredith, 607-278-5744. www.hanfordmills.org

JOSEPH L. POPP JR. BUTTERFLY CONSERVATORY, 5802 Route 7, Oneonta, 607-435-2238. www.oneontabutterflies.com

JOSEPH L. POPP JR. BUTTERFLY CONSERVATORY, ONEONTA

NORTHEAST CLASSIC CAR MUSEUM, 24 Rexford Street (Route 23), Norwich, 607-334-2886. www.classiccarmuseum.org

Dining and Nightlife

Utica

BELLA REGINA, 239 Genesee Street, Utica, 315-732-2426.

GINGERBREAD BAKE SHOP, 3991 Oneida Street, New Hartford (Utica), 315-737-5460.

HOLLAND FARMS DELI & BAKERY, 50 Oriskany Boulevard, Utica, 315-736-6044. www.hollandfarms.com

NAIL CREEK PUB & BREWERY, 720 Varick Street, Utica, 315-793-7593. www.nailcreekpub.com

OCEAN BLUE RESTAURANT AND OYSTER BAR, 118 Columbia Street, Utica, 315-735-2583. www.oceanbluerestaurant.com

O'SCUGNIZZO'S, 614 Bleecker Street, Utica, 315-732-6149. www.uticapizza .com

THE TAILOR & THE COOK, 94 Genesee Street, Utica, 315-793-7444. www .thetailorandthecook.com

Richfield Springs

CASSIDY'S DINER, 35 West Main Street, Richfield Springs, 315-858-2124.

Cooperstown and Fly Creek

BREWERY OMMEGANG, 656 Route 33, Cooperstown, 607-544-1800. www .ommegang.com

COOPERSTOWN BEVERAGE EXCHANGE, 73 Main Street, Cooperstown, 607-282-4374. www.cooperstowndistillery.com/beverage-exchange.html

COOPERSTOWN DINER, 136½ Main Street, Cooperstown, 607-547-9201. www.cooperstowndiner.com

DOUBLEDAY CAFÉ, 93 Main Street, Cooperstown, 607-547-5468.

FLY CREEK CIDER MILL & ORCHARDS, 288 Goose Street, Fly Creek, 800-505-6455. www.flycreekcidermill.com

JERRY'S PLACE, 6635 Route 28, Hartwick (Fly Creek), 607-547-1037. Open May–October. www.jerrysplaceny.com

MEL'S AT 22, 22 Chestnut Street, Cooperstown, 607-435-7062. www.melsat22.net

LAKE FRONT RESTAURANT, 10 Fair Street, Cooperstown, 607-547-8188. www.lakefrontcooperstown.com

SCHNEIDER'S BAKERY 157 Main Street, Cooperstown, 607-547-9631.

Oneonta

BROOKS' HOUSE OF BAR-B-Q, 5560 Route 7, Oneonta, 607-432-1782. www.brooksbbq.com

THE FARMHOUSE AT EMMONS, 5649 Route 7, Oneonta, 607-432-7374. www.thefarmhouseatemmons.com

Hobart

COFFEE POT RESTAURANT, 581 Main Street, Hobart, 607-538-1800.

DINNER PLATE RESTAURANT, 645 Main Street, Hobart, 607-538-3003. www.dinnerplateofhobart.com

BROOKS' HOUSE OF BAR-B-Q, ONEONTA

Shopping

Utica

SAMMY AND ANNIE FOODS, 717 Bleecker Street, Utica, 315-896-2173. Open Monday–Friday 9:00 AM–4:00 PM.

Cooperstown and Fly Creek

COOPERSTOWN BAT COMPANY, 118 Main Street, Cooperstown, 607-547-2415. www.cooperstownbat.com

COOPERSTOWN BEVERAGE EXCHANGE, 73 Main Street, Cooperstown, 607-282-4374. www.cooperstowndistillery.com/beverage-exchange.html

FLY CREEK CIDER MILL & ORCHARDS, 288 Goose Street, Fly Creek, 800-505-6455. www.flycreekcidermill.com

PAIL SHOP VINEYARDS, 128 Goose Street, Fly Creek, 607-282-4035. www.pailshopvineyards.com

RUSTIC RIDGE WINERY, 2805 Route 80, Burlington Flats, 607-965-0626. www.rusticridgewinery.com

Hobart

BLENHEIM HILL BOOKS, 698 Main Street, Hobart, 607-538-9222.

CREATIVE CORNERS BOOKS, 607 Main Street, Hobart, 607-386-2525

HOBART BOOK VILLAGE, www.hobartbookvillage.com

LIBERTY ROCK BOOKS, 698 Main Street, Hobart, 607-538-1760. www.hobartbookvillage.com/liberty-rock-books.html

MURAL ON MAIN ART GALLERY, 631 Main Street, Hobart, 607-538-3002. www.muralartgallery.org

MYSTERIES & MORE, 688 Main Street, Hobart, 607-538-9788.

WM. H. ADAMS ANTIQUARIAN BOOKS, 602 Main Street, Hobart, 607-538-9080. www.whabooks.com

Other Contacts

CITY OF NORWICH, www.norwichnewyork.net/index.php

COOPERSTOWN BEVERAGE TRAIL, www.cooperstownbeveragetrail .com

HOBART BOOK VILLAGE

COOPERSTOWN & OTSEGO COUNTY, 20 Chestnut Street, Cooperstown, 607-322-4046. www.thisiscooperstown.com

ONEIDA COUNTY TOURISM, www.oneidacountytourism.com

OTSEGO COUNTY CHAMBER OF COMMERCE, www.otsegocc.com

VISIT ONEONTA, www.oneonta.ny.us

1935

WER.
FOREST FIRE
RONDACKS.

15

ADIRONDACK ADVENTURE

ESTIMATED LENGTH: 250 miles for all three sections

ESTIMATED TIME: 4–5 days or more for all three sections (Note: Section 3 will take the longest, as there are more attractions along the way)

HIGHLIGHTS: The Adirondack Park has 6 million acres, over 100 towns and villages, and hundreds of miles of scenic roads, along with 46 high peaks, all but four of which are over 4,000 feet in elevation. Unlike other parks, The Adirondack Park has no gate; there is just an imaginary line that surrounds it. About 135,000 people live in communities within the park.

One chapter in one book couldn't possibly cover all there is to see and do here. The three sections described in this chapter give you an overview of the Adirondacks, taking you to some of the more well-known communities as well as some places a little off the beaten path.

The first section of this chapter describes the trip from Utica to Blue Mountain Lake, taking you through the Village of Old Forge, past the Fulton Chain of Lakes and the National Historic Landmark Sagamore Lodge.

The second section starts in the eastern part of the state in Pottersville, where you can explore the Natural Stone Bridge and Caves. Next, stop at North Creek and visit the railroad station where then Vice President Theodore Roosevelt, boarded the train to head to Buffalo to be sworn in as President of the United States after the assassination of President William McKinley. One can even mine for garnets while in the North Creek area.

The third section of the journey begins in Blue Mountain Lake; be sure to take the time to visit the Adirondack Experience, The Museum on Blue Mountain Lake (formerly known as the Adirondack Museum). Next, head north to the Wild Center in Tupper Lake before heading to Saranac Lake and then on to Lake Placid, site of the 1932 and 1980 Olympics. Then head to Wilmington,

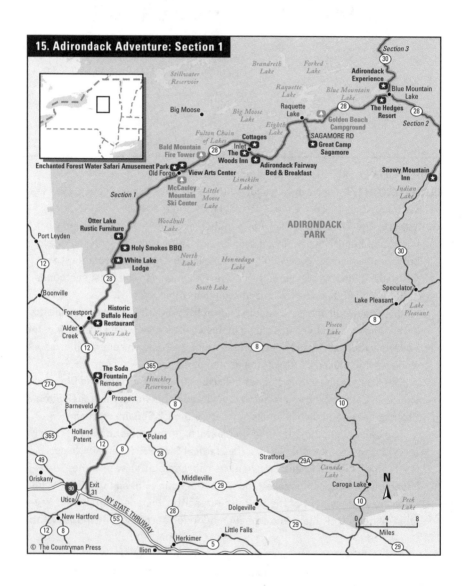

15. Adirondack Adventure: Section 1

where you can discover the natural beauty of High Falls Gorge, visit Santa at the North Pole, or take a scenic drive up Whiteface Mountain.

It will take at least five days to stop and explore the sites mentioned in this chapter, so you may want to pick one central location to stay or move around and stay overnight in a few different places along the way.

GETTING THERE: This particular drive is broken down into three sections; you can explore one, two, or all three depending on your interests and time available.

Section 1 Utica to Blue Mountain Lake: Start at Exit 31 off I-90 (New York State Thruway) and follow Route 12 north to Route 28 to Blue Mountain Lake.

Section 2 Pottersville to Blue Mountain Lake: Start at Exit 26 off I-87 (Adirondack Northway Expressway). Take Route 9 south to Route 8 to Route 28 west to Route 28/30 to Blue Mountain Lake.

Section 3 Blue Mountain Lake to Wilmington: From Blue Mountain Lake take Route 30 north to Route 3 east to Route 86 east to Wilmington.

SECTION 1

We will start this journey in Utica. If you want to know more about attractions in Utica, see Chapter 14. Note that the **Adirondack Scenic Railroad** (www .adirondackrr.com) offers scenic day trips from Utica from May through October to some of the towns described in this area. Begin driving north on Route 12. If you are looking for a place to enjoy American fare like meat loaf and chicken and biscuits, check out **The Soda Fountain**, a 1950s-themed restaurant on Route 12 in Remsen. Route 12 turns into Route 28, also called the Central Adirondack Scenic Byway; this is also a bike route, so be sure to share the road.

As you continue on Route 28, you'll pass a couple interesting restaurants and inns in the village of Forestport, which is often referred to the Gateway to the Adirondacks. The **Historic Buffalo Head Restaurant** features generous portions in an Adirondack atmosphere. Legend has it that when immigrant logging crews were brought to this area in the 1920s, one of them had a stuffed buffalo head that his wife wanted removed from their apartment, so he brought it here and nailed it on a post at the train depot. After that, when asked where they wanted to get off the train, the immigrants, who spoke little English, would tell the conductor "Buffalo head." The restaurant is located across from the old train depot.

Also in Forestport is **Holy Smokes BBQ**, which has smoked pulled pork, beef brisket, and homemade coleslaw on the menu. Overnight accommodations include the **White Lake Lodge**, located on White Lake, which has six different cabins and lodges of various sizes. A good place to shop in this area is **Otter Lake Rustic Furniture**, which has rustic Adirondack furniture, home decor, gift items, and souvenirs.

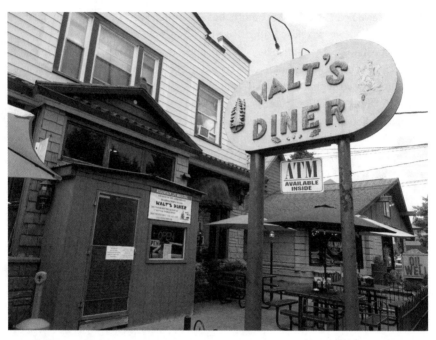

WALT'S DINER, OLD FORGE

The next town, Old Forge, has lots of things to see and do. If you like shopping, there is a plethora of stores along and near Main Street, including **Old Forge Hardware**, established in 1900, which has an array of books, clothing, gourmet foods, houseware, yarn, and yes, hardware too. The **Old Forge Department Store**, which also has hardware, carries toys, souvenirs, and gifts. **Maxon House** has a variety of books, primitives, quilts, and artwork, while the nearby **Dragonfly Cottage** has art, antiques, and vintage items.

There are also a number of restaurants in town, including **The Old Mill Restaurant**, which has upscale yet homestyle menu choices; soup, salad, and bread are served family-style. There's **Walt's Diner**, which features homemade diner food; be sure to try their hot turkey sandwich. Next door to Walt's, **Billy's Italian American** serves up your favorite Italian dishes. **Sisters Bistro**, open seasonally, features dishes made from locally grown organic ingredients.

If you have kids in tow, the **Enchanted Forest Water Safari Amusement Park** is a great place to spend the day. It is New York State's largest water-themed park, with over 50 rides, including 32 heated outdoor water rides.

You can also take a boat cruise with **Old Forge Lake Cruises**, following an old steamboat route through the first four lakes in the Fulton Chain of Lakes. Some of the cruises to choose from include a two-hour sight-seeing cruise or a three-hour mail boat ride.

Prefer the mountains over the lake? Take a scenic chairlift ride up

McCauley Mountain, June through October. If you're here during the winter months, you can enjoy skiing at family-friendly **McCauley Mountain Ski Center**, which has 21 trails for all levels of skiers.

If art is more your thing, check out the **View Arts Center**, which has a number of galleries featuring changing exhibits of works by living artists, as well as musical performances, workshops, and more. History buffs may want to visit the **Goodsell Museum**, which houses the Town of Webb Historical Association and exhibits on local Adirondack history.

Hikers will want to visit **Bald Mountain Fire Tower**, just off Route 28 on Rondaxe Road. It is a popular, easy hike, taking about an hour to get to the fire tower, which you can climb to get a panoramic view of the Adirondack countryside.

There are many places to stay in and near Old Forge, such as the **Water's Edge Inn**, which is open year-round and is within walking distance of village shops and restaurants as well as the Enchanted Forest. If you prefer more rustic accommodations, there's **Old Forge Camping Resort**, which offers year-round camping in cabins, cottages, RV sites, and tent sites, as well as vacation home rentals. There is also the **Great Pines Resort** (formerly the North Woods Inn) which was updated and renovated in 2016.

There are also many cottages and other lodging along Route 28 as you head toward Blue Mountain Lake, especially in the town of Inlet. Some of these include **Peter's Cottages, Lakeside Cottages,** and **Nelson's Cottages.**

NATURAL STONE BRIDGE AND CAVES, POTTERSVILLE

NATURAL STONE BRIDGE AND CAVES, POTTERSVILLE

For more information see www.inletny.com. Perhaps you'd like to stay at **The Woods Inn,** the only fully restored, turn-of-the-century inn located near the water's edge on the Fulton Chain of Lakes. It has a great view of Fourth Lake from the wraparound porch. The inn has 20 cozy rooms decorated with woodsy camp-style furniture; they all have private baths, but no phones or TV's, making it a true getaway reminiscent of another era. Other available accommodations include Adirondack guide tents with queen beds and a two-bedroom cabin. Another place to stay in Inlet is **Adirondack Fairway Bed & Breakfast,** which is located on the 18th fairway of the Inlet Golf Club, where one can enjoy golf in the warmer months and cross-country skiing in the winter. The inn has two large guest rooms furnished with Stickley furniture.

While in Inlet, stop at shops and restaurants like **Mary's Gift Shop,** which is one of the oldest gift shops in the Adirondacks. Open year-round, they have a large selection of Adirondack souvenirs. Mary's also has eight bed & breakfast rooms for overnight accommodations. The **Inlet Department Store** has a variety of gift items along with household items, clothing, and items for campers. **The Screamen Eagle & Matt's Draft House** is a great place to stop for pizza, wings, and subs.

Near Seventh Lake you'll see a sign for **Payne's Seaplane Rides**. For over 50 years they have been offering sight-seeing tours of the Adirondacks from the sky. Continue east toward **Great Camp Sagamore** in Raquette Lake. This 27-building National Historic Landmark, which was built in the 1890s, was the Adirondack summer home of the Alfred Vanderbilt family from 1901 to 1954. Many celebrities, politicians, and world leaders visited this Adirondack camp during that time.

Visitors can take a guided walking tour of the site from May to October. There are also programs and overnight retreats offered throughout the season, with accommodations offered in several of the rustic buildings; most rooms have two twin beds and share a bathroom in the hallway. There are no phones or TVs in the rooms, and cell phone reception is not good, so it is truly a getaway to enjoy the great outdoors.

Also in Raquette Lake is **Golden Beach Public Campground**, located on the shores of Raquette Lake. It offers 205 tent and trailer campsites, as well as a swimming beach, boat launch, hiking trails, and picnic areas. If you're not camping, you can pay a day-use fee to use the beach or boat launch.

Just before the intersection of Routes 28 and 30 is the popular **The Hedges** resort. If you want to stay here, make reservations at least a year in advance, as many people return here year after year. Open since the 1920s, this private, rustic, resort hotel, once an Adirondack Great Camp, is open from May through October. They have a variety of accommodations ranging from rooms in the lodge to large, four-bedroom cabins. A full breakfast and a four-course dinner are included in the room rate. They have a variety of recreational facilities, including tennis courts, a game room, canoes, kayaks, fishing, and swimming.

MINING FOR GEMSTONES, NATURAL STONE BRIDGE AND CAVES, POTTERSVILLE

This concludes this section of the drive. You can continue on either Route 28/30 east (Section 2) and head toward North Creek and Pottersville, or head north on Route 28N/30 (Section 3) toward Blue Mountain Lake, Tupper Lake, Lake Placid, and eventually Wilmington.

SECTION 2

If you are beginning this drive as a continuation of Section 1 or 3, you will have to read it in reverse. If you are beginning

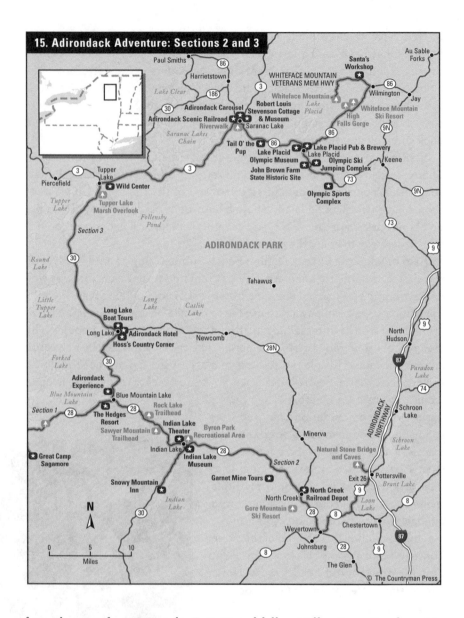

from the east, from I-87, take Exit 26 and follow Valley Farm Road west to Route 9 north and look for the signs pointing to the **Natural Stone Bridge and Caves** on Stonebridge Road.

This privately owned geological wonder has as its centerpiece a huge stone bridge arch, which has been determined to be the largest marble cave entrance in the east, measuring 166 feet wide and 32 feet high. One can easily spend three or four hours exploring this adventure park, which has been managed by the same family for five decades. The land was originally given to an ancestor of the current owners as a land grant in the 1700s.

Hiking boots or rubber-soled shoes are a must; a walking stick is really helpful (walking sticks are provided at the beginning of the hike). Even though the 0.75-mile trail is marked, you still have to climb many stairs and walk over uneven surfaces. Be sure to bring your camera, as there are many scenic spots along the way.

After your trek, visit their large gift shop, which has an extensive collection of rocks and minerals, as well as Adirondack-themed items. Kids of all ages can also enjoy gemstone mining; purchase a bag filled with sand that is also hiding gems, stones, shark teeth, and arrowheads, then pour the contents into a screened tray by the water trough and let the water wash away the sand to reveal your treasures.

As you leave the area, be sure to stop at the family's ice cream stand down the road, at the corner of Stonebridge Road and Route 9. There are 40 flavors of soft-serve ice cream to choose from.

Travel south on Route 9, past Loon Lake; look for Route 8 and follow it to Route 28, also known as the Central Adirondack Scenic Byway, heading west toward North Creek. If you enjoy skiing, **Gore Mountain Ski Resort** is located in this area. The family-friendly resort, which attracts skiers from all along the East Coast, has 109 trails on four peaks. During the off-season, folks can enjoy scenic gondola rides, which are very popular during the fall foliage season.

Continue west on Route 28 to Route 28N, turn right, then left on Main

NORTH CREEK RAILROAD STATION

Street and head into the village of North Creek, where there are a number of stores and restaurants. Some of these include **Barkeater Chocolates**, which has handcrafted gourmet chocolates, **Moose Mud Fudge**, which features sweets and homemade fudge, and **Hudson River Trading,** which has home decor items.

Restaurants include **Izzy's Deli**, whose sandwiches have been rated the best in the Adirondacks, and **Bar Vino**, a wine and tapas bar featuring locally grown, seasonal items on the menu.

Of course the most interesting and historic place to visit in North Creek is the **North Creek Railroad Depot**, which is open June through October; days vary. It was built in 1874 as the northern terminus to the Adirondack Railroad. It is here, at the North Creek Railroad station, where Vice President Theodore Roosevelt boarded a train on September 14, 1901, to head toward Buffalo, New York, where he would be sworn in as the 26th US President after the assassination of President William McKinley at the Pan American Exposition in Buffalo. Roosevelt had been vacationing with family in the Adirondacks when he received word to come to Buffalo, as President McKinley, who doctors thought previously would recover from his wounds, took a turn for the worse and was dying.

After visiting the railroad depot, or just reading the outside signage if you're there when it's not open, head west on Main Street back to Route 28 and travel in the direction of Indian Lake. The river running along the right-hand side of the road is the Hudson River; there are several small parking areas along this route that have information panels with different facts about the river.

An interesting place to stop along the way is the **Garnet Mine Tours**, where you can learn all about garnet mining history and geology. Garnet has been the official gemstone of New York State since 1969. Barton Mining, established in 1878, is the longest-running family-owned mine in the mining industry. Tours have been offered since 1933; visitors get to hunt for garnets in the open mine, which is similar to a quarry. It is one of the largest garnet deposits in the world.

Continue along Route 28; when you get to Lake Abankee be sure to notice the great scenery. Also very scenic is the **Byron Park Recreational Area** in Indian Lake; there is an overlook parking area right by the lake.

A good place to stop is the **Pines Country Store**, which has a little bit of everything: hardware, camping and fishing supplies, sporting goods, and sweatshirts. You may also want to stop at the **Indian Lake Restaurant and Tavern**, which has a number of innovative menu choices for a small-town restaurant, or the **Adirondack Smokehouse Barbecue Company** for chicken, ribs, prime rib, steak, and seafood.

The **Indian Lake Theater**, which originally opened in 1937 as the Lake Theater, shows new and classic films, and serves as a multipurpose venue for theater productions, concerts, and community events. It had closed in 2006, but it was re-opened two years later thanks to community support and state grants. Learn about the history of Indian Lake at the **Indian Lake Museum**, located in an 1865 home, one of the oldest in the community.

Accommodations in the area include the **Snowy Mountain Inn**, overlooking Indian Lake, with cute little cottages with knotty pine interiors furnished with white cedar Adirondack furniture. An annual event in Indian Lake is the Great Adirondack Moose Fest, held the fourth weekend in September. Events include guided hikes, locally made crafts, and family activities.

As you drive on most main roads in the Adirondacks, notice the brown signs with yellow lettering that point out places to park to hike a trail or see a scenic view. For example, the Sawyer Mountain Trail, which is located between Indian Lake and Blue Mountain Lake, about 4.5 miles west of Indian Lake, offers a 2.5-mile round-trip hike to the top of Sawyer Mountain. The trail climbs 650 feet from the trailhead, located along Route 28, to the summit, where you can get a great view of the surrounding area. Yellow marks posted by the New York State Department of Environmental Conservation will help keep you on course. Allow about an hour to hike the trail.

Also along Route 28 is the Rock Lake Trail, a short hike on flat ground through the forest to Rock Lake, which is popular with fishermen and bird-

ADIRONDACK EXPERIENCE, BLUE MOUNTAIN LAKE

TOP: ADIRONDACK EXPERIENCE, BLUE MOUNTAIN LAKE
BOTTOM: VIEW FROM FIRE TOWER, ADIRONDACK EXPERIENCE, BLUE MOUNTAIN LAKE

ers. It is great to snowshoe on the trail in the winter. In addition, there is a nice parking area right across the street from Lake Durant that has picnic tables; you can access a hiking trail along the lake from here.

This drive concludes in this area. You can either continue west on Route 28, which is described in Section 1 of this chapter, or continue north along Route 30, which will be described in the next section.

SECTION 3

This part of the journey starts in Blue Mountain Lake, which, looking at a map, is pretty much the center of The Adirondack Park. You have arrived in Blue Mountain Lake either from the west (Section 1) or the east (Section 2).

No visit to Blue Mountain Lake would be complete without going to the **Adirondack Experience The Museum on Blue Mountain Lake** (formerly the Adirondack Museum), which has over two dozen buildings with exhibits telling the history and culture of the Adirondacks. Located on 120 acres, the museum, which has been open since 1957, collects, preserves, and exhibits objects made or used in the Adirondacks.

After paying your admission in the visitors center, head to the boating exhibit, which explains the essential role that boats played in transportation in the Adirondacks. You can even see a professional boatbuilder crafting authentic Adirondack guide boats.

In the next building, sit on a stool and view historic photos on the mueum's photobelt, a unique exhibit the museum has used for over 40 years as a way to display photos from their collection of over 68,000 images. Another one of the buildings on the grounds has an exhibit on logging in the Adirondacks. Adjacent to this building is the circa 1919 observation tower that once stood on Whiteface Mountain and was used to watch for forest fires. Visitors can climb to the top to get a great view of the museum grounds with the mountains in the distance.

However, the most impressive exhibit building in the museum complex is the 19,000-square-foot "Life in the Adirondacks" which opened in May 2017 to kick off the museum's 60th anniversary year. The building has many hands-on interactive exhibits, along with new and familiar artifacts from the museum's collection. You can even get a bite to eat at the museum's Lake View Café, which overlooks Blue Mountain Lake.

After leaving the museum, head north on Route 30/28N toward Tupper Lake. This is a winding, tree-lined route with mountain views in the background. It is also a bike route, so keep an eye out for bicyclists.

The next town is Long Lake. Besides the beautiful lake, one of the must-see attractions here is **Hoss's Country Corner**, which has two floors with a variety of items, including gifts, jewelry, lots of books about the Adirondacks, toys, and camping supplies. While in the area you can even take a two-hour, 22-mile round-trip boat tour of Long Lake with **Long Lake Boat Tours.**

If you'd like to spend more time in this picturesque area, there are a variety of accommodations to choose from, including the historic **Adirondack Hotel,** which has two verandas overlooking the lake. The hotel has a formal Victorian dining room as well as the casual Lake Street Café.

Other accommodations in Long Lake include the **Lodge at Long Lake,** which has 14 guest rooms; **Journey's End Cottages,** which has four cottages plus a large lake house; and **The Shamrock Hotel and Cottages,** just to name a few.

Travel about 20 tree-lined miles until you reach Tupper Lake. The road will cross over the Raquette River, which has a large area of marshland. The Tupper Lake Marsh Overlook, a.k.a. Moody Marsh, on Route 30 just south of the village, is a great spot to stop to bird-watch.

One of the must-see attractions in Tupper Lake is the **Wild Center,** which focuses on exploring the natural world of the Adirondacks. There is so much to see and do here, both indoors and outdoors, that your admission is good for two consecutive days.

The most popular thing to do at the Wild Center is to take a walk on the Wild Walk, an elevated treetop walk with over 1,000 feet of bridges, walkways, and platforms over the forest. While the museum itself is open year-round, the Wild Walk is open seasonally, May–October. Climb up into the Eagles Nest

WILD WALK, WILD CENTER, TUPPER LAKE

to get a view of the surrounding mountains, and then walk across a huge spider web suspended 24 feet above the ground. Once you're back on the ground, take a nature hike to Oxbow Marsh.

Indoors there is 34,000 square feet of exhibit space with many hands-on exhibits, live animals, and films to view, as well as a museum store stocked with a variety of nature-themed items.

ADIRONDACK CAROUSEL, SARANAC LAKE

Places to eat in Tupper Lake include **Skyline Ice Cream**, which serves burgers and broasted chicken, in addition to homemade soft-serve ice cream; and **Raquette River Brewing,** which has pub fare and craft brews. Overnight accommodations in the area include the **Northwood Cabins.**

From Tupper Lake, head east on Route 3 toward Saranac Lake; this route is part of the 170-mile-long Olympic Byway, which runs from Keenesville, near Lake Champlain in the east, all the way to Henderson Harbor on Lake Ontario. This route is very desolate—all you see are trees; there are no houses, businesses, or street lights in sight. You will, however, see sev-

ADIRONDACK SCENIC RAILROAD, SARANAC LAKE

eral places to pull off for fishing access. It's also a designated bike route, so remember to share the road.

However, as you approach the Village of Saranac Lake, there are signs of civilization. The village has a number of interesting and unique attractions to check out, including the **Adirondack Carousel**, which opened in 2012. It has hand-carved figures of animals that one would find in the Adirondacks, like beavers, largemouth bass, bobcats, black flies, and salamanders. The panels decorating the carousel were hand-painted by local artists.

Down the street, at Saranac Lake's circa 1904 Union Depot, one can take a scenic 6-mile ride on the **Rail Explorers** railbikes from Saranac Lake to Lake Clear Junction. You can also catch a ride on the **Adirondack Scenic Railroad.**

Fans of the author Robert Louis Stevenson, best known for the book *Treasure Island,* can visit the **Robert Louis Stevenson Cottage and Museum**, which is preserved to reflect the winter of 1887, when Stevenson and his family lived in Saranac Lake while he was recovering from tuberculosis. The museum has the largest collection of Stevenson items in the United States.

Be sure to take a stroll along **Saranac Lake's Riverwalk**. Park your car in the lot behind the town hall, 3 Main Street, and follow the 1.5-mile-long multiuse trail along the Saranac River through the downtown area to Church Street. There are signs along the trail with historical information about Saranac Lake.

When walking though the downtown area, you may want to check out some

ROBERT LOUIS STEVENSON COTTAGE, SARANAC LAKE

SARANAC LAKE RIVERWALK

of the shops and restaurants, including **The Left Bank Café**, which has a porch overlooking the river. The café serves French café foods like crêpes and tartines.

Shop for reasonably priced household items at **Another's Treasures**, which is operated by Lakeside House, an organization that works with people with mental illnesses. Across the street, **Two Horse Trade Company** has unique gift items and locally made crafts and jewelry.

A reasonably priced and centrally located place to stay in Saranac Lake is the **Best Western Saranac Lake,** located across the street from Lake Flower. For breakfast or lunch, **McKenzie's Grille**, adjacent to the hotel, has been known for their pancakes and waffles for over 25 years. Look for the wood-carved bear statue holding a stack of pancakes. There are several other excellent restaurants just down the street from the Best Western, including the **Blue Line Brewery,** a brew pub which is located in a former car wash building. They are noted for their thin-crust personal pizzas as well as burgers and sandwiches. **La Bella Ristorante** is a great place to enjoy traditional Italian food in a casual atmosphere, while **Casa del Sol** has some of the best Mexican cuisine and margaritas in the Adirondacks.

Traveling along Route 86 between Saranac Lake and Lake Placid, you'll come across one of the more unique places in the Adirondacks: **Tail O' the Pup.** Opened in 1927, they have a casual restaurant with outdoor seating under tents. The menu features lobster, oysters, a raw bar, house-smoked barbecue, and ice cream. They even have live music! If you feel you can't get enough of this place and don't want to leave, you don't have to, as they have six rental cabins available.

Continue on this tree-lined route to Lake Placid, which could be considered the big city compared to some of the other places you've been driving though. There is a lot to see and do here; this book will just cover some of the high points, as well as some of the out-of-the-way attractions to check out.

First, there is little, if any, free parking to be found, so pay to park in one of the large municipal parking lots found along Main Street and walk to the places located within the village. Because Lake Placid hosted two Winter Olympics, 1932 and 1980, you can visit some of the Olympic sites in town, including the **Lake Placid Olympic Museum** located at the Olympic Center. This museum has all sorts of memorabilia from both Olympics, including ice skating costumes and skates from legendary figure skaters, a display of Olympic torches, and bobsleds visitors can sit in for photos. You can even watch highlights from the 1980 "Miracle on Ice" hockey game between the US and Soviet teams. Plus, you can see with your own eyes the ice rink where that game took place, the Herb Brooks Arena, which is still in use today.

Outside the Olympic Center, even if it's the middle of July, there's real snow piled up in front of a sign proclaiming, IT'S NO MIRACLE, IT'S REAL SNOW. LAKE PLACID IN THE ADIRONDACKS. OK, it's probably what's scraped off the ice with the Zamboni machine, but it's fun for kids, and adults, to make snowballs in the summer.

Next door to the Olympic Center, that cement oval in front of the Lake Placid High School was the oval used for Olympic speed skating. During the winter months you can actually skate here; skate rentals are available.

One of the hidden gems in Lake Placid is the **Olympic Torch Tower**; the flame was lit on top of this tower on February 13, 1980. This site isn't widely publicized as a place to see. In fact, you may be the only one there when you visit. It's located south of the village on Cascade Road between the **Lake Placid Horse Show Grounds** and the football field for Lake Placid High School. (Note: Do not plan on visiting during the annual Horse Show week in July; it will be crowded and you have to pay admission to the grounds at that time).

Just down the road from the torch site is the **Olympic Jumping Complex**, used for ski jumping during the 1980 Olympics and now a year-round training facility for ski jumpers and freestyle skiers. Visitors can ride an elevator to the top of the tower.

Ambitious visitors may want to head to the **Olympic Sports Complex**, where they can take a ride on the Lake Placid Bobsled Experience. It's open year-round; the bobsleds have blades in the winter and wheels in the warmer months.

History buffs may want to check out **John Brown Farm State Historic Site,** which is located in this area. This site was the home of well-known abo-

MIRROR LAKE, LAKE PLACID

litionist John Brown, whose gravesite is also on the grounds. Guided tours are offered of the home, and there are several hiking trails on the grounds.

There are plenty of places to shop, eat, and stay right in the village of Lake Placid. You can browse through shops like **Adirondack Popcorn**, with its many flavors of popcorn; get some Adirondack-themed items for your home at **Adirondack Decorative Arts & Crafts**; buy books about the Adirondacks at **The Bookstore Plus**; or pick up some locally handcrafted items at **Moon Tree Design**, just to name a few things.

There are also many great places to eat in town, including the **Lake Placid Pub & Brewery**, which overlooks Mirror Lake. They brew their own beer and always have six house brews on tap. The menu features pub classics like burgers, barbecue, wings, and fish-and-chips. Be sure to save room for dessert, specifically their signature s'mores dessert featured in *USA Today*. You get to toast your own marshmallows on a tiny tabletop fire pit before placing them between graham crackers and chocolate. The mini version feeds four. They also have other desserts which are made locally at Cake Placid Bakery. When you're done eating, head across the street and take a stroll along the beach at Peacock Park on Mirror Lake.

Another spot to eat in Lake Placid is **Big Mountain Deli & Crêperie**. Their claim to fame is the list of 46 sandwiches on the menu, each named after one of the 46 Adirondack high peak mountains. They also serve breakfast, along with soups, salads, and smoothies. The **Good Bite Kitchen** is a tiny restaurant located in a former storage hallway measuring a mere 6 feet by 35 feet, with seating for only eight people. Popular for take-out, it features vegetarian food made in-house. There are many more great restaurants in the village, from very casual to fine dining.

There are also dozens of places to stay overnight, from inexpensive to very high end. For a complete listing, visit www.lakeplacid.com/lodging. Some of the more reasonably priced hotels right in the village include the **Hampton Inn & Suites,** which overlooks Mirror Lake and is right next door to the Lake Placid Pub & Brewery; the **Best Western Adirondack Inn;** and the **Crowne Plaza.**

From Lake Placid take a short drive east to Wilmington along Route 86, as there are several attractions of note to check out. **High Falls Gorge,** located about 8 miles east of Lake Placid, is a privately owned nature park on 22 acres along the Ausable River. Visitors first started coming here to view the gorge in the 1890s. You can view four waterfalls from paths, bridges, and walkways along the gorge; one overlook even has a glass floor to stand on to look down at the rushing water below your feet. The journey through this area takes about an hour; because there is a lot of walking and many steps, closed-toe tied shoes are recommended. There's also a nature trail through the woods. The **Riverview Café,** in the visitors center, serves soups, sal-

HIGH FALLS GORGE, WILMINGTON

ads, sandwiches, and appetizers, along with regional craft beers and New York State wines.

Other places to explore in Wilmington include **Santa's Workshop** in the hamlet of North Pole, a perfect place to visit if you have youngsters in tow. In operation since 1949, it's one of the first theme parks in the country. Open June to December, it has a variety of special events, especially as Christmas approaches.

Of course the biggest thing in Wilmington, literally and figuratively, is **Whiteface Mountain**, at 4,865 feet, the fifth-highest mountain in New York State. It is one of the premier destinations in the Adirondacks. During the winter it is known for world-class skiing. In fact, the Olympic skiing competitions were held here!

You can ride the **Cloudsplitter Gondola**, not only during the ski season but

STANDING ON THE GLASS FLOOR OVERLOOK, HIGH FALLS GORGE, WILMINGTON

during other times of the year, to take in the spectacular view. Another way to enjoy the scenery is to take the 5-mile drive up to the top of Whiteface Mountain on the **Whiteface Veterans Memorial Highway**, which is open from May to mid-October. There are nine places along the drive where you can pull over to admire the view.

This section concludes in Wilmington. You can either return the way you came, back toward Blue Mountain Lake, or continue on Route 86 to Route 9N to connect with the I-87 expressway.

IN THE AREA

Accommodations

Section 1

ADIRONDACK FAIRWAY BED & BREAKFAST, 314 Route 28, Inlet, 315-357-2550. www.adirondackfairwaybedandbreakfast.wordpress.com. $.

GOLDEN BEACH PUBLIC CAMPGROUND, Route 28, Raquette Lake, 315-354-4230. $.

GREAT PINES RESORT, 4920 Route 28, Old Forge, 315-369-6777. www .greatpineslodge.com. $$$.

THE HEDGES RESORT, 1 Hedges Road, 518-352-7325. Open from the end of May to mid-October. www.thehedges.com. $$$$.

LAKESIDE COTTAGES, 120 Route 28, Inlet, 315-357-2110. www.inletlake sidecottages.com. **.

MARY'S GIFT SHOP, 125 Route 28, Inlet, 315-357-5170. **.

NELSON'S COTTAGES, 128 Route 28, Inlet, 315-357-4111. www.nelsons cottages.com. $$.

OLD FORGE CAMPING RESORT, 3347 Route 28, Old Forge, 315-369-6011. www.oldforgecamping.com. $.

PETER'S COTTAGES, 100 Route 28, Inlet, 315-357-3862. www.peterscottages .com. **.

WATER'S EDGE INN, 3188 Route 28, Old Forge, 315-369-2484. www.waters edgeinn.com. $$.

WHITE LAKE LODGE, 12973 Route 28, Forestport, 315-392-3493 (summer only), 973-452-3960 (year-round). www.whitelakelodges.com. **.

THE WOODS INN, 148 Route 28, Inlet, 315-357-5300. www.thewoodsinn .com. $$.

Section 2

SNOWY MOUNTAIN INN, 5088 Route 30, Indian Lake, 518-648-5995 or 877-669-9466. Open year-round. www.snowyinn.com. **.

Section 3

ADIRONDACK HOTEL, 1245 Main Street, Long Lake, 518-624-4700. www .adirondackhotel.com. $$.

BEST WESTERN ADIRONDACK INN, 2625 Main Street, Lake Placid, 518-523-2424. $$.

BEST WESTERN SARANAC LAKE, 487 Lake Flower Avenue, Saranac Lake, 518-891-1970. www.bwmountainlakeinn.com. $$.

CROWNE PLAZA, 101 Olympic Drive, Lake Placid, 518-523-2556. $$$.

HAMPTON INN & SUITES, 801 Mirror Lake Drive, Lake Placid, 518-523-9505. $$$.

JOURNEY'S END COTTAGES, 94 Deerland Road, Long Lake, 518-624-5381. www.journeysendlodging.com. $.

LODGE AT LONG LAKE, 681 Deerland Road, Long Lake, 518-624-2862. $$.

NORTHWOOD CABINS, 2775 Route 30, Tupper Lake, 800-727-5756. www .tupperlake.com/lodging/northwood-cabins. **.

THE SHAMROCK MOTEL AND COTTAGES, 1055 Deerland Road, Long Lake, 518-624-5381. www.shamrockmotellonglake.com/motel.html. $$.

TAIL O' THE PUP, 1186 Route 86, Ray Brook, 518-891-0777. Open seasonally May–mid-October. www.tailofthepupbbq.com. **.

Attractions and Recreation

Section 1

ADIRONDACK SCENIC RAILROAD, 877-508-6728. www.adirondackrr .com

BALD MOUNTAIN FIRE TOWER, Rondaxe Road off Route 28, Old Forge.

ENCHANTED FOREST WATER SAFARI AMUSEMENT PARK, 3183 Route 28, Old Forge, 315-369-6145. www.watersafari.com

GOODSELL MUSEUM, 2993 Route 28, Old Forge, 315-369-3838. Open Tuesday–Saturday 10:00 AM–3:00 PM. www.webbhistory.org

GREAT CAMP SAGAMORE, 1 Sagamore Road, Raquette Lake, 315-354-5311. www.greatcampsagamore.com

MCCAULEY MOUNTAIN SKI CENTER, 300 McCauley Road, Old Forge, 315-369-3225. www.mccauleyny.com

OLD FORGE LAKE CRUISES, 3210 Route 28, Old Forge, 315-369-6473. www.oldforgelakecruises.com

PAYNE'S SEAPLANE RIDES, 431 Route 28, Inlet, 315-357-3971. www.paynesairservice.com

VIEW ARTS CENTER, 3273 Route 28, Old Forge, 315-369-6411. www.viewarts.org

Section 2

BYRON PARK RECREATIONAL AREA, Route 28, Indian Lake, 518-648-6483.

GARNET MINE TOURS, 1126 Barton Mines Road, North River, 518-251-2706. Open late June–Labor Day. www.garnetminetours.com

GORE MOUNTAIN SKI RESORT, 793 Peaceful Valley Road, North Creek, 518-251-2411. www.goremountain.com

INDIAN LAKE MUSEUM, Main Street at Crowe Hill Road, Indian Lake. Open Memorial Day–mid-October Saturday–Sunday 1:00–4:00 PM.

INDIAN LAKE THEATER, 13 West Main Street, Indian Lake, 518-648-5950. www.indianlaketheater.org

NATURAL STONE BRIDGE AND CAVES, 535 Stone Bridge Road, Pottersville, 518-494-2283. Open late May–mid-October 10:00 AM–5:00 PM; open mid-December–March for snowshoeing. www.stonebridgeandcaves.com

NORTH CREEK RAILROAD DEPOT, 5 Railroad Place, North Creek, 518-251-5842. Free admission. Open June Saturday–Sunday 12:15–4:00 PM, July–October Friday–Tuesday 12:15–4:00 PM. www.northcreekdepotmuseum.com

Section 3

ADIRONDACK CAROUSEL, 2 Depot Street, Saranac Lake, 518-891-9521. Open daily May–October, weekends November–May. www.adirondackcarousel.org

ADIRONDACK EXPERIENCE, THE MUSEUM ON BLUE MOUNTAIN LAKE, 9097 Route 30, Blue Mountain Lake, 518-352-7311. Open late May–mid-October 10:00 AM–5:00 PM. daily. www.theadkx.org

ADIRONDACK SCENIC RAILROAD, 800-819-2291. www.adirondackrr.com

CLOUDSPLITTER GONDOLA, www.whiteface.com/activities/cloudsplitter-gondola-ride

HIGH FALLS GORGE, 4761 Route 86, Wilmington, 518-946-2278. Open daily May–October, closed November, open December–April Friday–Tuesday. www.highfallsgorge.com

JOHN BROWN FARM STATE HISTORIC SITE, 115 John Brown Road, Lake Placid, 518-523-3900. www.nysparks.com/historic-sites/29/details.aspx

LAKE PLACID OLYMPIC MUSEUM, 2634 Main Street, Lake Placid, 518-302-5326. www.lpom.org

LONG LAKE BOAT TOURS, 1240 Main Street, Long Lake, 518-624-3911.

OLYMPIC MUSEUM, LAKE PLACID

OLYMPIC JUMPING COMPLEX, 5487 Cascade Road, Lake Placid, 518-523-2202.

OLYMPIC SPORTS COMPLEX, 220 Bobsled Run Lane, Lake Placid, 518-523-4436.

OLYMPIC TORCH TOWER/LAKE PLACID HORSE SHOW GROUNDS, 5514 Cascade Road, Lake Placid.

RAIL EXPLORERS RAILBIKES, 42 Depot Street, Saranac Lake. Open mid-June–November 1, Wednesday–Sunday 11:30 AM–7:00 PM. www.rail explorers.net

ROBERT LOUIS STEVENSON COTTAGE AND MUSEUM, 44 Stevenson Lane, Saranac Lake, 518-891-1462.

SANTA'S WORKSHOP, 324 Whiteface Mountain Memorial Highway, Wilmington, 518-946-2211. Open June–December, hours vary. www.northpoleny .com

SARANAC LAKE'S RIVERWALK, parking lot and access from behind 3 Main Street, Saranac Lake.

WHITEFACE MOUNTAIN, www.whiteface.com

WHITEFACE VETERANS MEMORIAL HIGHWAY, Open mid-June–mid-October. www.whiteface.com/activities/whiteface-veterans-memorial -highway

WILD CENTER, 45 Museum Drive, Tupper Lake, 518-359-7800. Museum open year-round, hours vary according to season. Wild Walk open seasonally May–October. www.wildcenter.org

Dining and Nightlife

Section 1

BILLY'S ITALIAN AMERICAN, 3047 Route 28, Old Forge, 315-369-2001. www.billysrestaurant.org

HISTORIC BUFFALO HEAD RESTAURANT, 10626 North Lake Road, Forestport, 315-393-6607. www.buffaloheadrestaurant.com

HOLY SMOKES BBQ, 13532 Route 28, Forestport, 315-223-1674. Open Thursday–Sunday 11:30 AM–6:00 PM.

THE OLD MILL RESTAURANT, 2888 Route 28, Old Forge, 315-369-3662.

THE SCREAMEN EAGLE & MATT'S DRAFT HOUSE, 172 Route 28, Inlet, 315-357-6026. www.screameneaglepizza.com

SISTERS BISTRO, 3046 Main Street, Old Forge, 315-369-1053. Open seasonally, Memorial Day–Columbus Day. www.sistersbistro.com

SODA FOUNTAIN, 9698 Main Street, Remsen, 315-831-8400. www.thesoda-fountain.com

WALT'S DINER, 3047 Route 28, Old Forge, 315-369-2582.

Section 2

ADIRONDACK SMOKEHOUSE BARBECUE COMPANY, (at the Snowy Mountain Inn), 5088 Route 30, Indian Lake, 877-669-9466. www.adkbbq.com

BAR VINO, 272 Main Street, North Creek, 518-251-3000. www.barvino.net

INDIAN LAKE RESTAURANT AND TAVERN, 2 West Main Street, Indian Lake, 518-648-5115.

IZZY'S DELI, 282 Main Street, North Creek, 518-251-3000.

Section 3

BIG MOUNTAIN DELI & CRÊPERIE, 2475 Main Street, Lake Placid, 518-523-3222. Open 8:00 AM–4:00 PM. www.simplygourmetlakeplacid.com/46-sandwiches

BLUE LINE BREWERY, 555 Lake Flower Avenue, Saranac Lake, 518-354-8114. www.bluelinebrew.com

CASA DEL SOL, 513 Lake Flower Avenue, Saranac Lake, 518-891-2271. www.casadelsolsaranac.com

LAKE PLACID PUB & BREWERY

GOOD BITE KITCHEN, 2501 Main Street, Lake Placid, 518-637-2860. www.thegoodbitekitchen.com

LA BELLA RISTORANTE, 564 Lake Flower Avenue, Saranac Lake, 518-891-1551.

LAKE PLACID PUB & BREWERY, 813 Mirror Lake Drive, Lake Placid, 518-523-3813. www.ubuale.com

THE LEFT BANK CAFÉ, 36 Broadway, Saranac Lake, 518-354-8166. www.leftbankcafe36.com

MCKENZIE'S GRILLE, 148 Lake Flower Avenue, Saranac Lake, 518-891-2574.

RAQUETTE RIVER BREWING, 11 Balsam Street, Tupper Lake, 518-359-5219. Open Tuesday–Saturday 11:00 AM–6:00 PM, Sunday 12:00–6:00 PM. www.raquetteriverbrewing.com

RIVERVIEW CAFÉ, (at High Falls Gorge), 4761 Route 86, Wilmington, 518-946-2278. www.highfallsgorge.com

SKYLINE ICE CREAM, 1976 Route 30, Tupper Lake, 518-359-7288. www.skylineicecream.com

TAIL O' THE PUP, 1186 Route 86, Ray Brook, 518-891-0777. Open seasonally May–mid-October. www.tailofthepupbbq.com

Shopping

Section 1

DRAGONFLY COTTAGE, 2987 Main Street, Old Forge, 315-327-9007.

INLET DEPARTMENT STORE, 167 Route 28, Inlet. www.inletace.com

MARY'S GIFT SHOP, 152 Route 28, Inlet, 315-357-5170.

MAXON HOUSE, 3035 Route 28, Old Forge, 315-882-4402.

OLD FORGE DEPARTMENT STORE, 3085 Route 28, Old Forge, 315-369-6609.

OLD FORGE HARDWARE, 104 Fulton Street, Old Forge, 315-369-6100. www.oldforgehardware.com

OTTER LAKE RUSTIC FURNITURE, 13977 Route 28, Otter Lake, 315-369-6530. Open 10:00 AM–5:00 PM. www.otterlakerustics.com

Section 2

BARKEATER CHOCOLATES, 3235 Route 28, North Creek, 518-251-4438. www.barkeaterchocolates.com

HUDSON RIVER TRADING, 292 Main Street, North Creek, 518-251-4461. www.hudsonrivertradingco.com

MOOSE MUD FUDGE, 276 Main Street, North Creek, 518-260-3251. www.moosemudfudge.com

THE LEFT BANK CAFÉ, SARANAC LAKE

SHOPPING IN LAKE PLACID

PINES COUNTRY STORE, 1 Main Street, Indian Lake, 518-648-5212. www .pinescs.com

Section 3

ADIRONDACK DECORATIVE ARTS & CRAFTS, 2512 Main Street, Lake Placid, 518-523-4545. www.adktrade.com

ADIRONDACK POPCORN, 2520 Main Street, Lake Placid, 518-837-5277. www.adirondackpopcorn.com

ANOTHER'S TREASURES, 14 Broadway, Saranac Lake, 518-891-6021.

THE BOOKSTORE PLUS, 2491 Main Street, Lake Placid, 518-523-2950. www .thebookstoreplus.com

HOSS'S COUNTRY CORNER, 1142 Main Street, Long Lake, 518-624-2481. www.hossscountrycorner.com

MOON TREE DESIGN, 2422 Main Street, Lake Placid, 518-523-1970. www .moontreedesign.com

TWO HORSE TRADE COMPANY, 15 Broadway, Saranac Lake, 518-891-4055. www.twohorsetrade.com

Other Contacts

ADIRONDACKS INFORMATION, www.visitadirondacks.com

INLET INFORMATION OFFICE, 160 Route 28, Inlet, 315-357-5501. www .inletny.com

LAKE PLACID, www.lakeplacid.com

OLD FORGE/TOWN OF WEBB VISITORS INFORMATION CENTER, 3140 Route 28, Old Forge, 315-369-6983 or 1-877-OLDFORGE. www.oldforgeny .com

SARANAC LAKE, www.saranaclake.com

TUPPER LAKE, www.tupperlakeny.gov or www.tupperlake.com

WHITEFACE REGION, www.whitefaceregion.com

YADDO GARDENS, SARATOGA SPRINGS

16

ROUTE 9

From Troy to Lake George

ESTIMATED LENGTH: 60 miles

ESTIMATED TIME: 1–4 days, depending what you want to see and do.

HIGHLIGHTS: In Troy, you will learn about the "real" Uncle Sam, Sam Wilson, at the Rensselaer County Historical Society. You can even visit his final resting place, just outside of town. Afterward, drive up Route 9 through a number of small towns until you reach Saratoga Springs, which has a number of interesting and unique attractions. While some of the towns mentioned in this chapter, like Saratoga Springs and Lake George, are a bit more "touristy" than places visited in some of the other chapters in this book, they do offer some hidden gems along with the more well-known attractions. After visiting Saratoga Springs, travel through Glens Falls, then on to Lake George.

GETTING THERE: This drive starts just north of Albany in Troy. To get there from the New York State Thruway (I-90), take Exit 23 north to I-787 north to Exit 8, and then cross the Hudson River to downtown Troy.

We will begin this drive in Troy, which is located a few miles north of Albany, the state capital. While Troy may not be a place on most travelers' radars, it does have a few attractions that are worth the trip.

Troy was home to the real Uncle Sam, Sam Wilson (1766–1854), who played a significant role in the development of the character of Uncle Sam, who represents the whole country. Pay a visit to the **Rensselaer County Historical Society** in downtown Troy and visit the permanent exhibit, "Uncle Sam, the Man in Life and Legend," which chronicles the life of Wilson. While Wilson was recognized during his lifetime as the real person behind the symbol of Uncle Sam, it wasn't until 1961 that he was officially recognized as Uncle Sam by an Act of Congress.

Start by watching a short film about his life and how he became known

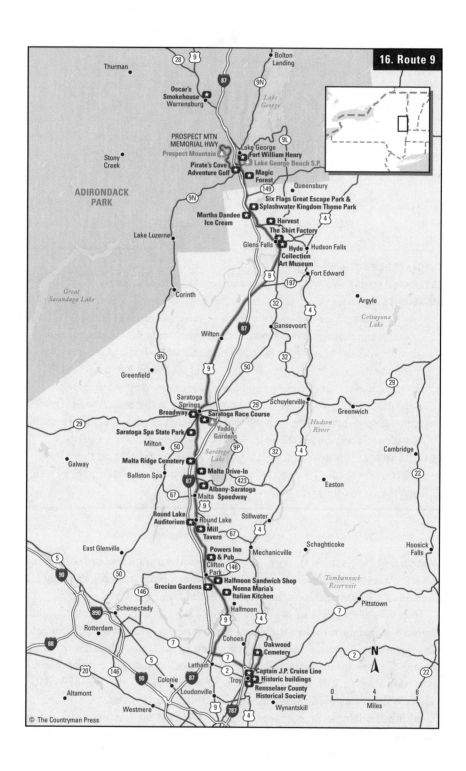

16. Route 9

Thurman

Bolton Landing

28 · 9

87

9N

Oscar's
Smokehouse ★
Warrensburg

Lake George

PROSPECT MTN
MEMORIAL HWY
Prospect Mountain ▲

9L

Lake George
★ Fort William Henry
Lake George Beach S.P.

Stony
Creek

Pirate's Cove ★
Adventure Golf

★ Magic
Forest

Queensbury

149

**ADIRONDACK
PARK**

9N

Six Flags Great Escape Park &
★ Splashwater Kingdom Theme Park

Martha Dandee ★
Ice Cream

★ Harvest
The Shirt Factory

4

Lake Luzerne

Glens Falls

★ Hyde · Hudson Falls
Collection
Art Museum

Fort Edward

9

197

*Great
Sacandaga Lake*

Corinth

Argyle

*Cossayuna
Lake*

32

4

87

Gansevoort

Wilton

9N

9

50

32

Greenfield

29

Saratoga
Springs
Broadway ★ · ★ Saratoga Race Course

29 · Schuylerville

*Hudson
River*

Greenwich

Saratoga Spa State Park ★

Yaddo
Gardens

29

Milton

50

*Saratoga
Lake*

9P

32

4

Cambridge

Galway

Malta Ridge Cemetery ★

Ballston Spa

87

★ Malta Drive-In

423

Easton

22

67

★ Albany-Saratoga
Malta Speedway

9

Round Lake
Auditorium ★ · ★ Round Lake
★ Mill
Tavern

67

Stillwater

4

East Glenville

Powers Inn
★ & Pub
Clifton
Park

146

Schaghticoke

Hoosick
Falls

5

90

50

Mechanicville

*Tombannock
Reservoir*

146

Grecian Gardens ★

★ Halfmoon Sandwich Shop
★ Nonna Maria's
Italian Kitchen

7

Pittstown

890

Schenectady

Halfmoon

Rotterdam

7

9

4

88

Cohoes

5

7

Oakwood
★ Cemetery

2

N

20

146

90

Latham

2

Captain J.P. Cruise Line

22

Colonie

87

Troy

★ Historic buildings
Rensselaer County
Historical Society

Altamont

Loudonville

9

787

Wynantskill

0   4   8

Westmere

4

Miles

© The Countryman Press

UNCLE SAM EXHIBIT, RENSSELAER COUNTY HISTORICAL SOCIETY, TROY

as Uncle Sam, not only to the people who worked for him but to the entire nation. On display are all sorts of pieces of Uncle Sam memorabilia, including folk art, costumes, toys, photos, and posters. In the museum's foyer is a 1937 mural depicting Uncle Sam.

Just a short walk from the historical society, at the junction of Third, Fulton, and River Streets, is a large metal statue of Uncle Sam, a local landmark that was dedicated in 1980. A plaque near the statue describes the Uncle Sam Trail; if time permits, take a walking tour to various spots in Troy where Wilson's homes and businesses once stood. Walk through nearby Riverfront Park, which is the site of many local events, including the **Troy Waterfront Farmers' Market**, open Saturday 9:00 AM–2:00 PM year-round and featuring over 80 food growers and bakers. During the summer months you can take a sight-seeing cruise on the Hudson River aboard the **Captain J. P. Cruise Line**, which docks at State and Front Streets.

As you stroll through downtown Troy, notice

RENSSELAER COUNTY HISTORICAL SOCIETY, TROY

UNCLE SAM STATUE, TROY

its unique architecture; it has one of the most well-preserved 19th-century downtown areas in the country, including two National Historic Landmark buildings. The first is the Gurley building at the corner of Fifth and Fulton Streets, a Classic Revival-style building that once housed a business which produced military products during the Civil War. The second is the Troy Savings Bank at 32 Second Street. Inside is the Troy Savings Bank Music Hall, which has the original seats and stage from when it was built in 1845. As you walk around the city you'll see a number of businesses that have Uncle Sam as part of their name, and you'll also notice Uncle Sam's image on everything from police cars to recycling bins.

There are several well-known places to eat in Troy, including **Famous Lunch**, a diner which has been known for its miniature hot dogs since 1932, as well as their breakfast fare. The **Cookie Factory** has a lot more than cookies; they also sell a variety of breads, cakes, and even tiramisu. A newer restaurant in town, **The Ruck**, has been voted the best beer bar in the United States by craftbeer.com.

Before leaving Troy, take a slight detour north of the city on Route 40 to **Oakwood Cemetery** to pay your respects to Sam Wilson. Once inside the gates, follow the signage to Wilson's grave; look for the large flagpole. Just a note: it may be a bit tricky finding your way out of the cemetery, as the roads are very narrow and winding; too narrow to make a U-turn and go back the way you came in.

Head back into Troy, cross over the Hudson River via Route 7, head east to Route 9, and travel north. You'll pass through a number of small towns, including Halfmoon, which is part of the town of Clifton Park. There are several restaurants of note here, including the **Halfmoon Sandwich Shop**, known for their variety of sandwiches, panini, and salads; **Nonna Maria's Italian Kitchen**, a small restaurant noted for their authentic Italian dishes (reservations are a must); and **Grecian Gardens**, which has Greek specialties along with homemade soups and specialty pizzas. You might also want to check out the **Powers Inn & Pub**, which has craft beer selections along with shepherd's pie, homemade meat loaf, fish-and-chips, and burgers.

The next village is **Round Lake**, which gets its name from the round lake located here. As you drive through this area, notice the great view of the lake from the road, especially right by the Round Lake boat launch.

The village has interesting architecture, including the **Round Lake Auditorium**, which hosts summer programs, concerts, and other performances. Inside is a very rare 1847 Ferris Tracker organ, which has 1,900 pipes. It is the oldest and largest organ of its kind in the country.

If you're looking for a bite to eat, the Adirondack-themed **Mill Tavern** serves up typical pub fare like burgers. Their outdoor patio, which includes a fire pit, has been named the best outdoor dining area in the Capital region.

The Village of Malta, just a few miles up the road, was the home of George Crumm, who is credited with inventing the potato chip at the Moon Lake House in Saratoga Springs in 1853. A customer

UNCLE SAM GRAVESITE, TROY

had ordered fried potatoes and sent them back to the kitchen because they weren't crispy enough. Mr. Crumm, the cook, sliced up a new batch of paper-thin potatoes and fried them in oil; they were an instant hit. Stop by **Malta Ridge Cemetery** to pay your respects to Mr. Crumm. Note that nearby Saratoga Springs holds a chip festival each July (www.thechipfestival.com).

The **Malta Drive-In**, which shows first-run movies, has been in continuous operation since 1949. The **Albany-Saratoga Speedway**, with a 0.36-mile oval track, can also be found in Malta.

Restaurants in Malta include the **Publik House**, known for specialty sandwiches, pizza, ribs, and clams; the **Ripe Tomato**, which offers cooked-to-order, from-scratch Italian-American fare; and the **Dunning Street Station Bar & Grill** which has eclectic offerings like fig and goat cheese flatbread, lobster mac and cheese, chopped salad, and specialty french fries.

Continue north on Route 9 to Saratoga Springs, which will seem like the big city compared to some of the places you've just driven through. It actually is the fifth-largest city in New York State by geographic size, at 28 square miles. Saratoga Springs is considered one of America's best small cities.

A whole book could probably be written about Saratoga Springs, as there is so much to see and do here. What follows are some of the must-see sights, as well as a few hidden gems that visitors might overlook.

Saratoga Springs, as the name implies, is known for its many naturally carbonated mineral springs. There are 21 public mineral springs located throughout the city, the majority of them in the 2,500-acre **Saratoga Spa State Park**. Visitors to Saratoga Springs can taste the water at all the various springs, as each has a unique taste due to different mineral compositions. There is signage in the park pointing out the locations of the springs and information about the taste.

The Iroquois Indians recognized the healing powers of the waters long before settlers came to the area. Later, during the 19th century, visitors would flock here to "take the cure," by drinking the various mineral waters and taking mineral baths and other hydrotherapy treatments. The city also became a resort destination and a place to "be seen," with gambling and horse racing as popular pastimes.

However, the water supply became threatened in the early 1900s, when entrepreneurs wanted to take the carbon dioxide out of the water for carbonated beverages. To prevent the depletion of the springs, legislation was enacted in 1909 to create the Saratoga State Reservation (now the state park) to protect the land. Many of the buildings in the park were constructed in the 1930s, when the park was being developed into a health spa.

The **Roosevelt Baths & Spa** were first established by President Franklin Roosevelt in 1935 to preserve the springs in Saratoga. Today soaks in the naturally effervescent spring waters are still offered by reservation only to spa guests, along with traditional spa treatments such as massages, facials, scrubs, and wraps. Reservations can be made through the park's **Gideon Putnam Hotel**, which offers luxurious accommodations.

Also in the park are two swimming pools, as well as 18-hole and 9-hole golf courses. Hiking trails throughout the park are also used in the winter for cross-country skiing. The **Saratoga Performing Arts Center**, a performance venue that celebrated 50 years in 2016, is located within the park, as are two museums. The **National Museum of Dance**, established in 1986, is the only museum in the country dedicated to the art of dance, while the **Saratoga Automobile Museum** is located in the former water-bottling plant.

Head to downtown Saratoga Springs and stop by the **Saratoga Springs Heritage Area Visitor Center**, which is located in a historic 1915 beaux-arts former trolley station for the Hudson Valley Railway Company. It was later a "drinking hall" from 1941 to 1965, a place where people could purchase and drink bottles of spring water. At the visitor center you can get maps and brochures about the area, including self-guided walking tour maps of the various neighborhoods in the city.

Across the street from the visitor center is **Congress Park**, which has a couple of noted attractions, including the **Canfield Casino**, a National Historic Landmark that was used for gambling in the 19th century; today it

ROOSEVELT BATHS AND SPA, SARATOGA SPA STATE PARK

is a venue for weddings and other events. The **Saratoga Springs History Museum** is located on the second floor.

The **Congress Park Carousel** was built in 1910 and had been located at several sites throughout the region before being purchased by the City of Saratoga and restored between 1987 and 2012. There are four mineral springs located in Congress Park: Congress Spring, Deer Park Spring, Columbian Spring, and Hathorn Spring No. 1.

After visiting Congress Park, head down Union Avenue (Route 9P) to see the historic **Saratoga Race Course**, which first opened in 1863 and has been in almost continuous use since. It is one of horse racing's most well-known tracks. The 40-day race season runs from late July to Labor Day.

Just past the race course you'll see a sign for **Yaddo Gardens,** which is one of the hidden gems of the area. Pull in and follow the very narrow winding road; park in the small parking lot and walk toward the gardens. The mansion high on the hill is a private retreat house for guest artists, writers, and composers.

The gardens, which are open to the public, were a gift to author Katrina Trask from her husband Spencer in 1899. There is a formal rose garden, with terraces, marble steps, and statuary. There is also a rock garden that uses differently shaped rocks and perennial plants. Guided tours of the gardens take place on summer weekends.

Another attraction in Saratoga Springs is the **Saratoga & North Creek**

GIDEON PUTNAM HOTEL, SARATOGA SPA STATE PARK

Railroad, which takes passengers on a two-hour ride in vintage dome cars from Saratoga Springs to North Creek during spring, summer, and fall. In the winter they offer a "snow train," which includes a free shuttle ride to the Gore Mountain Ski Area near North Creek.

Broadway in Saratoga Springs has been voted one of the 10 best main streets in the country. There are many shops, restaurants, and inns along Broadway, as well as on Phila and Caroline Streets. Some of the shops include **Impressions of Saratoga**, a locally owned shop which since 1978 has carried everything Saratoga-related, including souvenirs, gifts, local artwork, locally produced foods, and horse- and racing-themed items; the **Crafters Gallery**, which carries items made by local artists; and down the street, **Northshire Bookstore**, which has books, gifts, cards, and toys and also hosts weekly author events. In addition, be sure to stop by the **Saratoga Marketplace**, home to over a dozen local businesses, including gift shops, clothing stores, and restaurants.

Restaurants include the iconic **Hattie's**, which has been a Saratoga Springs favorite since 1938. Their fried chicken has been voted the best in the US by *Food & Wine* magazine. The menu features authentic southern comfort foods like creole jambalaya, gumbo, and hush puppies; desserts are made in-house.

Other spots to dine include **Ravenous Crêperie**, which features savory and sweet crêpes for lunch, dinner, and weekend brunch. The **Stadium Café**

SARATOGA AUTOMOBILE MUSEUM

on Broadway makes homemade potato chips, just like the ones George Crumm made back in 1853 at the Moon Lake House. **Caffé Lena** is a well-known coffee house and entertainment venue, while the **Country Corner Café**, known for its omelets and homemade pastries and jams, is a favorite with locals. The Food Network named it one of the best mom-and-pop restaurants in America.

There are also many places to stay in Saratoga Springs, from inexpensive hotels to upscale inns. Here is just a sampling of what the city has to offer: the **Spring Motel** has clean, comfortable rooms at a reasonable price; nearby, the **Carriage House Inn** offers deluxe rooms and queen canopy beds in a circa 1875 building; **The Inn at Saratoga**, built in 1848, is the oldest operating hotel in town, with 42 guest rooms and suites and a complimentary breakfast each morning; **Anne's Washington Inn** has a huge wrap-around porch with rocking chairs, as does the **Saratoga Arms**, which was built in 1870; and the upscale **Batcheller Mansion Bed & Breakfast** is in a Gothic Victorian mansion.

Leaving Saratoga Springs, head north on Route 9 toward Glens Falls, which has an up-and-coming downtown area. Art lovers will enjoy the **Hyde Collection Art Museum**, a world-class collection of art housed in an Italianate-style mansion. Featured in the collection are works by Picasso, Rembrandt, Renoir, and Seurat.

There are also shops and restaurants in Glens Falls you may want to check out. **The Shirt Factory,** a four-story historic 1902 building that once housed a shirt manufacturer, is a retail and art complex that includes artist studios, shops, galleries, and services. Some of the original machinery and clothing made here are on display.

For the best-tasting bread and soup in town, stop by the **Rockhill Bakehouse Café.** If you want some craft brews, check out **Davidson Brothers Brewing** or **Cooper's Cave Ale Company**; both are open for lunch and dinner. If health food is your thing, **FX3 Fit Food Fast** offers tasty alternatives to beef burgers like veggie burgers and black bean burgers.

A short distance away from Route 9 is **Harvest,** an Italian-American restaurant that is popular with locals as well as visitors. It is one of Food Network star Rachael Ray's favorite restaurants. Ray is a native of Glens Falls and grew up in nearby Lake George. The restaurant even named a pizza after her; it's topped with hot cherry peppers, green peppers, and onions.

Driving north on Route 9 toward Lake George, you'll see an increased number of businesses, motels, and restaurants. Admittedly, Lake George is a resort area and not really a "backroads" destination. However, there are a few unique attractions here that make the stop worthwhile, even if you have to deal with throngs of people.

Before getting into town, you'll see a sign for the **Magic Forest**, an amusement park that is perfect for families with young children. Even if you're not planning on visiting the park, pull into the parking lot to check out the **World's Tallest Uncle Sam** towering over the lot. (Don't worry, parking is free!) This 38-foot-tall, 4,500-pound Uncle Sam is made of fiberglass. He was brought here in 1982 from the Danbury Connecticut Fair.

If you're traveling with older kids, you might want to check out **Six Flags Great Escape Park & Splashwater Kingdom Theme Park.** You can even bring a picnic lunch into the park. Afterward, be sure to stop for ice cream at **Martha Dandee Ice Cream** just across the street; this well-known ice cream spot, a landmark in Lake George for over 50 years, has over 95 flavors of ice cream. They have even been mentioned on *The Today Show*. Why the rooster on the sign? The business originally started out as a chicken farm and restaurant; the ice cream stand was added as an afterthought. Although now only ice cream is served, the rooster remains on the sign.

Another kid-friendly attraction is the 18-hole **Pirate's Cove Mini Golf,** which has been voted the best mini golf course in the Capital region. You may also want to check out **Around the World Mini Golf** on Beach Road, right in Lake George village. It has two courses; one takes you around the United States; the other takes you around the world.

However, in keeping with this book's focus of backroads and byways, one of the most scenic things to do in Lake George is to take the drive up the **Prospect Mountain Veterans Memorial Highway**; it is definitely worth the $10 fee per car. The highway was built in 1969 and dedicated in honor of

American war veterans. If you're ambitious, you can save 10 bucks and hike the rather strenuous 2.7-mile out-and-back trail to the top of the mountain.

The 5.5-mile drive up the mountain has three scenic overlooks before you get to the large parking lot near the top. Park your car, then ride the shuttle bus to the summit, where you'll get a panoramic, 100-mile view of the surrounding area. At 2,030 feet, Prospect Mountain has great views of Lake George and the Adirondacks. You can bring a picnic lunch if you want, as there are a number of picnic tables and a covered shelter at the summit.

WORLD'S TALLEST UNCLE SAM, MAGIC FOREST, LAKE GEORGE

VIEW FROM PROSPECT MOUNTAIN VETERANS MEMORIAL HIGHWAY, LAKE GEORGE

While you are at the summit, read historic information about the Prospect Mountain House Hotel, which was located here in the late 1800s; guests could stay here for $3 a day, meals included. To get here back then, people would have to take a horse-drawn carriage ride over rough roads or ride the Prospect Mountain Inclined Railroad, which was in operation between 1895 and 1903. It was the longest and steepest inclined railroad in the country at the time. It cost 50 cents to ride, which was expensive for the day, considering wages were about $3 a week. Today you can see the bull wheel and masonry ruins from the railroad.

Once you come down from the mountain, stop for a bite to eat at the **Lake George A&W**, located just a short distance north of the Prospect Mountain Memorial Highway entrance. You can either stay in your car and get carhop service or get table service at one of the outdoor tables; the restaurant is open seasonally. Enjoy hot dogs, burgers, and more. Be sure to wash your meal down with an A&W root beer in a frosted souvenir glass or perhaps an A&W root beer float. Across the street, the **Prospect Mountain Diner**, open year-round, is another good place for breakfast, lunch, dinner, or late-night snacks.

Stop by the **Lake George Visitor Center**, where you can get area information as well as view exhibits on the area's environment. But what you really want to do is go to the area behind the visitor center. Find the large, circular cement area with a big X in the middle. Stand in the X and shout; you'll hear an echo like you are inside a cone. This is the **Lake George Mystery Spot.** Why does this happen? No one is really sure.

Fort William Henry, on the south shore of the lake, was constructed by the British in 1775. Today it is a living history museum that is open daily for guided tours. In the same general area, one can even take a steamboat ride on Lake George with the **Lake George Steamboat Company,** which offers daytime, lunch, and evening cruises. Just be aware the boat's whistle is very loud when it blows!

While Main Street is a bustling place, you can get away from the crowds at **Shepard Park,** located right on Main Street overlooking the lake, with a nice swimming beach. The park is the site of annual events, especially during the summer, when they have live entertainment and weekly fireworks. There is a Jazz Festival in September and a Winter Festival in February. Another park in Lake George is **Lake George Beach State Park,** which includes Million Dollar Beach, the largest and most popular beach in the area. People also enjoy ice fishing on the lake in this area during the winter.

There are numerous shops, restaurants, and accommodations located along Route 9. Here is just a sampling of the restaurants: **Bella's Delicatessen** has the best sandwiches in town as well as salads and coffee; the **Adirondack Pub & Brewery** offers American comfort food and craft beers in an Adirondack lodge setting; if you're craving Mexican, stop by **S. J. Gar-**

RUINS OF PROSPECT MOUNTAIN INCLINE RAILROAD, LAKE GEORGE

cia's for authentic cuisine; those wanting Italian should stop by **MezzaLuna**, which has been serving pizza and Italian dishes for over 40 years; coffee lovers need to stop at **Caffe Vero**, which has a wonderful bakery, a great breakfast, and a long list of specialty coffees like *cup-a-cabana*, coffee with mocha coconut flavor; and just south of the village, the **Barnsider BBQ Restaurant** has a great selection of barbecue items.

There are probably close to 100 hotels and other accommodations in the Lake George area, from very basic, inexpensive chain hotels to more upscale resorts. Some of them include the **Tiki Resort**, which has a Polynesian-themed dinner show; the **Lake George Courtyard Marriott**, which has 119 rooms with Adirondack decor, a rooftop terrace, and a bistro restaurant; the **Fort William Henry Resort Hotel**, which has three separate buildings—the upscale grand hotel, a premium east wing, and the west motel—as well as an indoor pool and an Olympic-sized outdoor pool; and the **Quality Inn** on Canada Street, which is so close to the village that you can leave your car there and walk to most places, and which includes a free continental breakfast in your stay. For more information about places to stay in Lake George, visit www.lakegeorge.com.

There are also a number of ever-changing shops along Beach Avenue in the village, as well as the Lake George Outlets located south of the village on Route 9. If you liked smoked meats and cheeses, take a drive to **Oscar's Smokehouse** in Warrensburg, about 6 miles north of Lake George. They have the best bacon in the Adirondacks, according to area native Rachael Ray.

VIEW OF LAKE GEORGE FROM PROSPECT MOUNTAIN

LAKE GEORGE WATERFRONT

This drive concludes in Lake George. You can continue north on Route 9 to Pottersville and start the Adirondack drive (See Chapter 15, Adirondack Adventure) or head to the I-87 expressway to return to points north or south.

IN THE AREA

Accommodations

Saratoga Springs

ANNE'S WASHINGTON INN, 111 S. Broadway, Saratoga Springs, 518-584-9807. www.anneswi.com. $$$.

BATCHELLER MANSION BED & BREAKFAST, 20 Circular Street, Saratoga Springs, 518-584-7012. www.batchellermansioninn.com. $$$$.

CARRIAGE HOUSE INN, 198 Broadway, Saratoga Springs, 518-584-4220. www.carriagehouseinnsaratoga.com. $$$.

GIDEON PUTNAM HOTEL, 24 Gideon Putnam Road, Saratoga Springs, 518-584-3000. www.gideonputnam.com. $$.

THE INN AT SARATOGA, 231 Broadway, Saratoga Springs, 518-583-1890. www.theinnatsaratoga.com. $$.

SARATOGA ARMS, 497 Broadway, Saratoga Springs, 518-584-1775. www .saratogaarms.com. $$$$.

SPRING MOTEL, 189 Broadway, Saratoga Springs, 518-584-6336. www .springsmotel.com. $$.

Lake George

FORT WILLIAM HENRY RESORT HOTEL, 48 Canada Street, Lake George, 518-668-3081. www.fortwilliamhenry.com. $$$.

LAKE GEORGE COURTYARD MARRIOTT, 365 Canada Street, Lake George, 518-761-1150. $$$.

QUALITY INN, 57 Canada Street, Lake George, 518-668-3525. $$.

TIKI RESORT, 2 Canada Street, Lake George, 518-668-5744. www.tikiresort .com. $$.

Attractions and Recreation

Troy

THE CAPTAIN J. P. CRUISE LINE, 278 River Street, Troy, 518-270-1901. www.captainjpcruise.com

OAKWOOD CEMETERY, 50 101st Street, Troy (for GPS use address 186 Oakwood Avenue, Troy), 518-272-7520. Open daily 8:00 AM–7:00 PM. www .oakwoodcemetery.org

RENSSELAER COUNTY HISTORICAL SOCIETY, 57 Second Street, Troy, 518-272-7232. Open Thursday–Saturday, 12:00–5:00 PM, February– December. www.rchsonline.org

TROY WATERFRONT FARMERS' MARKET, Riverfront Park, Troy. Open Saturdays 9:00 AM–2:00 PM. www.troymarket.org

Round Lake and Malta

ALBANY-SARATOGA SPEEDWAY, 2671 Route 9, Malta, 518-587-0220. www.albany-saratogaspeedway.com

MALTA DRIVE-IN, 2785 Route 9, Malta, 518-587-6077. Open April–September. www.maltadrivein.com.

MALTA RIDGE CEMETERY, Route 9, Malta.

ROUND LAKE AUDITORIUM, 2 Wesley Avenue, Round Lake. www.round lakeauditorium.org

Saratoga Springs

CANFIELD CASINO, in Congress Park, 1 East Congress Street, Saratoga Springs.

CONGRESS PARK, 1 East Congress Street, Saratoga Springs.

CONGRESS PARK CAROUSEL, 5 Lake Avenue, Saratoga Springs, 518-587-3550. www.saratoga.com/news/carousel.cfm

NATIONAL MUSEUM OF DANCE, 99 South Broadway, Saratoga Springs, 518-584-2225. www.dancemuseum.org

ROOSEVELT BATHS & SPA, 30 Roosevelt Drive, Saratoga Springs, 518-226-4790. www.gideonputnam.com/roosevelt-baths-and-spa

SARATOGA & NORTH CREEK RAILROAD, 26 Station Lane, Saratoga Springs, 877-726-7245. www.sncrr.com

SARATOGA AUTOMOBILE MUSEUM, 110 Avenue of the Pines, Saratoga Springs, 518-587-1935. www.saratogaautomuseum.org

SARATOGA PERFORMING ARTS CENTER, 108 Avenue of the Pines, Saratoga Springs, 518-584-9330. www.spac.org

SARATOGA RACE COURSE, 207 Union Avenue, Saratoga Springs, in-season 518-584-6200, off-season 718-641-4700. www.saratogaracetrack.com

SARATOGA SPA STATE PARK, 19 Roosevelt Drive, Saratoga Springs, 518-584-2535. www.nysparks.com/parks/saratogaspa

SARATOGA SPRING HISTORY MUSEUM, Canfield Casino in Congress Park, 1 East Congress Street, Saratoga Springs, 518-584-6920. www.saratoga history.org

YADDO GARDENS, 312 Union Street, Saratoga Springs, 518-584-0746. www .yaddo.org

Glens Falls and Lake George

AROUND THE WORLD MINI GOLF, Beach Road, Lake George, 518-668-2531. www.aroundtheworldgolf.com/mini-golf.asp

FORT WILLIAM HENRY, 48 Canada Street, Lake George, 518-668-5471. www.fwhmuseum.com

HYDE COLLECTION ART MUSEUM, 161 Warren Street, Glens Falls, 518-792-1761. www.hydecollection.org

LAKE GEORGE BEACH STATE PARK, Beach Road and Cedar Lane, Lake George. Open seasonally, late May–Labor Day.

LAKE GEORGE MYSTERY SPOT, Route 9 at Beach Road, behind visitor center.

LAKE GEORGE STEAMBOAT COMPANY, 57 Beach Road, Lake George, 800-553-2628. www.lakegeorgesteamboat.com

MAGIC FOREST/WORLD'S TALLEST UNCLE SAM, 1912 Route 9, Lake George, 518-688-2448. www.magicforestpark.com

PIRATE'S COVE MINI GOLF, 1089 Route 9, Queensbury (Lake George), 518-745-1887. www.piratescove.net

PROSPECT MOUNTAIN MEMORIAL HIGHWAY, Entrance located a half mile south of village of Lake George, 518-668-5471. Open May–October, 9:00 AM–5:00 PM. daily.

SHEPARDS PARK, Route 9, Lake George, 518-668-2864.

SIX FLAGS GREAT ESCAPE PARK & SPLASHWATER KINGDOM THEME PARK, 89 Six Flags Drive, Queensbury (Lake George), 518-824-6000. www.sixflags.com/greatescape

Dining and Nightlife

Troy

COOKIE FACTORY, 520 Congress Street, Troy, 518-268-1060. Open Tuesday–Saturday 9:00 AM–7:00 PM, Sunday 7:00 AM–5:00 PM. www.cookiefactoryllc.com

FAMOUS LUNCH, 111 Congress Street, Troy, 518-272-9481. www.famouslunch.org/welcome.html

THE RUCK, 104 Third Street, Troy, 518-273-1872.

Halfmoon/Clifton Park

GRECIAN GARDENS, 1612 Route 9, Clifton Park, 518-373-9950. Open daily 11:00 AM–9:30 PM. www.greciangardensny.com

HALFMOON SANDWICH SHOP, 1613 Route 9, Clifton Park. www.halfmoonsandwichshop.com

NONNA MARIA'S ITALIAN KITCHEN, 1505 Route 9, Halfmoon, 518-952-7201. www.nonnamariasitaliankitchen.com

POWERS INN & PUB, 130 Meyer Road, Clifton Park, 518-406-5561. www.powersinnandpub.com

Malta/Round Lake/Ballston Spa

DUNNING STREET STATION BAR & GRILL, 2853 Route 9, Malta, 518-587-2000. www.dunningstreetstation.com

MILL TAVERN, 2121 Route 9, Round Lake, 518-899-5253. www.myfavoritetaverns.com/taverns/the-mill

PUBLIK HOUSE, 2727 Route 9, Malta, 518-581-1530. www.publikhouse.net

RIPE TOMATO, 2721 Route 9, Ballston Spa, 518-581-1530. www.ripetomato
.com

Saratoga Springs

CAFFÉ LENA, 47 Phila Street, Saratoga Springs, 518-583-0022. www.caffe
lena.org

COUNTRY CORNER CAFÉ, 25 Church Street, Saratoga Springs, 518-583-
7889. Open Monday–Friday 7:00 AM–2:00 PM, Saturday–Sunday 7:00 AM–
3:00 PM. www.countrycornercafe.net

HATTIE'S, 45 Phila Street, Saratoga Springs, 518-584-4790. Open for dinner at 5:00 PM daily, and also Saturday–Sunday 9:00 AM–2:00 PM for brunch.
www.hattiesrestaurant.com

RAVENOUS CRÊPERIE, 21 Phila Street, Saratoga Springs, 518-581-0560.
www.ravenouscrepes.com

STADIUM CAFÉ, 389 Broadway, Saratoga Springs, 518-226-4437. Open
daily 11:00 AM–9:00 PM. www.saratogastadium.com

Glens Falls and Lake George

ADIRONDACK PUB & BREWERY, 33 Canada Street, Lake George, 518-668-
0002. www.adkbrewery.com/pub

BARNSIDER BBQ RESTAURANT, 2112 Route 9, Lake George, 518-668-
5268. www.barnsider.com

BELLA'S DELICATESSEN, 176 Main Street, Lake George, 518-668-3354.
www.bellasdeli.com

CAFFE VERO, 1 Canada Street, Lake George, 518-668-5800. Open daily
6:30 AM–6:00 PM. www.caffevero.net

COOPER'S CAVE ALE COMPANY, 2 Sagamore Street, Glens Falls, 518-792-
0007. www.cooperscaveale.com

DAVIDSON BROTHERS BREWING, 184 Glen Street, Glens Falls, 518-743-9026. www.davidsonbrothers.com

FX3 FIT FOOD FAST, 682 Upper Glen Street (Route 9), Glens Falls, 518-832-4443. www.fx3fitfoodfast.com

HARVEST, 4 Cronin Road, Queensbury, 518-793-6233. Open 11:00 AM–10:00 PM daily.

LAKE GEORGE A&W, 2208 Route 9, Lake George, 518-668-4681. Open seasonally.

MARTHA DANDEE ICE CREAM, 1133 Route 9, Queensbury, 518-793-0372. www.marthasicecream.com

MEZZALUNA, 157 Canada Street (Route 9) Lake George, 518-668-9090.

PROSPECT MOUNTAIN DINER, 2205 Canada Street (Route 9), Lake George, 518-668-9721.

ROCKHILL BAKEHOUSE CAFE, 19 Exchange Street, Glens Falls, 518-615-0777. www.rockhillbakehouse.com

S. J. GARCIA'S, 192 Canada Street (Route 9), Lake George, 518-668-5111. www.sjgarcias.com

Shopping

CRAFTERS GALLERY, 427 Broadway, Saratoga Springs, 518-583-2435. www.craftersgallerysaratoga.com

IMPRESSIONS OF SARATOGA, 368 Broadway, Suite C, Saratoga Springs, 518-587-0666. www.impressionssaratoga.com

NORTHSHIRE BOOKSTORE, 424 Broadway, Saratoga Springs, 518-682-4200. www.northshire.com

OSCAR'S SMOKEHOUSE, 22 Raymond Lane, Warrensburg, 800-627-3431. www.oscarsadksmokehouse.com

SARATOGA MARKETPLACE, 454 Broadway, Saratoga Springs. www.saratogamarketplace.com

LAKE GEORGE A&W

THE SHIRT FACTORY, 71 Lawrence Street, Glens Falls, 518-907-4478. www .shirtfactorygf.com

Other Contacts

CITY OF GLENS FALLS, www.cityofglensfalls.com

CITY OF TROY, www.troyny.gov

LAKE GEORGE GUIDE, www.lakegeorgeguide.com

LAKE GEORGE VISITOR CENTER, Beach and Canada Streets. www .visitlakegeorge.com

RENSSELAER COUNTY TOURISM, www.renscotourism.com

ROUND LAKE, www.roundlakevillage.org

SARATOGA CHAMBER OF COMMERCE, www.saratoga.org

SARATOGA COUNTY, www.saratogacountyny.gov

SARATOGA SPRINGS HERITAGE AREA VISITOR CENTER, 297 Broadway, Saratoga Springs. www.saratogaspringsvisitorscenter.com

WARREN COUNTY, www.warrencountyny.gov (Lake George area)

17

WOODSTOCK AND VICINITY
Music, Art, and Shopping in the Catskills

ESTIMATED LENGTH: 25 miles; add an additional 55 miles for side trip to Bethel Woods, site of the 1969 Woodstock Music Festival

ESTIMATED TIME: Day trip

HIGHLIGHTS: This trip takes you on a visual and musical creative journey. Start out at Opus 40, a 6-acre monumental sculpture created by one man. Then it's on to Woodstock, not the music festival site but the town that inspired it. (You can visit the actual festival site in a separate side trip, described at the end of this chapter.) Then head to Mount Tremper to experience the world's largest kaleidoscope. Finish your drive in Phoenicia, a small town with several unique shops and restaurants.

GETTING THERE: This is a short drive beginning in Saugerties (Exit 20 off the I-87 expressway). However, allow at least a full day or more, as there are many things to see and do. You can also take a side trip to Bethel Woods, about 1.5 hours away. Alternately, Bethel Woods could be a separate day trip.

We will start this drive in Saugerties at **Opus 40**. To get to Opus 40, from I-87 Exit 20 take Route 212 west, turn left onto Fish Creek Road, turn right onto Highwoods Road, and then right onto Fite Road.

Opus 40 is a very unique outdoor environmental sculpture created by the late Harvey Fite (1903–76) over a period of 37 years. The 6-acre site, formerly a quarry, is made of tons of pieces of bluestone fitted together stone by stone. This is a sculpture you can walk on, through, and around. There are stairways, walkways, subterranean passageways, and natural quarry pools.

LEFT: OPUS 40, SAUGERTIES

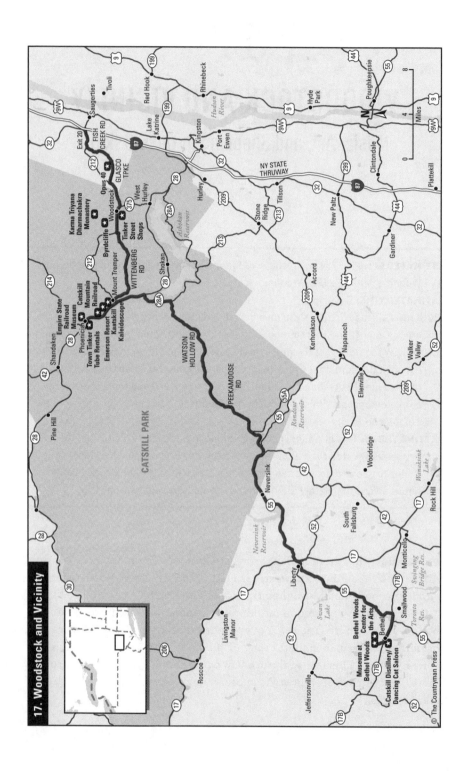

17. Woodstock and Vicinity

CATSKILL PARK

Hudson River

Ashokan Reservoir

Rondout Reservoir

Neversink Reservoir

Swan Lake

Toronto Res.

Swinging Bridge Res.

Wanaksink Lake

Poughkeepsie

Hyde Park

Rhinebeck

Red Hook

Tivoli

Saugerties

Lake Katrine

Kingston

Port Ewen

NY STATE THRUWAY

Stone Ridge

Hurley

West Hurley

Woodstock

Opus 40

Karma Triyana Dharmachakra Monastery

Byrdcliffe

Tinker Street Shops

WITTENBERG RD

Mount Tremper

Catskill Mountain Railroad

Empire State Railroad Museum

Phoenicia

Town Tinker Tube Rentals

Emerson Resort

Kaatskill Kaleidoscope

Shandaken

Pine Hill

WATSON HOLLOW RD

PEEKAMOOSE RD

Shokan

Accord

Kerhonkson

Napanoch

Ellenville

Walker Valley

Woodridge

South Fallsburg

Rock Hill

Monticello

Liberty

Smallwood

Bethel

Bethel Woods Center for the Arts

Museum at Bethel Woods

Catskill Distillery/ Dancing Cat Saloon

Neversink

Livingston Manor

Roscoe

Jeffersonville

New Paltz

Gardiner

Clintondale

Plattekill

Tillson

GLASCO TPKE

FISH CREEK RD

Exit 20

Miles

N

© The Countryman Press

Fite, who was the founder of the Bard College Art Department, was originally going to use the site as a backdrop for his large stone carvings. However, when the background became the focal point, he moved his sculptures to the lawn that surrounds the entrance to the sculpture.

The centerpiece of Opus 40 is the monolith: a 9-ton, 13-foot-high stone that Fite found in a nearby streambed and brought here by truck. He used ancient techniques to raise it into position.

Note that the site has no railings and there are many steep drop-offs along with several deep pools of water. It goes without saying that if you come here with small children, they must hold your hand when exploring the sculpture.

Fite used traditional quarryman tools, like hammers, drills, and chisels, to create the site. The second floor of the admissions/gift shop building houses the Quarryman's Museum, which contains Fite's collection of tools

OPUS 40, SAUGERTIES

OPUS 40, SAUGERTIES

and artifacts. Opus 40 can be rented for wedding ceremonies; occasionally concerts and other performances are held here.

From Opus 40, take the Glasco Turnpike to Route 212 and then go west, toward the town of Woodstock, which has been a magnet for creative types since the early 1900s, when the arts and crafts colony called **Byrdcliffe** was formed. Today Byrdcliffe, located just north of town, is still a center for the arts in Woodstock. Listed on the National Register of Historic Places, it offers art exhibits, music, theater, and more. Visitors can even take a walking tour of the grounds.

Allow several hours to explore the town on foot, so park your car in one of the several parking lots in town. The ones farther out are free, while the one closer lot charges a nominal fee.

Stroll up and down Tinker Street, the main street in town, which has all sorts of shops, art galleries, and restaurants. Some of the shops include **Freewheel Pottery**, which has a lot more than just pottery; the **Golden Notebook**, an independent bookstore since 1978; and **Legends**, which has all sorts of vintage and tie-dyed clothing. As you stroll through the town, you'll even see a few "hippies" who look like they stepped out of 1969.

SHOP AT LEGENDS IN WOODSTOCK

Some of the restaurants in Woodstock include **Joshua's Café**, a fixture on Tinker Street for over 40 years known for its farm-to-table cuisine; **Provisions Deli,** noted for its freshly made sandwiches; and **Bread Alone Café**, which was voted the best bakery in the Catskills.

Be sure to try some of Jane's Homemade Ice Cream, an award-winning artisan ice cream made in nearby Kingston, from **Taco Juan's,** which also serves Mexican fare. The coconut almond ice cream tastes just like an Almond Joy candy bar, and the pistachio ice cream has real pistachios in it. You can also enjoy cupcakes from **Peace, Love and Cupcakes**, which has signature tie-dyed cupcakes, along with others named after famous Woodstock performers like Jimi Hendrix and Janis Joplin.

To see something unique, take a drive up Meads Mountain Road to the **Karma Triyana Dharmachakra Monastery**. Tours of this Buddhist monastery are offered on Saturday and Sunday afternoons. If you are visiting Woodstock on a weekend, be sure to check out **Mower's Flea Market**, a Woodstock tradition for over 40 years.

Overnight accommodations in Woodstock include the **Village Green Bed & Breakfast,** which is located right in town across from the village green.

JOSHUA'S RESTAURANT, WOODSTOCK

Another option is the **Hotel Dylan**, a boutique hotel that captures the essence of the Woodstock Music Festival; rooms are named after musical performers. You can even borrow a vinyl album to listen to; each room comes equipped with a record player.

The next stop on the drive is the **Kaatskill Kaleidoscope** at the Emerson Resort at Mount Tremper, about 10 miles west of Woodstock. (Take Tinker Street west to Wittenberg Road, to Route 212, to Route 28.) The kaleidoscope, certified by the Guinness Book of World Records as the world's largest kaleidoscope, was created in 1996 inside a 60-foot-tall silo.

For the reasonable price of $5 a person, you can watch the 10-minute, multimedia *Kaleidoshow*, which is an amazing display of color and sound. Stand against one of the padded boards and lean back to view the show; or, if you're the only ones at the show, lay on the floor to view it, as it is the best way to get the full effect.

Afterward, browse through the gift shop, which has one of the largest selections of kaleidoscopes in the country. While they have a number of

KAATSKILL KALEIDOSCOPE, MOUNT TREMPER

The iconic 1969 Woodstock Music Festival was not held in the town of Woodstock, but 60 miles away in the town of Bethel. The promoters, who were from Woodstock, had hoped to have the festival in Woodstock, but there was no venue large enough. Fortunately, prominent dairy farmer Max Yasgur had 600 acres of farmland in Bethel that they were able to use for the concert. Over 400,000 people gathered for a three-day music festival featuring the who's who of rock and roll, including Jimi Hendrix, The Who, the Grateful Dead, and Janis Joplin.

(To reach Bethel from Phoenicia, take Route 28 to 28A, head south on Watson Hollow Road and Peekamoose Road to Route 55 to 17B west.)

A visit to the **Museum at Bethel Woods Center for the Arts** will not only tell you about the festival and performers, it will educate you about culture and society during the 1960s. There are a number of multimedia exhibits that include footage from the festival.

MUSEUM AT BETHEL WOODS CENTER FOR THE ARTS

After viewing the exhibits on both floors and visiting the gift shop, head outside to the grounds next to the museum. Here you'll see the Bethel Woods Performing Arts Center, a state-of-the-art venue that can seat about 15,000 for outdoor summer concerts. Continue walking until you are looking down a hill over a vast lawn. This is the site of the 1969 Woodstock Music Festival.

(continued on next page)

There is a commemorative monument along the road at the bottom of the hill; you can either walk to it along a footpath or hop in your car and drive there (there's a small parking lot by the monument). From the monument you can see the spot where the festival stage was set up.

Afterward, stop by the **Catskill Distillery** and sample some spirits, with Woodstock-inspired names like Peace Vodka and Most Righteous Bourbon, made from locally grown grains and fruit. The adjacent **Dancing Cat Saloon** has a variety of menu items from burgers to steaks, along with signature cocktails with names like Summer of '69 and Ricky Don't Call My Number.

inexpensive ones to bring home, they also have some worth hundreds of dollars for serious kaleidoscope collectors.

The **Emerson Resort** offers a variety of accommodations, from reasonably priced to very upscale. There is a large country store located adjacent to the kaleidoscope and dining at the **Woodnotes Grille**, which features locally sourced foods and handcrafted cocktails.

Also located in Mount Tremper is the **Catskill Mountain Railroad**, which takes you on a scenic train ride along Esopus Creek. Travel in a restored 1920s coach or ride in the open gondola car. The train operates from the end of May to September for scenic rides and from late September to October for fall foliage rides.

BRIO PIZZERIA, PHOENICIA

The next stop along the drive is the town of Phoenicia, which has a nice selection of shops and restaurants. Phoenicia was actually named one of the coolest small towns in America in 2011 by Budget Travel. You can spend a lot of time browsing at **The Nest Egg**, an old-fashioned country store that has a large selection of jewelry, candy, puzzles, crafts, and more. Down the street, **The Mystery Spot** has all sorts of antique and vintage items. **Tenderland Home** has reasonably priced gift and home decor items, jewelry, soap, and locally crafted items.

Feeling ambitious? Then rent some equipment from **Town Tinker Tube Rentals** and experience white-water tubing on the Esopus Creek, which has Class II rapids. In addition, the shop also rents out inflatable kayaks.

If you visit Phoenicia on a weekend, stop by the **Empire State Railroad Museum,** located in a circa 1899 railroad depot. The mission of the museum is to tell the story of the people and towns in the Catskills that were served by the railroad. The museum is included as a layover as part of a ride on the Catskill Mountain Railroad.

Places to eat in Phoenicia include **Brio Pizzeria,** best known for their crispy thin-crust, Neapolitan-style pizza. They are open for breakfast, lunch, and dinner, so they also have a variety of other menu items to choose from. The **Phoenician Steakhouse** is the place in town to go if you want steak and chops, including filet mignon and rack of lamb.

The **Phoenicia Belle Bed & Breakfast** is within walking distance of shops and restaurants. They have four guest rooms: two with private baths, and they serve an organic breakfast each morning.

IN THE AREA

Accommodations

EMERSON RESORT, 5340 Route 28, Mount Tremper, 845-688-2828. www.emersonresort.com. $$$.

HOTEL DYLAN, 320 Maverick Road, Woodstock, 845-684-5422. www.thehoteldylan.com. $$$.

PHOENICIA BELLE BED & BREAKFAST, 73 Main Street, Phoenicia, 845-688-7226. www.phoeniciabelle.com. $$.

VILLAGE GREEN BED & BREAKFAST, 12 Tinker Street, Woodstock, 845-679-0313. www.villagegreenbb.com. $$.

Attractions and Recreation

CATSKILL MOUNTAIN RAILROAD, 5408 Route 28, Mount Tremper, 845-688-7400. www.catskillmtrailroad.com

EMPIRE STATE RAILROAD MUSEUM, 70 Lower High Street, Phoenicia, 845-688-7501. www.esrm.com

KAATSKILL KALEIDOSCOPE, 5340 Route 28, Mount Tremper, 845-688-2828. www.emersonresort.com

MUSEUM AT BETHEL WOODS CENTER FOR THE ARTS

KARMA TRIYANA DHARMACHAKRA MONASTERY, 335 Meads Mountain Road, Woodstock, 845-679-5906. www.kagyu.org

MUSEUM AT BETHEL WOODS CENTER FOR THE ARTS, 200 Hurd Road, Bethel, 866-781-2922. www.bethelwoodscenter.org

OPUS 40, 50 Fite Road, Saugerties, 845-246-3400. www.opus40.org

TOWN TINKER TUBE RENTALS, 10 Bridge Street, Phoenicia, 845-688-5553. www.towntinker.com

WOODSTOCK BYRDCLIFFE GUILD, 3 Upper Byrdcliffe Road, Woodstock, 845-679-2079. (Administrative offices, 34 Tinker Street.) www.woodstock guild.org

Dining and Nightlife

BREAD ALONE CAFÉ, 22 Mill Hill Road, Woodstock, 845-679-2108. www
.breadalone.com/woodstock

BRIO PIZZERIA, 68 Main Street, Phoenicia, 845-688-5370. www.brios.net

CATSKILL DISTILLERY/DANCING CAT SALOON, 2037 Route 17B, Bethel,
845-583-3141. www.catskilldistilling.com or www.dancingcatsaloon.com

JOSHUA'S CAFÉ, 51 Tinker Street, Woodstock, 845-679-5533. www.joshuas
woodstock.com

PHOENICIAN STEAKHOUSE, 10 Main Street, Phoenicia, 845-688-9800.
www.thephoeniciansteakhouse.com

PROVISIONS DELI, 65 Tinker Street, Woodstock, 845-546-DELI.

TACO JUAN'S, 31 Tinker Street, Woodstock, 845-679-9673.

WOODNOTES GRILLE, 5340 Route 28, Mount Tremper, 845-688-2828. www
.emersonresort.com

Shopping

FREEWHEEL POTTERY, 7 Tinker Street, Woodstock, 845-679-7478.

GOLDEN NOTEBOOK, 29 Tinker Street, Woodstock, 845-679-8000. www
.goldennotebook.com

LEGENDS, 74 Tinker Street, Woodstock, 845-679-4853.

MOWER'S FLEA MARKET, 1 Maple Lane, Woodstock. www.mowers
saturdayfleamarket.com

THE MYSTERY SPOT, 72 Main Street, Phoenicia, 845-688-7868. www
.mysteryspotvintage.com

THE NEST EGG, 84 Main Street, Phoenicia, 845-688-5851. www.thenest
eggcountrystore.com

PEACE, LOVE AND CUPCAKES, 54 Tinker Street, Woodstock, 845-247-3687. www.woodstockcupcakes.com

TENDERLAND HOME, 64 Main Street, Phoenicia, 845-688-7213. www.tenderlandhome.com

Other Contacts

THE CATSKILLS, www.visitthecatskills.com

DISCOVER SULLIVAN COUNTY, www.discoversullivancounty.com

WOODSTOCK MUSIC FESTIVAL SITE, BETHEL

SULLIVAN COUNTY CHAMBER OF COMMERCE, www.catskills.com

SULLIVAN COUNTY VISITOR ASSOCIATION, www.scva.net

ULSTER COUNTY CHAMBER OF COMMERCE, 214 Fair Street, Kingston, 845-338-5100. www.ulsterchamber.org

ULSTER COUNTY TOURISM, www.ulstercountyalive.com

WOODSTOCK CHAMBER OF COMMERCE, 10 Rock City Road, Wood-stock, 845-679-6234. www.woodstockchamber.com

HUDSON

18

THE HUDSON VALLEY PART 1

Historic Estates and More along Route 9, from Poughkeepsie to Kinderhook

ESTIMATED LENGTH: About 60 miles

ESTIMATED TIME: About 1.5 hours drive time; allow up to 5 days to explore sights along the way

HIGHLIGHTS: This route, which runs parallel to the Hudson River, takes you to mansions, presidential homes, and historic sites. One can also take a stroll 212 feet above the Hudson River on the Walkway Over the Hudson, enjoy gourmet food at the Culinary Institute of America, explore quaint small towns, learn about the Hudson River School of Art, and even stay overnight in the oldest inn in the country.

GETTING THERE: Poughkeepsie is located east of Exit 18 off the I-87 expressway. From New York City, you can also get to this area via Route 9.

This drive begins in Poughkeepsie. If you only have the time to do one thing in the area, the must-see attraction is the **Walkway Over the Hudson Historic State Park**, a former railroad bridge turned linear park that spans the Hudson River from Poughkeepsie to Highland. At 1.28 miles in length and 212 feet above the river, it is the longest elevated pedestrian bridge in the world.

The bridge first opened in 1888 as the Poughkeepsie-Highland Railroad Bridge, the only railroad bridge that crossed the Hudson between New York City and Albany. It was part of a key transportation route that brought goods and passengers across the river.

However, train traffic declined throughout the 20th century. After a fire in 1974 severely damaged the tracks, the bridge was abandoned. In 1992, a nonprofit group was organized to save the bridge and provide public access to it. Construction to transform it into a pedestrian walkway began in 2008, and the walkway officially opened in 2009. It is an outstanding example

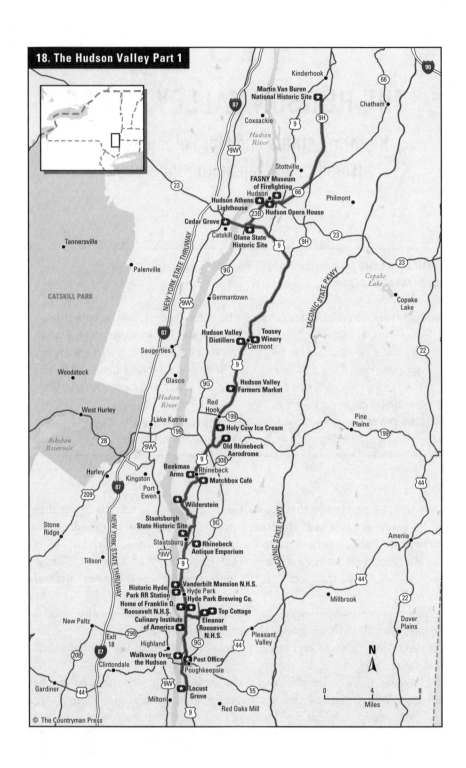

18. The Hudson Valley Part 1

Kinderhook

Martin Van Buren
National Historic Site ★

Chatham

87

Coxsackie

9H

9

Hudson River

9W

Stottville

FASNY Museum
of Firefighting

66

Hudson

Philmont

23

Hudson Athens
Lighthouse ★

23B

Hudson Opera House

Cedar Grove ★

Catskill

Olana State
Historic Site ★

9H

23

23

Tannersville

NEW YORK STATE THRUWAY

Copake Lake

Palenville

9G

Copake
Lake

CATSKILL PARK

9W

Germantown

TACONIC STATE PKWY

22

87

Hudson Valley
Distillers ★

Tousey
Winery ★

Clermont

Saugerties

9

Woodstock

Glasco

9G

Hudson Valley
Farmers Market ★

Hudson River

West Hurley

Red
Hook

199

Pine
Plains

Lake Katrine

Holy Cow Ice Cream ★

199

Ashokan Reservoir

28

9W

199

308

Old Rhinebeck
Aerodrome ★

Hurley

9

Rhinebeck

Kingston

Beekman
Arms ★

Matchbox Café ★

44

87

Port
Ewen

209

Wilderstein ★

Stone
Ridge

Staatsburgh
State Historic Site ★

9G

NEW YORK STATE THRUWAY

Amenia

Staatsburg

9W

Rhinebeck
Antique Emporium ★

TACONIC STATE PKWY

Tillson

9

44

Historic Hyde ★
Park RR Station ★

Vanderbilt Mansion N.H.S. ★
Hyde Park
Hyde Park Brewing Co. ★

Millbrook

22

Home of Franklin D.
Roosevelt N.H.S. ★

Top Cottage ★★

New Paltz

Culinary Institute
of America ★

Eleanor
Roosevelt
N.H.S. ★

Dover
Plains

Exit
18

299

Highland

9G

44

Pleasant
Valley

208

87

Walkway Over ★
the Hudson

Clintondale

Post Office ★

N

Poughkeepsie

Gardiner

44

9W

Locust
Grove ★

55

0   4   8

Milton

Miles

9

Red Oaks Mill

© The Countryman Press

of adaptive reuse; it was named a National Historic Civil Engineering Landmark.

The walkway, which connects to 16 miles of rail trails on both sides of the river, is open from 7 AM to dusk. It can be accessed from the east side of the river from a parking lot along Parker Avenue, from stairs on Washington Street, or from a 21-story, glass-enclosed elevator in Poughkeepsie's Riverfront Park. Access on the west side of the river is off Haviland Road in Highland.

Another point of interest in Poughkeepsie is the **Poughkeepsie Post Office**. The Colonial Revival–style building, which was completed in 1946, is a designated National Historic Landmark. Inside the post office are five murals depicting historic occasions in local and national history. The murals were painted by Olin Dowes, assisted by Works Progress Administration

WALKWAY OVER THE HUDSON, POUGHKEEPSIE

(WPA) artists. Hundreds of artists throughout the country created paintings, murals, and sculptures through the government-funded federal arts project of the WPA as part of Franklin Delano Roosevelt's New Deal Program.

POUGHKEEPSIE POST OFFICE

Another National Historic Landmark in Poughkeepsie is **Locust Grove**, located just south of the downtown area on Route 9. This 180-acre estate was the summer home of Samuel Morse, an artist and scientist who invented the telegraph and Morse Code. The estate includes a 25-room Italianate-style villa, formal gardens, and walking trails. There is a gallery of his paintings and sculptures, as well as a display on communications.

After exploring Poughkeepsie, head north on Route 9 toward Hyde Park. The large collection of buildings you'll notice on the left is the **Culinary Institute of America**, one of the premier schools for those in the food and hospitality industry. You can make dining reservations to eat at one of several restaurants on campus, where foods are prepared by the students. Reservations must be made several weeks in advance, except for the Apple Pie Bakery Café, which takes walk-ins.

For more casual fare, travel a bit up Route 9 to the **Eveready Diner**, a 1950s-style diner known for its comfort foods and apple pie. The diner's pancakes have been featured on the Food Network.

Hyde Park's most famous son was President Franklin D. Roosevelt. Visit the **Home of Franklin D. Roosevelt National Historic Site** and take a guided tour of his family home, Springwood, a National Historic Landmark; as well as a self-guided tour of the **FDR Presidential Library and Museum**, which opened in 1941, the nation's first presidential library. Be sure to stop at Franklin and Eleanor's gravesite in the rose garden. Plan on spending at

CULINARY INSTITUTE OF AMERICA, HYDE PARK

HOME OF FRANKLIN D. ROOSEVELT NATIONAL HISTORIC SITE, HYDE PARK

least three hours touring the entire facility; a café in the visitors center is open seasonally April to October.

Also in the same vicinity are two other Roosevelt homes, **Eleanor Roosevelt National Historic Site (Val-kill)** and **Top Cottage**. Val-kill, a Dutch-style stone cottage, was Eleanor's personal retreat; it is the only National Historic Site dedicated to a first lady. Top Cottage was the hilltop retreat of FDR and he also used it as a place to meet privately with foreign dignitaries. Both sites are open seasonally, May to October.

A great place to eat is the **Hyde Park Brewing Company Restaurant and Brewery,** located across the street from the Home of Franklin D. Roosevelt National Historic Site. The brewery specializes in handcrafted ales and lagers; the restaurant has an extensive menu featuring ribs, schnitzel, seafood, burgers, and more, including some vegetarian items.

Continuing north along Route 9, you'll see a sign for the **Historic Hyde Park Railroad Station**. The 1914 station, located on the banks of the Hudson River, was used quite a bit by Roosevelt when he was governor of New York. Regular passenger service to it was discontinued in 1953. It was later acquired by the Hudson Valley Railroad Society and restored to be used as a railroad museum.

The next point of interest is the **Vanderbilt Mansion National Historic Site**, which was the spring and summer country home of Frederick and Louise Vanderbilt from 1896 to 1938. Frederick was the grandson of Cornelius

GARDENS AT VANDERBILT MANSION, HYDE PARK

Vanderbilt, a shipping and railroad tycoon in the mid-1800s. This lavish, 54-room, beaux-arts mansion, designed by McKim, Mead, and White and is considered opulent by most people. But it's actually modest by Vanderbilt standards. Frederick's brother, George, built the 250-room Biltmore Mansion in Asheville, North Carolina; that structure is America's largest home.

Note that the mansion is in the final stages of a multiyear restoration project. However, you can still take a guided tour of the interior of the home, which is very ornate. Be sure to take a stroll in the formal gardens, which have multiple tiers, over 2,000 rose bushes, several fountains, and multiple sitting areas. Guests of the Vanderbilts were served Japanese tea in the *loggia*, an open-sided garden house, after touring the gardens.

Another mansion in the area that you may want to tour is **Staatsburgh State Historic Site,** also known as the Mills Mansion, as it was the country home of Ogden and Ruth Mills in the late 1800s and early 1900s. Their daughter donated it to New York State in 1938. It is open seasonally for tours and special events; the 65-room beaux-arts mansion is decorated for the holidays during the Christmas season.

Accommodations in the area include the **Journey Inn Bed & Breakfast,** which is located across the street from the Vanderbilt estate.

The next town along Route 9 is Rhinebeck, which has many beautiful, well-preserved homes. If you're craving something sweet be sure to stop by the **Matchbox Café**, which is noted for their cookies. Their chocolate chip cookie has won "Best Cookie in America" several years in a row at the International Fancy Food Show, and their red velvet cake is on Oprah's list of favorite things. The café also serves an all-day breakfast, as well as lunch and dinner. The **Rhinebeck Antique Emporium**, located just south of town, is a good place to shop. There are about 40 vendors in this 7,000-square-foot store; items are nicely arranged and reasonably priced.

While in Rhinebeck stop to tour **Wilderstein**, which was the home of Margaret (Daisy) Suckley, cousin to Franklin Roosevelt. The Queen Anne–style mansion, located on 40 acres, is open for guided tours from May to October and also for holiday tours in November and December. The grounds of the mansion were designed by noted landscape architect Calvert Vaux, and all the items in the site's collection (textiles, art, and clothing) are original to the estate, amassed by the Suckley family during the 140 years they lived there.

If you're interested in vintage aircraft, check out the **Old Rhinebeck Aerodrome** in Rhinebeck. It has one of the largest collections of early aircraft in the world, including a 1909 Bleriot, the oldest flying aircraft in the country.

Of course, no visit to Rhinebeck is complete without stopping at the **Beekman Arms,** America's oldest operating inn. Located in the center of town, it has 23 guest rooms located in the original inn, with an additional 50 guest rooms located a block away in their Delamater Inn. Even if you can't stay the night, you can dine in their tavern restaurant, which is open for lunch, dinner, and Sunday brunch.

Other restaurants in Rhinebeck include **Foster's Coach House Tavern**, which features home-style cooking in an 1890 tavern, and the **Terrapin Restaurant Bistro and Bar**, which has a menu of seasonally inspired items using local and organic ingredients. The **Liberty Public House** serves American comfort food in a landmark 1860s building.

There are also a number of great places to eat in nearby Red Hook, including **Holy Cow Ice Cream**, which was named one of the top 10 ice cream shops in America by TripAdvisor. Be sure to try their signature flavor, Holy Cow: vanilla with peanut butter and mini peanut butter cups.

There are also two diners in town if you're craving comfort food. The family-owned **Red Hook Diner**, which opened in 2014, is the new kid on the block. Then there is the **Historic Village Diner**, located in a 1927 Silk City Diner. When you walk in, you feel like you've stepped back in time. Placed on the National Historic Register in 1988, it has been named one of the top 20 diners in the nation by *Country Living*.

For more upscale dining, stop by the **Flatiron Restaurant,** which uses locally grown and organic foods as much as possible; menu items

HISTORIC VILLAGE DINER, RED HOOK

include seafood, steak, and burgers. In warmer weather you can dine outdoors on their patio.

If you visit Red Hook on a Saturday, stop by the **Hudson Valley Farmers Market** at the Greig Farm, which is open year-round. As you continue traveling north on Route 9 you'll see the **Hudson Valley Distillers**, which offers tours of their facilities and tastings of their products, including their Spirit Grove Vodka, made from apples. Also in the same area is **Tousey Winery**, which offers a variety of wines for tasting and purchasing.

Be sure to allow time to stop in the village of Hudson, which has a downtown area full of shops, including about 50 antiques stores and dozens of art galleries. The **Hudson Opera House** on Warren Street, built in 1875, is the oldest surviving theater in New York State. Abandoned in 1962, it sat vacant until the 1990s, when it was transformed into an arts and cultural center. It is currently undergoing an $8.5 million restoration.

Also located on Warren Street is **Spotty Dog Books and Ale**, a combination bar and bookstore. If you want to eat where the locals go, stop by **The Cascades**, a very busy take-out deli, which also has a dining room. They are known for their soups and sandwiches. Another popular place to eat is **American Glory**, a barbecue restaurant specializing in comfort food. Other restaurants include **Tanzy's**, a small café and gift shop serving breakfast, lunch, and afternoon tea, owned by a pair of sisters and named after their father; and **Baba Louie's**, known for pizza and soup.

Another attraction in Hudson is the **Hudson Athens Lighthouse**, the northernmost lighthouse on the Hudson River. It can be viewed from Henry Hudson Riverfront Park, and tours are offered the second Saturday of the month, July through October. The **FASNY Museum of Firefighting**, also located in Hudson, has interactive exhibits, along with over 60 pieces of fire-fighting equipment on display.

There are a number of premier lodging properties to stay at in Hudson, including the **Barlow Boutique Hotel** on Warren Street. For a complete listing of places to stay, visit www.hudsonarealodging.com.

Just north of downtown Hudson, **Olana State Historic Site** was the home of Frederic Church (1826–1900), the leading painter of American landscapes in the mid-19th century. The Persian-style home, which overlooks the Hudson River, is considered one of the most important artistic residences in the country. It took Church over 40 years to create Olana and the 250 landscaped acres surrounding it. He considered it to be a work of art. The house, which can be visited by guided tour only, has the original furnishings, including Church's paintings.

Cross the Hudson River to visit **Cedar Grove**, the home of Thomas Cole (1801–48), who is regarded as the founder of the Hudson River School, America's first major art movement, and the "Father of American Landscape Painting." The site, a designated National Historic Landmark, features guided tours of the 1815 home and Cole's art studio.

The last stop on this drive is Kinderhook, which is about 22 miles south of Albany. **The Martin Van Buren National Historic Site**, the home of President Martin Van Buren (1782–1862), the eighth president of the United States, is located here. First, watch the 10-minute film in the visitors center, which gives you an overview of the site, and then go on a ranger-guided tour of the house, called Lindenwald. Van Buren, a native of Kinderhook, lived in this home after leaving public office. He is buried at the Kinderhook Dutch Reform Cemetery on Albany Avenue in the Village of Kinderhook.

CEDAR GROVE, HOME OF THOMAS COLE, CATSKILL

MARTIN VAN BUREN NATIONAL HISTORIC SITE, KINDERHOOK

IN THE AREA

Accommodations

BARLOW BOUTIQUE HOTEL, 542 Warren Street, Hudson, 518-828-2100. www.thebarlowhotel.com. $$$.

BEEKMAN ARMS, 6387 Mill Street, Rhinebeck, 845-876-7077. www.beek mandelamaterinn.com. $$$.

HUDSON AREA LODGING, 800-558-8584. www.hudsonarealodging.com. $$$.

JOURNEY INN BED & BREAKFAST, 1 Sherwood Place, Hyde Park, 845-229-8972. www.journeyinn.com. $$$.

Attractions and Recreation

CEDAR GROVE, 218 Spring Street, Catskill, 518-943-7465. www.thomascole .org

ELEANOR ROOSEVELT NATIONAL HISTORIC SITE (VAL-KILL), 56 Val-kill Park Road, Hyde Park, 845-229-9422. www.nps.gov/elro

FASNY MUSEUM OF FIREFIGHTING, 117 Harry Howard Avenue, Hudson, 518-822-1875. www.fasnyfiremuseum.com

HISTORIC HYDE PARK RAILROAD STATION, 34 River Road, Hyde Park, 845-229-2338. www.hydeparkstation.com

HOME OF FRANKLIN D. ROOSEVELT NATIONAL HISTORIC SITE, Route 9, Hyde Park, 800-FDR-VISIT. www.nps.gov/hofr

HUDSON ATHENS LIGHTHOUSE, 518-828-5294, www.hudsonathenslight house.org. For tour reservations call 518-348-8993 or 888-764-1844. www .hudsoncruises.com

HUDSON OPERA HOUSE, 327 Warren Street, Hudson, 518-822-1438. www .hudsonoperahouse.org

HUDSON VALLEY DISTILLERS, 1727 Route 9, Clermont, 518-537-6820. www.hudsonvalleydistillers.com

BEEKMAN ARMS, RHINEBECK

LOCUST GROVE, 2683 South Road, Poughkeepsie, 845-454-4500. www
.lgny.org

THE MARTIN VAN BUREN NATIONAL HISTORIC SITE, 1013 Old Post
Road, Kinderhook, 518-758-9689. www.nps.gov/mava

OLANA STATE HISTORIC SITE, 5720 Route 9G, Hudson, 518-828-0135.
www.olana.org

OLD RHINEBECK AERODROME, 9 Norton Road, Red Hook, 845-752-3200.
www.oldrhinebeck.org

POUGHKEEPSIE POST OFFICE, 55 Mansion Street, Poughkeepsie, 845-452-
5297. Open Monday–Friday 9:00 AM–5:30 PM, Saturday 9:00 AM–2:30 PM.

STAATSBURGH STATE HISTORIC SITE, 75 Mills Mansion Road, Staatsburgh, 845-889-8851. www.nysparks.com/historic-sites/25/details.aspx

TOP COTTAGE, Open May–October. www.nps.gov/hofr/planyourvisit/
top-cottage.htm

TOUSEY WINERY, 1774 Route 9, Germantown, 518-567-5462. www.tousey
winery.com

VANDERBILT MANSION NATIONAL HISTORIC SITE, 119 Vanderbilt
Park Road, Hyde Park, 845-229-7770. www.nps.gov/vama

WALKWAY OVER THE HUDSON HISTORIC STATE PARK, 845-454-9649.
www.walkway.org

WILDERSTEIN, 330 Morton Road, Rhinebeck, 845-876-4818. Grounds are
open year-round, daily 9:00 AM–4:00 PM; guided tours are offered May–
October, with holiday tours in November and December. www.wilderstein
.org

Dining and Nightlife

AMERICAN GLORY RESTAURANT, 342 Warren Street, Hudson, 518-822-
1234. www.americanglory.com

BABA LOUIE'S, 517 Warren Street, Hudson, 518-751-2155. www.babalouies
pizza.com

OLANA, HOME OF FREDERIC CHURCH, HUDSON

CASCADES, 407 Warren Street, Hudson, 518-822-9146. www.thecascades hudson.com

CULINARY INSTITUTE OF AMERICA, 1946 Campus Drive, Hyde Park, 845-452-9600. www.ciachef.edu

EVEREADY DINER, 4184 Route 9, Hyde Park, 845-229-8100. www.the evereadydiner.com

FLATIRON RESTAURANT, 7488 South Broadway, Red Hook, 845-758-8260. www.flatironsteakhouse.com

FOSTER'S COACH HOUSE TAVERN, 6411 Montgomery Street, Rhinebeck, 845-876-8052. www.fosterscoachhouse.com

HISTORIC VILLAGE DINER, 7550 North Broadway, Red Hook, 845-758-6232. www.historic-village-diner.com

HOLY COW ICE CREAM, 7270 South Broadway, Red Hook, 845-758-5959.

HYDE PARK BREWING COMPANY RESTAURANT AND BREWERY, 4076 Albany Post Road, Hyde Park, 845-229-8277. www.hydeparkbrewing.com

LIBERTY PUBLIC HOUSE, 6417 Montgomery Street, Rhinebeck, 845-876-1760. www.libertyrhinebeck.com

MATCHBOX CAFÉ, 6242 Route 9, Rhinebeck, 845-876-3911. Open Thursday–Tuesday 9:30 AM–8:00 PM.

RED HOOK DINER, 7329 South Broadway, Red Hook, 845-758-5000. www.theredhookdiner.com

TANZY'S, 223 Warren Street, Hudson, 518-828-5165. www.tanzyshudson.com

TERRAPIN RESTAURANT BISTRO AND BAR, 6426 Montgomery Street, Rhinebeck, 845-876-3330. www.terrapinrestaurant.com

Shopping

HUDSON VALLEY FARMERS MARKET, Greig Farm, Red Hook, 845-758-1234. www.greigfarm.com/hudson-valley-farmers-market.html

HISTORIC VILLAGE DINER, RED HOOK

RHINEBECK ANTIQUE EMPORIUM, 5229 Albany Post Road (Route 9), 845-876-8168. www.rhinebeckantiqueemporium.com

SPOTTY DOG BOOKS AND ALE, 440 Warren Street, Hudson, 518-671-6006. www.thespottydog.com

Other Contacts

COLUMBIA COUNTY, 401 State Street, Hudson, 800-724-1846 or 518-828-3375. www.columbiacountytourism.org

DUTCHESS COUNTY, 3 Neptune Road, Poughkeepsie, 845-463-4000 or 800-445-3131. www.dutchesstourism.com

HUDSON INFORMATION, www.gotohudson.net

2250

MOTORCYCLEPEDIA

LOOK · EXPLORE · LEARN

MOTORCYCLE MUSEUM

500 MOTORCYCLES *from* 1867

LOOK ★ EXPLORE ★ LEARN

OPEN FRI.-SUN. 10-5

#1
tripadvisor.com

19

THE HUDSON VALLEY PART 2
Chopper Art to Sculptures

ESTIMATED LENGTH: 10 miles

ESTIMATED TIME: Day trip

HIGHLIGHTS: This day trip takes you to two extremes, from motorcycle art and history in the somewhat gritty city of Newburgh to more than 100 sculptures and other installations located on 500 acres of fields and woodlands at the Storm King Art Center.

GETTING THERE: This area of the Lower Hudson Valley is accessible from Exit 17 off the I-87 expressway, which runs north to south along the eastern portion of New York State from Canada to Pennsylvania. This area is about 90 minutes north of New York City. You can also access this area from the I-84 expressway, which runs east to west through the area. Route 9W also runs through this area.

Begin this day trip at the **Motorcyclepedia Museum** on Lake Avenue in Newburgh. This 85,000-square-foot museum, which opened in 2011, has almost 550 motorcycles on display on two floors, including the largest collection of Indian motorcycles in the world. The museum is only open Friday, Saturday, and Sunday, so plan your visit accordingly. As you walk through the museum you'll realize that most these bikes are not merely motorcycles, but works of art, especially some of the custom bikes.

There are a couple of motorcycles with sidecars near the entrance; feel free to climb aboard and take some photos. However, be aware that you can't touch or sit on most of the motorcycles in the museum, just the ones that have the photo opportunity signs by them.

As you stroll through the museum you'll notice how nicely the bikes and

LEFT: MOTORCYCLEPEDIA MUSEUM, NEWBURGH

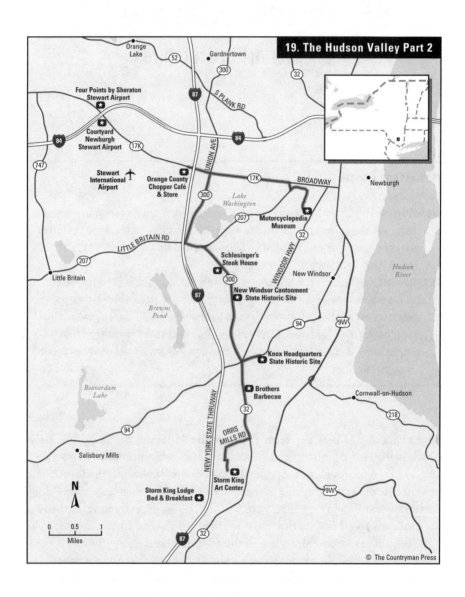

19. The Hudson Valley Part 2

Orange Lake
Gardnertown
52
300
32
Four Points by Sheraton
Stewart Airport
87
S PLANK RD
Courtyard
Newburgh
Stewart Airport
84
84
17K
UNION AVE
747
Stewart
International
Airport
Orange County
Chopper Café
& Store
17K
BROADWAY
Newburgh
300
Lake
Washington
207
Motorcyclepedia
Museum
32
LITTLE BRITAIN RD
Schlesinger's
Steak House
WINDSOR HWY
207
Little Britain
300
New Windsor
Hudson
River
87
New Windsor Cantonment
State Historic Site
Browns
Pond
94
9W
Knox Headquarters
State Historic Site
Beaverdam
Lake
Brothers
Barbecue
Cornwall-on-Hudson
NEW YORK STATE THRUWAY
32
218
94
ORRS
MILLS RD
Salisbury Mills
Storm King
Art Center
9W
N
Storm King Lodge
Bed & Breakfast
0   0.5   1
Miles
87
32

© The Countryman Press

MOTORCYCLEPEDIA MUSEUM, NEWBURGH

other items are displayed; they're not too crowded and clearly labeled. The museum is the private collection of Gerald A. Doering and his son, Ted. The pair amassed their collection over several decades. The elder Mr. Doering has a special fondness for Indian motorcycles, as his first bike was an Indian Scout. Indian, which was in business between 1901 and 1953, was the world's largest motorcycle manufacturer before Harley-Davidson came along.

Displays in the museum include an exhibit dedicated to the memory of "Indian" Larry DeSmedt, a custom motorcycle builder and stuntman who got the nickname "Indian" from the motorcycle he rode when he was young. Another exhibit focuses on motorcycles that were used in movies, including replicas of Captain America and Billy's bike, which appeared in the movie *Easy Rider*, starring Peter Fonda and Dennis Hopper. The museum also has a large gallery of bikes on loan from private collectors.

Downstairs there are some early models of motorcycles, as well as police and military motorcycles. Of special interest is one of the Harley-Davidson motorcycles from President Kennedy's motorcade on the day he was assassinated in Dallas. It was used in the 1991 film *JFK*. Also on this level are two motordromes, commonly referred to as the "wall of death." In the early 1900s these were part of a traveling carnival.

Your next stop on this drive is the **Orange County Choppers Café** for lunch. From the museum, take Lake Street north to Route 17K to Crossroads Court. A custom Orange County Choppers Café bike is on display near the

TOP AND BOTTOM: MOTORCYCLEPEDIA MUSEUM, NEWBURGH

entrance of the café. The menu features sandwiches, burgers, wraps, and salads. The sandwich buns come branded with the Orange County Choppers logo. The café has a full bar, along with a small game area that includes arcade machines and a four-lane bowling alley.

After lunch, wander over to the adjacent **Orange County Choppers Retail Store**, which has more than a dozen "choppers" on display that were featured on the *Orange County Choppers* television show.

ORANGE COUNTY CHOPPERS CAFÉ, NEWBURGH

Included is a space shuttle tribute bike honoring the crews of the space shuttle program and a New York Yankees bike that was originally built for Yankee catcher Jorge Posada. Don't forget to allow some time to shop for some souvenirs of your visit.

Next we will head toward the Storm King Art Center; take 17K east to Route 300. When you get to New Windsor, you will pass **Schlesinger's Steak House**, a highly rated restaurant which is noted for its steaks, seafood, and baby back ribs, as well as its apple pie and deep-dish key lime pie. They also have a cigar bar, making this one of the only bars in the state that allows smoking. However, the restaurant is only open for dinner, so keep it in mind to eat here later.

There are a couple of historic sites in this area you may want to check out. However, if you do this, you may want to add an extra day to your itinerary. The **New Windsor Cantonment State Historic Site** is where the Continental Army spent its last winter and spring of the Revolutionary War under the command of General George Washington. Costumed interpreters demonstrate 18th-century skills like blacksmithing and musket drills. There are several Revolutionary War encampments by reenactors during the year. Also on the grounds is the **National Purple Heart Hall of Fame**, which preserves the stories of Purple Heart recipients from all branches of the service.

Located nearby is **Knox Headquarters State Historic Site**, where Major General Henry Knox established the military headquarters for the American artillery in 1782.

Continue driving south on Route 300 to Route 32 South. Another place to eat along here is **Brothers Barbecue**, which is known for their homestyle southern barbecue fare. Turn right onto Route 20 and then follow the signs to **Storm King Art Center**. This 500-acre open-air art center, founded by H. Peter Stern and Ralph E. Ogden, opened in 1960. It is one of the world's largest sculpture parks, with over 100 sculptures located on the grounds. Placement of larger works was determined by the landscape. You could easily spend the entire day here if you wanted to, or at least the entire afternoon. Plan on visiting on a Saturday or Sunday during the summer, when they stay open until 8:00 PM.

The best way to explore the grounds is on foot, as there are many walking paths, trails, and open fields, but there is also a tram that runs every half hour, giving visitors a 40-minute tour of the grounds. Bicycles are available for rent on a first-come, first-serve basis; however, the grounds are quite hilly, so riding can be somewhat challenging.

Storm King Art Center, which was named after Storm King Mountain located to the east of the art center, is divided into four areas: *The North Woods*, which has smaller-scale works; *The Meadows*, which features several larger-scale sculptures; *The Museum Building*, which has the museum's administration building with indoor exhibits and a gift shop, along with some of the museum's earlier pieces displayed outside the building; and the largest section, *The South Fields*, with numerous walking paths and large-scale works.

As you walk through the grounds you'll see a variety of sculptures, including some so big they give you the feeling that a giant had momentarily stepped away from playing with his building toys. *Acoustiguides*, small handheld devices with headphones to listen to an audio tour of the sculptures, are available to rent at the visitor center for a nominal fee.

There are 10 large sculptures in the south field created by artist Mark DiSuvero. Nearby, in the pond area, you'll find a mermaid on the hull of a

STORM KING ART CENTER, NEW WINDSOR

boat, which was originally on the yacht *Young America* that raced in the America's Cup in 1995. Another installation of note is the Storm King Wall by Andy Goldsworthy. The wall snakes through the area, even going in and out of a small pond.

The fountain on Museum Hill, right by the main building of the art center, is an abstract bronze and steel sculpture by Linda Benglis. It is a very picturesque spot, especially with the tall columns just beyond it.

While it seems tempting to touch or climb on many of the large sculptures and installations, it is not permitted, as over time the sculptures could be damaged. However, there are several select works visitors are allowed to touch, like *Gazebo for Two Anarchists* by Siah Armajani and *Butterfly Chair* by Johnny Swing. See the map given to you at admissions for a complete list of "touchables."

The art center has a small café, open 11:00 AM–4:30 PM and serving light fare, located near the north parking lot. The center also offers special events during the season, which runs from April to November, including walking tours, art exhibits, and family events.

While this drive is written as a day trip, if you want to stay overnight there are numerous chain hotels near Stewart Airport in Newburgh, including the **Courtyard Newburgh Stewart Airport** and the **Four Points by Sheraton Stewart Airport**. There is also the **Storm King Lodge Bed & Breakfast**, located a short distance from the Storm King Art Center.

IN THE AREA

Accommodations

COURTYARD NEWBURGH STEWART AIRPORT, 4 Governor Drive, Newburgh, 845-567-4800. $$$.

FOUR POINTS BY SHERATON STEWART AIRPORT, 5 Lakeside Road, Newburgh, 845-567-0567. $$$.

STORM KING LODGE BED & BREAKFAST, 100 Pleasant Hill Road, Mountainville, 845-534-9421. www.stormkinglodge.com. $$$.

Attractions and Recreation

KNOX HEADQUARTERS STATE HISTORIC SITE, 289 Old Forge Hill Road, New Windsor, 845-561-5498. www.nysparks.com/historic-sites/5/details.aspx

MOTORCYCLEPEDIA MUSEUM, 250 Lake Street, Newburgh, 845-569-9065. Open Friday–Sunday 10:00 AM–5:00 PM. www.motorcyclepedia museum.org

NEW WINDSOR CANTONMENT STATE HISTORIC SITE/NATIONAL PURPLE HEART HALL OF FAME, 374 Temple Hill Road, New Windsor, 845-561-1765. www.nysparks.com/historic-sites/22/details.aspx or www.nysparks.com/historic-sites/38/details.aspx

STORM KING ART CENTER, 1 Museum Road, New Windsor, 845-534-3115. Open April–early December, Wednesday–Sunday. www.stormking.org

Dining and Nightlife

BROTHERS BARBECUE, 2402 Route 32, Cornwall, 845-534-4227. www.the brothersbarbecue.com

ORANGE COUNTY CHOPPERS CAFÉ, 14 Crossroads Court, Newburgh, 845-522-5222. Open Sunday–Thursday 11:00 AM–10:00 PM, Friday–Saturday 11:00 AM–2:00 AM. www.orangecountychoppers.com

SCHLESINGER'S STEAK HOUSE, 475 Temple Hill Road (Route 300), New Windsor, 845-561-1762. www.schlesingerssteakhouse.com

Shopping

ORANGE COUNTY CHOPPERS RETAIL STORE, 14 Crossroads Court, Newburgh, 845-522-5222. Open Monday–Saturday 9:00 AM–9:00 PM, Sunday 10:00 AM–6:00 PM. www.orangecountychoppers.com

Other Contacts

CITY OF NEWBURGH, 83 Broadway, Newburgh, 845-567-7300. www.city ofnewburgh-ny.gov

NEWBURGH, www.newburghonhudson.com

ORANGE COUNTY TOURISM, 845-615-3860. www.orangetourism.org

SCENIC OVERLOOK NEAR ELLENVILLE

20

THE SHAWANGUNK MOUNTAIN SCENIC BYWAY

ESTIMATED LENGTH: 90 miles

ESTIMATED TIME: 1–2 days

HIGHLIGHTS: This drive, which travels around and through the Shawan-gunk Mountains, or "Gunks," as the locals say, is truly a drive that can be described as backroads! While the drive starts out in New Paltz, a fairly large college town, home to SUNY New Paltz, you travel to more rural areas rather quickly. You can discover delightful small towns, farmers' markets, unique historic sites, and scenic vistas overlooking the mountains. For the more ambitious, there are hiking trails galore, especially in the Mohonk Preserve and Minnewaska State Park Preserve.

GETTING THERE: The Shawangunk Mountain Scenic Byway, which was desig-nated a Scenic Byway in 2006, can be accessed from several routes. For the purposes of this book, we will be starting our drive in New Paltz, which is Exit 18 off the I-87 expressway. Take Route 299 west to Springtown Road to get to the byway. Note that if you look at the byway's website, the drive is split into four sections. We will drive three of these sections in a loop, and then we will have to do a bit of backtracking to get to the fourth section along Route 44/55. In recent years this fourth section has been closed periodically due to forest fires in the mountains during extremely dry weather.

From New Paltz, head west on Route 299 until Springtown Road (Route 7), then head north through rural farmland. You'll pass Mountain Rest Road and see the sign for the **Mohonk Mountain House**, a National Historic Land-mark luxury resort on 1,325 acres in the mountains which has been in oper-ation since 1869. However, unless you are a guest at the inn (guest rooms average about $700 per night, meals included) or have dining reservations,

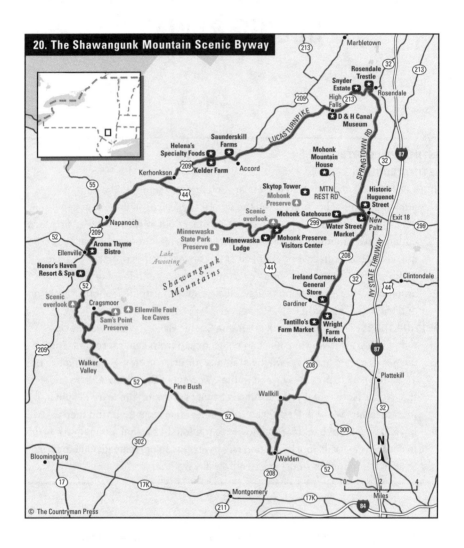

20. The Shawangunk Mountain Scenic Byway

Marbletown

213

32

213

Rosendale
Trestle

Snyder
Estate ⭐

Rosendale

209

High
Falls

213

⭐ D & H Canal
Museum

LUCAS TURNPIKE

SPRINGTOWN RD

87

32

Saunderskill
Farms

Helena's
Specialty Foods ⭐

Mohonk
Mountain
House ⭐

209

⭐ Kelder Farm

Accord

Kerhonkson

55

44

Skytop Tower ⭐

Mohonk
Preserve ⬆

MTN
REST RD

Historic
Huguenot
Street ⭐

Scenic
overlook

Mohonk Gatehouse ⭐

New
Paltz

Exit 18

299

Napanoch

52

209

Minnewaska
State Park
Preserve ⬆

Lake
Awosting

Minnewaska
Lodge ⭐

299

Water Street
Market ⭐

299

Mohonk Preserve
Visitors Center ⭐

208

Aroma Thyme
Bistro ⭐

Ellenville ⭐

Honor's Haven
Resort & Spa ⭐

52

Shawangunk
Mountains

44

Ireland Corners
General
Store ⭐

32

44

Clintondale

Gardiner

Scenic
overlook ⬆

Cragsmoor

Sam's Point
Preserve ⬆

⬆ Ellenville Fault
Ice Caves

Tantillo's
Farm Market ⭐

⭐ Wright
Farm
Market

209

Walker
Valley

208

Plattekill

NY STATE THRUWAY

87

52

Pine Bush

Wallkill

32

52

300

302

N

Bloomingburg

Walden

208

52

0   2   4

Miles

17

17K

Montgomery

211

17K

84

© The Countryman Press

1850 HOUSE INN & TAVERN, ROSENDALE

you have to park near the entrance and hike a rather strenuous trail to the inn to purchase a day pass to hike the grounds.

The first stop on this drive will be the small town of Rosendale, just slightly off the byway, which has a number of places to explore. First, we will explore the shops and restaurants in the tiny downtown, which has colorful houses and businesses lining Main Street. If you're looking for overnight accommodations or a bite to eat, the **1850 House Inn & Tavern** is a boutique inn and restaurant that offers guest rooms with views of the Rondout Creek and Rosendale's Main Street. The rooms have custom linens, flat-screen TVs and WiFi. The tavern offers a pub menu with items like lobster rolls and black bean burgers. In warmer weather, you can dine outdoors on the deck overlooking the creek.

Shops in Rosendale include **Perry's Pickles and Country Accents**, which has all sorts of natural gourmet pickled products, including sauerkraut and kimchi, as well as a variety of pickled vegetables. Rosendale even has a pickle festival every November that includes a home pickling contest, a pickle-eating contest, and even a pickle-tossing contest (www.rosendalechamber.org/pickle-festival). Another shop, **Visions of Tibet**, specializes in handicrafts from Tibet, Nepal, and India. The **Rosendale Farmers Market** takes place on Sundays.

Head west on Route 213 and you will see a railroad trestle 150 feet above the road and Rondout Creek. Known as the **Rosendale Trestle**, this 940-foot continuous truss bridge, constructed in 1895, is part of the Wallkill Valley Trail. The Wallkill Valley Land Trust acquired the bridge in 2009 and opened the trail over it in 2013. To access the trestle, turn down Binnewater Road, then right by the trestle, and travel up the road about 0.25 mile to the Binnewater Kiln parking lot; the trail is across the street from the parking lot.

The next stop in Rosendale is the **Snyder Estate/Century House Historical Society/Widow Jane Mine**. Rosendale was known as the center for natural cement in the 19th century because the limestone deposits in the area were perfect for producing natural cement. The 275-acre Snyder Estate Natural Cement Historic District was the location of five cement plants that produced Rosendale Cement between 1825 and 1970. The grounds, which include the Widow Jane Mine, are open free to the public, May to September from dawn to dusk, for self-guided tours. The Century House Historical Society is open Sundays from 1:00–4:00 PM. The grounds are also a venue for concerts, performances, and cultural events.

The next town along the drive is High Falls. There is a cute little shop, **Green Cottage Gifts and Floral**, which has a nice selection of gifts, jewelry,

GREEN COTTAGE GIFTS AND FLORAL, HIGH FALLS

and accessories in addition to their floral items. Looking for a bite to eat? Stop by the **Kitchenette Restaurant**, a cozy little restaurant featuring locally sourced produce. Along with tasty entrées, they also have homemade breads and desserts. If you want to stay overnight in the area, **Captain Schoonmaker's Bed & Breakfast** has four guest rooms. It is named after Captain Frederick Schoonmaker, a Revolutionary War hero who built the stone house in 1760.

A short distance from Route 213 on Mohonk Road, the **D&H Canal Museum** focuses on the history of the Delaware & Hudson Canal, which once went through this area. Visitors can walk along the towpath to see the remains of five locks that were part of the canal.

Continue along Route 213 to Lucas Turnpike (Route 1) to Route 209. When you get to the town of Accord, **Saunderskill Farms** is a great place to stop for homegrown produce, as well as sandwiches, salads, baked goods, and ice cream.

CHOMSKY, WORLD'S THIRD LARGEST GARDEN GNOME, KELDER FARM, KERHONKSON

A few miles away in Kerhonkson, there are a couple of attractions that are definitely the definition of backroads! As you approach **Kelder Farm**, look to your left to see Chomsky, a 13½-foot-tall garden gnome. Pull into the driveway and visit the farm. Of course, the first thing you'll want to do is snap a photo with Chomsky. When he was built in 2006, he was the world's tallest garden gnome. However, since then, two other gnomes, a 15-foot-tall one located at Iowa State University and an 18-foot one in Poland, have surpassed him in height.

There are a number of activities to enjoy at Kelder Farm, including their unique Homegrown Mini-Golf course, which has edible plants throughout the course that players can sample—for example, chives, lettuce, kale, cabbage, and even a root beer tree. The bark of the tree is used in making root beer; guests are encouraged to pull off a twig and chew on it for that familiar root beer flavor. The farm also has a jumping pillow, a corn maze, and U-pick fruits and vegetables, as well as a farm market with produce and locally produced items. Inside the market is a display of antique farm equipment and historic information about the farm. Outside, the view of the mountains in the distance is spectacular.

One of the area's best-kept secrets is located just across the street from Kelder Farm. If you like pierogies, be sure to stop at **Helena's Specialty**

HOMEGROWN MINI-GOLF, KELDER FARM, KERHONKSON

Foods, which is run by Ukrainian American Anna Samko. The business, which opened in 1995, is named after her mother-in-law.

Pull into the parking lot for the trailer rental place; now look at the left side of the building. If Helena's is open, you'll see an open door with a hand-lettered sign for pierogies. Step inside and place your order at the window; there will be a selection of pierogies to choose from, whatever happens to be being made that day. You order by the dozen, cash only. You can also order kielbasa by the pound. While you wait, watch Anna, along with her daughter and cousin, make the pierogies. They make about 700 to 1,000 pierogis by hand daily.

This is strictly a no-frills operation. Most locals buy the pierogies in bulk to take home. However, you can eat here; there are two tiny tables inside and a picnic table outside, and Anna will give you paper plates and plastic cutlery. The pierogis are served to you in a plastic bag; it's up to you to divvy them up among your family.

Continue along Route 209 to the Village of Ellenville, which will seem like the big city compared to some of the places you just traveled through. There are a few restaurants of note here, including **Aroma Thyme Bistro**, which features organic, American fare, including steaks, seafood, and vegetarian dishes. They also have one of the best-stocked bars in the area, with 300 craft beers and 300 wines. If you prefer classic Italian dishes and brick-oven pizza, stop by **Tony & Nick's Italian Kitchen**. Down the street, **Gaby's Café** has authentic Mexican cuisine. If you're here on a Sunday, the **Ellenville Farmers Market** can be found on Market Street from mid-June to late October. If you want to stay overnight in Ellenville, **Honor's Haven Resort and Spa** offers 232 rooms and suites in a picturesque 200-acre setting with gorgeous gardens, three hiking trails, and waterfalls on the property.

Take Route 52 east out of Ellenville; be sure to stop by the scenic overlook just beyond Ellenville, where you can get a great view of the Shawangunk Ridge State Forest and the mountains in the distance. Nearby is **Sam's Point Preserve**, a 4,600-acre site that is part of Minnewaska State Park. Sam's Point is the name of a panoramic vista within the park. Also in this area are the **Ellenville Fault Ice Caves**, which were designated a National Historic Landmark in 1957. The Ellenville Fault is the largest known open fault with ice caves in the country. You can hike to the ice caves during the summer, but you need to obtain a permit to do so. There might also be restrictions due to wildfires; check the park's website for the latest conditions (www.nysparks.com/parks/193).

Continue along the byway; the road will be very curvy as you travel

HELENA'S SPECIALTY FOODS, KERHONKSON

through several smaller towns, like Pine Bush and Wallkill, where there are a lot of horse farms. Head up Route 208 toward Gardiner, where you will find two long-standing farm markets. **Tantillo's Farm Market** has been in the same family for four generations, since 1932. Open June to October, they sell produce, jams, jellies, cookies, and award-winning pies, along with their apple cider doughnuts, which have been voted the best apple cider doughnuts in the Hudson Valley.

Just down the road is **Wright Farm Market**, a five-generation farm which has been a fixture in this area since 1903. In September and October you can pick your own apples and pumpkins. Their farm market is open year-round, and they also have a bakery with pies, cookies, and cider doughnuts.

On Route 208, just past the intersection of Route 44/55, the **Ireland Corners General Store**, a small convenience store, is known for its submarine and deli sandwiches. Most folks get them to go, but there are a few small tables on the front porch if you want to eat there.

Continue north on Route 208 until you arrive back in New Paltz. Because it is a college town, you'll find a number of shops and restaurants concentrated along Main Street, Church Street, and North Front Street, includ-

HISTORIC HUGUENOT STREET, NEW PALTZ

ing the **Main Street Bistro**, known for comfort diner food. There's also **P&G's**, a cornerstone of New Paltz that offers inexpensive fine dining in a family atmosphere. **A Travola** has homemade pastas and desserts like tiramisu and gelato.

A nice place to shop is the **Water Street Market**, a "village" of independently owned and operated shops, including antiques stores, clothing boutiques, gourmet food shops, and several small cafés.

A must-see attraction in New Paltz is **Historic Huguenot Street**, which is the oldest authentic museum street in the country and the most intact architectural concentration of late 17th-century and early 18th-century stone houses. This 10-acre National Historic Landmark district has buildings that date back to 1677. You can walk along the street and view the houses from the outside for free.

Stop by the visitor center and museum shop, which is located in the circa 1705 DuBois Fort. You can watch a 10-minute film about Huguenot history and experience hands-on exhibits. If time permits, take the one-hour guided tour of the interior of the historic homes.

If it's early enough in the day, you may want to continue driving on the Route 44/55 portion of the byway. However, it does go through the mountains, so if you don't think you'll get done before dark, you might want to drive this section another day. If you want to stay overnight in New Paltz, there are several chain motels. You could also stay at the previously mentioned inns, 1850 House Inn in Rosendale (6 miles away) or Captain Schoonmaker's in High Falls (9 miles). You could also book a room at the **Minnewaska Lodge**, a boutique inn on Route 44/55 with 26 cozy rooms decorated in Mission style. The rooms have a great view of the mountains, and breakfast is included.

To get to the last portion of the byway, from New Paltz take Route 299 west. Before you get to Route 44/55, you may want to stop and look at the picturesque Mohonk Gatehouse, located on Gatehouse Road. It was the gatehouse for the Mohonk Mountain House from 1908 to 1935.

Continue on to Route 44/55 and head toward the Mohonk Preserve and Minnewaska State Park Preserve. The 8,000-acre **Mohonk Preserve**, which is New York State's largest nature preserve, has a mission to protect the Shawangunk Mountain region and to help people care for and explore nature. Admission to the visitors center is free; however, if you want to hike, bike, or horseback ride on the more than 75 miles of trails, you have to either be a member or purchase a day pass. The "Gunks" are considered a world-class climbing destination; cliffs can be accessed from the West Trapps trailhead.

One of the most challenging hikes in the preserve is one referred to as the Labyrinth or Lemon Squeeze to Skytop Tower. This trail can be accessed from the preserve or from the Mohonk Mountain House. It is a 5-mile roundtrip, very strenuous, four-hour hike that involves squeezing through some

MOHONK PRESERVE GATEHOUSE

very tight spaces before getting to the summit where Skytop Tower is located. Built in 1921, the tower is a memorial to Albert K. Smiley, who was one of the founders of the Mohonk Mountain House. From the top of the tower, there is a spectacular view of the mountains and the Mohonk Mountain House.

From the Mohonk Preserve, continue driving west on Route 44/55; you will go around a hairpin turn before coming to a scenic overlook, where you can get a view of the surrounding mountains. Continue on to **Minnewaska State Park Preserve**, a day-use park which has 22,275 acres along the Shawangunk Ridge. The park, which is open year-round, has several waterfalls and hiking trails with mountain views. Lake Awosting, which is a 3-mile hike from the entrance, has a swimming beach.

There are two more scenic overlooks along Route 44/55 before the road becomes residential and you arrive at Route 209 in Kerhonkson. You can turn around and return the way you came or loop back on the byway following the route described earlier in the chapter.

IN THE AREA

Accommodations

1850 HOUSE INN & TAVERN, 435 Main Street, Rosendale, 845-658-7800. www.the1850house.com. $$$.

CAPTAIN SCHOONMAKER'S BED & BREAKFAST, 913 Route 213, High Falls, 845-687-7946. www.captainschoonmakers.com. $$.

HONOR'S HAVEN RESORT, 1195 Arrowhead Road, Ellenville, 845-210-1600 or 877-969-4283. www.honorshaven.com. $$$.

MINNEWASKA LODGE, 3116 Route 44/55, Gardiner, 845-442-1010. www .minnewaskalodge.com. $$$$.

MOHONK MOUNTAIN HOUSE, 1000 Mountain Rest Road, New Paltz, 855-883-3798. www.mohonk.com. $$$$.

HISTORIC HUGUENOT STREET, NEW PALTZ

Attractions and Recreation

D&H CANAL MUSEUM, 23 Mohonk Road, High Falls, 845-687-2000. Open May–October, Saturday and Sunday 11:00 AM–5:00 PM.

HISTORIC HUGUENOT STREET, 81 Huguenot Street, New Paltz, 845-255-1889. Open Tuesday–Thursday 10:00 AM–5:00 PM; evening tours on Fridays 4:00–8:00 PM. Guided tours $10–15. www.huguenotstreet.org

KELDER FARM, 5755 Route 209, Kerhonkson, 845-626-7137. Growing season open daily 10:00 AM–6:00 PM, winter open Monday, Wednesday, Friday, and Saturday 10:00 AM–4:00 PM. www.kelderfarm.com

MINNEWASKA STATE PARK PRESERVE, 5281 Route 44/55. Kerhonkson, 845-255-0752. www.parks.ny.gov/parks/127/details.aspx

ROSENDALE TRESTLE, open dawn to dusk, access from Binnewater Kiln parking lot on Binnewater Road.

SAM'S POINT PRESERVE/ELLENVILLE FAULT ICE CAVES, 400 Sam's Point Road, Cragsmoor, 845-647-7989. www.nysparks.com/parks/193

SNYDER ESTATE/CENTURY HOUSE HISTORICAL SOCIETY/WIDOW JANE MINE, 668 Route 213, Rosendale, 845-658-9900. Grounds open dawn to dusk, May–September; Century House is open Sundays 1:00–4:00 PM. www.centuryhouse.org

Dining and Nightlife

1850 HOUSE INN AND TAVERN, 435 Main Street, Rosendale, 845-658-7800. www.the1850house.com

AROMA THYME BISTRO, 165 Canal Street, Ellenville, 845-647-3000. www.aromathymebistro.com

A TRAVOLA, 46 Main Street, New Paltz, 845-255-1426. www.atavolany.com

GABY'S CAFÉ, 150 Canal Street, Ellenville, 845-647-7620. www.gabyscafe.com

HELENA'S SPECIALTY FOODS, 5754 Route 209, Kerhonkson, 845-626-2958. Open Thursday–Monday 12:00–5:00 PM. www.helenaspecialtyfoods.com

IRELAND CORNERS GENERAL STORE, 551 Route 208, Gardiner, 845-255-8883.

KITCHENETTE RESTAURANT, 1219 Route 213, High Falls, 845-687-7464. www.kitchenetterestaurant.com/home.html

MAIN STREET BISTRO, 59 Main Street, New Paltz, 845-255-7766. www.mainstreetbistro.com

P&G'S, 91 Main Street, New Paltz, 845-255-6161. www.pandgs.com

TONY & NICK'S ITALIAN KITCHEN, 162 Canal Street, Ellenville, 845-210-1040. www.tonyandnicksitaliankitchen.com

Shopping

ELLENVILLE FARMERS MARKET, Market Street, Ellenville. Open Sundays 10:00 AM–2:00 PM, mid-June–late-October.

GREEN COTTAGE GIFTS AND FLORAL, 1204 Route 213, High Falls, 845-687-4810. www.thegreencottage.com

PERRY'S PICKLES AND COUNTRY ACCENTS, 424 Main Street, Rosendale, 845-633-3890. www.perryspicklesonline.com

ROSENDALE FARMERS MARKET, 1055 Route 32, community center parking lot, Rosendale. Open Sundays 8:00 AM–2:00 PM.

SAUNDERSKILL FARMS, 5100 Route 209, Accord, 845-626-2676. Open Tuesday–Sunday 7:00 AM–6:00 PM. www.saunderskill.com.

TANTILLO'S FARM MARKET, 730 Route 208, Gardiner, 845-256-9109. Open daily 9:00 AM–6:00 PM. www.tantillosfarm.com

VISIONS OF TIBET, 378 Main Street, Rosendale, 845-658-3838. Open Wednesday–Monday 12:00–5:00 PM.

WATER STREET MARKET, 10 Main Street, New Paltz, 845-255-1403. www
.waterstreetmarket.com

WRIGHT FARM MARKET, 699 Route 208, Gardiner, 845-255-5300. www
.eatapples.com

Other Contacts

ELLENVILLE-WAWARSING CHAMBER OF COMMERCE, 124 Canal Street,
Ellenville, 845-647-4620. Open Tuesday–Saturday 10:00 AM–3:00 PM. www
.ewcoc.com

HIGH FALLS, www.highfallsnewyork.com

ROSENDALE CHAMBER OF COMMERCE, www.rosendalechamber.org

SHAWANGUNK MOUNTAIN SCENIC BYWAY, information about and
maps of the byway. www.mtnscenicbyway.org

TOWN OF NEW PALTZ, 52 Clearwater Road, New Paltz, 845-255-0604.
www.townofnewpaltz.org

TOWN OF ROSENDALE, www.townofrosendale.com

ULSTER COUNTY TOURISM, 20 Broadway, Kingston, 845-340-3566 or
800-342-5826. www.ulstercountyalive.com

Index